JavaScript™

Your visual blueprint for building dynamic Web pages

by Kelly L. Murdock

Visual

From
maranGraphics™

&

IDG BOOKS

IDG Books Worldwide, Inc.
An International Data Group Company
Foster City, CA • Indianapolis • Chicago • New York

JavaScript™: Your visual blueprint for building dynamic Web pages

Published by
IDG Books Worldwide, Inc.
An International Data Group Company
919 E. Hillsdale Blvd., Suite 400
Foster City, CA 94404

www.idgbooks.com (IDG Books Worldwide Web Site)

Library of Congress Catalog Card No.: 00-107552
ISBN: 0-7645-4730-5
Printed in the United States of America
10 9 8 7 6 5 4 3 2 1

1V/TR/QY/QQ/IN

Distributed in the United States by IDG Books Worldwide, Inc.

Distributed by CDG Books Canada Inc. for Canada; by Transworld Publishers Limited in the United Kingdom; by IDG Norge Books for Norway; by IDG Sweden Books for Sweden; by IDG Books Australia Publishing Corporation Pty. Ltd. for Australia and New Zealand; by TransQuest Publishers Pte Ltd. for Singapore, Malaysia, Thailand, Indonesia, and Hong Kong; by Gotop Information Inc. for Taiwan; by ICG Muse, Inc. for Japan; by Intersoft for South Africa; by Eyrolles for France; by International Thomson Publishing for Germany, Austria and Switzerland; by Distribuidora Cuspide for Argentina; by LR International for Brazil; by Galileo Libros for Chile; by Ediciones ZETA S.C.R. Ltda. for Peru; by WS Computer Publishing Corporation, Inc. for the Philippines; by Contemporanea de Ediciones for Venezuela; by Express Computer Distributors for the Caribbean and West Indies; by Micronesia Media Distributor, Inc. for Micronesia; by Chips Computadoras S.A. de C.V. for Mexico; by Editorial Norma de Panama S.A. for Panama; by American Bookshops for Finland.
For corporate orders, please call maranGraphics at 800-469-6616.
For general information on IDG Books Worldwide's books in the U.S., please call our Consumer Customer Service department at 800-762-2974.
For reseller information, including discounts and premium sales, please call our Reseller Customer Service department at 800-434-3422.
For information on where to purchase IDG Books Worldwide's books outside the U.S., please contact our International Sales department at 317-572-3993 or fax 317-572-4002.
For consumer information on foreign language translations, please contact our Customer Service department at 800-434-3422, fax 317-572-4002, or e-mail rights@idgbooks.com.
For information on licensing foreign or domestic rights, please phone 650-653-7098.
For sales inquiries and special prices for bulk quantities, please contact our Order Services department at 800-434-3422.
For information on using IDG Books Worldwide's books in the classroom or for ordering examination copies, please contact our Educational Sales department at 800-434-2086 or fax 317-572-4005.
For press review copies, author interviews, or other publicity information, please contact our Public Relations department at 650-653-7000 or fax 650-653-7500.
For authorization to photocopy items for corporate, personal, or educational use, please contact Copyright Clearance Center, 222 Rosewood Drive, Danvers, MA 01923, or fax 978-750-4470.
Screen shots displayed in this book are based on pre-released software and are subject to change.

U.S. Corporate Sales	**U.S. Trade Sales**
Contact maranGraphics at (800) 469-6616 or fax (905) 890-9434.	Contact IDG Books at (800) 434-3422 or (650) 655-3000.

ABOUT IDG BOOKS WORLDWIDE

Welcome to the world of IDG Books Worldwide.

IDG Books Worldwide, Inc., is a subsidiary of International Data Group, the world's largest publisher of computer-related information and the leading global provider of information services on information technology. IDG was founded more than 30 years ago by Patrick J. McGovern and now employs more than 9,000 people worldwide. IDG publishes more than 290 computer publications in over 75 countries. More than 90 million people read one or more IDG publications each month.

Launched in 1990, IDG Books Worldwide is today the #1 publisher of best-selling computer books in the United States. We are proud to have received eight awards from the Computer Press Association in recognition of editorial excellence and three from Computer Currents' First Annual Readers' Choice Awards. Our best-selling ...*For Dummies*® series has more than 50 million copies in print with translations in 31 languages. IDG Books Worldwide, through a joint venture with IDG's Hi-Tech Beijing, became the first U.S. publisher to publish a computer book in the People's Republic of China. In record time, IDG Books Worldwide has become the first choice for millions of readers around the world who want to learn how to better manage their businesses.

Our mission is simple: Every one of our books is designed to bring extra value and skill-building instructions to the reader. Our books are written by experts who understand and care about our readers. The knowledge base of our editorial staff comes from years of experience in publishing, education, and journalism — experience we use to produce books to carry us into the new millennium. In short, we care about books, so we attract the best people. We devote special attention to details such as audience, interior design, use of icons, and illustrations. And because we use an efficient process of authoring, editing, and desktop publishing our books electronically, we can spend more time ensuring superior content and less time on the technicalities of making books.

You can count on our commitment to deliver high-quality books at competitive prices on topics you want to read about. At IDG Books Worldwide, we continue in the IDG tradition of delivering quality for more than 30 years. You'll find no better book on a subject than one from IDG Books Worldwide.

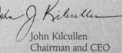

John Kilcullen
Chairman and CEO
IDG Books Worldwide, Inc.

*Eighth Annual
Computer Press
Awards ≷1992*

*Ninth Annual
Computer Press
Awards ≷1993*

*Tenth Annual
Computer Press
Awards ≷1994*

*Eleventh Annual
Computer Press
Awards ≷1995*

maranGraphics is a family-run business
located near Toronto, Canada.

At **maranGraphics**, we believe in producing great computer books — one book at a time.

maranGraphics has been producing high-technology products for over 25 years, which enables us to offer the computer book community a unique communication process.

Our computer books use an integrated communication process, which is very different from the approach used in other computer books. Each spread is, in essence, a flow chart — the text and screen shots are totally incorporated into the layout of the spread. Introductory text and helpful tips complete the learning experience.

maranGraphics' approach encourages the left and right sides of the brain to work together — resulting in faster orientation and greater memory retention.

Above all, we are very proud of the handcrafted nature of our books. Our carefully-chosen writers are experts in their fields, and spend countless hours researching and organizing the content for each topic. Our artists rebuild every screen shot to provide the best clarity possible, making our screen shots the most precise and easiest to read in the industry. We strive for perfection, and believe that the time spent handcrafting each element results in the best computer books money can buy.

Thank you for purchasing this book. We hope you enjoy it!

Sincerely,

Robert Maran
President
maranGraphics
Rob@maran.com
www.maran.com
www.idgbooks.com/visual

CREDITS

Acquisitions, Editorial, and Media Development

Project Editor
Dana Rhodes Lesh

Acquisitions Editor
Martine Edwards

Associate Project Coordinator
Lindsay Sandman

Copy Editor
Tim Borek

Proof Editor
Dwight Ramsey

Technical Editor
Angela Murdock

Permissions Editor
Carmen Krikorian

Associate Media Development Specialist
Megan Decraene

Editorial Manager
Rev Mengle

Media Development Manager
Heather Heath Dismore

Editorial Assistant
Candace Nicholson

Production

Book Design
maranGraphics™

Project Coordinator
Cindy Phipps

Layout
Barry Offringa, Jill Piscitelli, Kathie Schutte, Erin Zeltner

Proofreaders
Corey Bowen, Vicki Broyles

Indexer
York Production Services, Inc.

Special Help
Megan Decraene, Mark Harris, Jill Johnson, Beth Parlon, Marisa E. Pearman, Maureen Spears

ACKNOWLEDGMENTS

General and Administrative

IDG Books Worldwide, Inc.: John Kilcullen, CEO

IDG Books Technology Publishing Group: Richard Swadley, Senior Vice President and Publisher; Walter R. Bruce III, Vice President and Publisher; Joseph Wikert, Vice President and Publisher; Mary Bednarek, Vice President and Director, Product Development; Andy Cummings, Publishing Director, General User Group; Mary C. Corder, Editorial Director; Barry Pruett, Publishing Director

IDG Books Consumer Publishing Group: Roland Elgey, Senior Vice President and Publisher; Kathleen A. Welton, Vice President and Publisher; Kevin Thornton, Acquisitions Manager; Kristin A. Cocks, Editorial Director

IDG Books Internet Publishing Group: Brenda McLaughlin, Senior Vice President and Publisher; Sofia Marchant, Online Marketing Manager

IDG Books Production for Branded Press: Debbie Stailey, Director of Production; Cindy L. Phipps, Manager of Project Coordination, Production Proofreading, and Indexing; Tony Augsburger, Manager of Prepress, Reprints, and Systems; Shelley Lea, Supervisor of Graphics and Design; Debbie J. Gates, Production Systems Specialist; Robert Springer, Supervisor of Proofreading; Trudy Coler, Page Layout Manager; Kathie Schutte, Senior Page Layout Supervisor; Janet Seib, Page Layout Supervisor; Michael Sullivan, Production Supervisor

Packaging and Book Design: Patty Page, Manager, Promotions Marketing

The publisher would like to give special thanks to Patrick J. McGovern, without whom this book would not have been possible.

ABOUT THE AUTHOR

Kelly Murdock has been involved in numerous Internet-related titles, including most recently, *Master Visually HTML and XHTML, HTML Unleashed, Using FrontPage,* and the *FrontPage Bible.* He also works full-time managing a Web development team for Big Planet and is the creative force behind the children's Web site at www.animabets.com, which features a variety of JavaScript games.

AUTHOR'S ACKNOWLEDGMENTS

There are several individuals that I'd like to thank for their support on this project. First of all is my family. Thanks to Angela for helping me in the most stressful times during the development of this work and for her continual encouragement. Thanks to Eric and Thomas for being understanding while Dad was so busy.

Thanks to Chris Murdock for his work on the Animabets characters that are feature prominently throughout the book.

Thanks to Martine Edwards for directing me to this project and a big thanks to Dana Lesh for her expert editing and project guidance. Thanks also to all other IDG employees who were responsible for copy editing, proofreading, indexing, designing the cover, and producing the CD-ROM.

Thanks also to all the contributors who added value to the book's CD-ROM.

Never underestimate the power of a good game.

To Eric, 2000

TABLE OF CONTENTS

1) INTRODUCING JAVASCRIPT

2) USING VARIABLES AND ARRAYS

JAVASCRIPT:
Your visual blueprint for
building dynamic Web pages

3) CREATING EXPRESSIONS

4) CONTROLLING PROGRAM FLOW

TABLE OF CONTENTS

5) WORKING WITH FUNCTIONS

6) HANDLING EVENTS

7) USING OBJECTS

JAVASCRIPT:
Your visual blueprint for
building dynamic Web pages

8) WORKING WITH WINDOWS

TABLE OF CONTENTS

9) WORKING WITH STRINGS

10) WORKING WITH DATES AND TIMES

JAVASCRIPT:
Your visual blueprint for
building dynamic Web pages

11) USING THE MATH OBJECT

12) WORKING WITH FORMS

TABLE OF CONTENTS

JAVASCRIPT:
Your visual blueprint for
building dynamic Web pages

14) DETERMINING ENVIRONMENT PROPERTIES

15) DEBUGGING JAVASCRIPT

TABLE OF CONTENTS

JAVASCRIPT:
Your visual blueprint for
building dynamic Web pages

UNDERSTAND SCRIPTING

Web page files, written in the *Hypertext Markup Language* (HTML), define how elements such as text, tables, and images will appear when viewed in a browser. HTML deals only with static elements.

JavaScript is a scripting language that can co-exist with HTML in a Web page file. It can be used to add interactivity to a Web page.

This interactivity enables the Web page creator to dynamically control the Web page elements. You can also use JavaScript to change Web page elements as the user interacts with the Web page. For example, you can set the text displayed in a form's text box to update when the user clicks a button.

JavaScript can run in a browser without any additional tools.

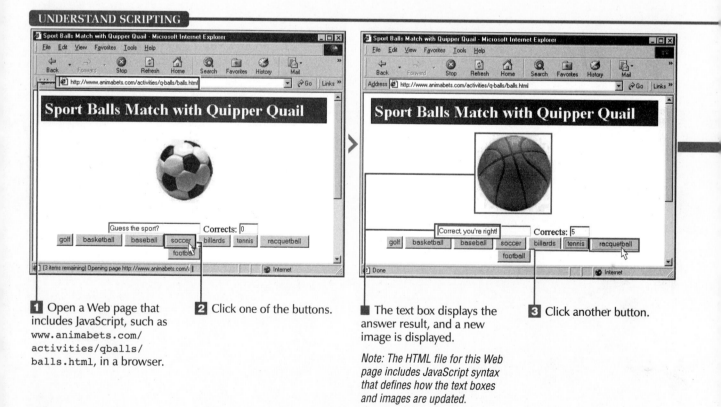

1 Open a Web page that includes JavaScript, such as `www.animabets.com/ activities/qballs/ balls.html`, in a browser.

2 Click one of the buttons.

■ The text box displays the answer result, and a new image is displayed.

Note: The HTML file for this Web page includes JavaScript syntax that defines how the text boxes and images are updated.

3 Click another button.

Extra

JavaScript is the most popular client-based Web scripting language because it is supported on both Netscape Navigator and Internet Explorer, but you can use other scripting languages to add interactivity to a Web page. Setting the `language` attribute for the `<script>` tag to `VBScript` specifies that VBScript is used as the scripting language. VBScript is similar in syntax to Visual Basic, but it is only supported on the Internet Explorer browser.

VBScript is very similar to the Visual Basic programming language, so the advantage of using it if you are familiar with Visual Basic is that VBScript may be easier for you to learn than JavaScript. The disadvantage is that VBScript works only in the Microsoft Internet Explorer browser.

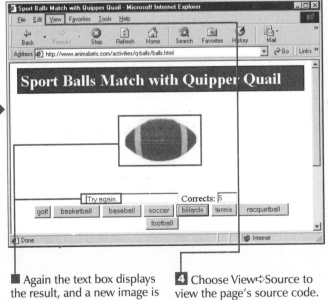

■ Again the text box displays the result, and a new image is displayed.

Note: The text box is logically updated depending on the answer.

4 Choose View⇨Source to view the page's source code.

5 Scroll down until you find the `<script>` tag.

■ Notice that the language attribute is set to javascript.

ENTER JAVASCRIPT STATEMENTS IN THE URL FIELD

JavaScript is composed of statements that when executed perform a desired function. For example, the JavaScript statement `document.write("hello")` displays the word *hello* in the browser.

Browsers can interpret and execute JavaScript statements. These statements can be found within a Web page file or entered directly into the browser's URL box.

To have the browser execute a JavaScript statement, type the javascript: keyword in the Address box of the browser, type the JavaScript statement, and then press the Enter key to execute the statement.

A semicolon (;) should be placed at the end of the JavaScript statement. Several different statements can be included together in the Address box by separating them with semicolons.

For example, if you enter `javascript: document.write("hello");` the browser displays the text "hello" when you press the Enter key.

ENTER JAVASCRIPT STATEMENTS IN THE URL FIELD

1 Open a browser.

2 In the Address box, type the **javascript:** keyword.

Extra

If a keyword is entered in the Address box, the browser normally searches for Web pages based on the keyword. If you want the browser to search for JavaScript Web pages instead of executing a JavaScript statement, just omit the colon after `javascript:` If you type the `javascript:` keyword in the browser's Address box without including a colon (`:`), the browser searches for Web pages that match the `javascript` keyword. The colon symbol tells the browser that the following text should be interpreted as JavaScript statements.

If you forget to include the `javascript:` keyword, the browser will think that the JavaScript statement you type is a Web page address. It will try to locate a Web page with that address, which it won't be able to find.

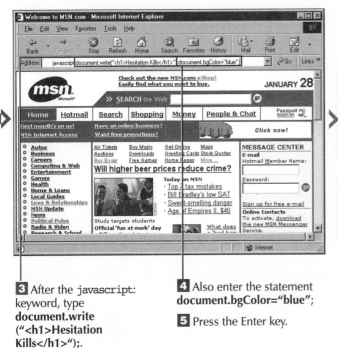

3 After the `javascript:` keyword, type **document.write ("<h1>Hesitation Kills</h1>");**.

4 Also enter the statement **document.bgColor="blue";**

5 Press the Enter key.

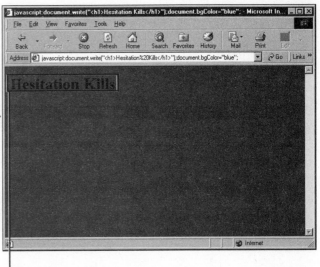

■ The JavaScript statements are executed in the browser.

EMBED JAVASCRIPT WITHIN AN HTML DOCUMENT

JavaScript can be included in a Web page within `<script>` tags. The JavaScript statements included within the `<script>` tags are executed when the Web page loads in a browser.

The `<script>` tags can appear anywhere within the `<head>` or `<body>` tags. A single Web page can include several sets of `<script>` tags.

The `<script>` tag accepts the `type` and `language` attributes. The `type` attribute can be set to a recognized MIME type, such as `text/javascript`. The `language` attribute is another way to specify the

scripting language to use. For JavaScript, it can be simply set to `javascript`.

If a JavaScript statement displays any text to the browser, the location of the text will be at the `<script>` tag's location in the Web page file. For example, if an HTML file has a heading followed by a `<script>` tag that outputs some text, then the JavaScript text will come immediately after the HTML heading.

This example uses the `skeleton.html` file found on the book's CD-ROM, but you can apply these steps to any file.

EMBED JAVASCRIPT WITHIN AN HTML DOCUMENT

```
js-skeleton.html - Notepad
File  Edit  Search  Help
<html>
<head>
</head>
<body>
  <script language="javascript">
  </script>
</body>
</html>
```

```
changebg.html - Notepad
File  Edit  Search  Help
<html>
<head>
</head>
<body>
  <script language="javascript">
  document.bgColor = "blue";
  </script>
</body>
</html>
```

1 Open the `skeleton.html` file.

2 Add a set of `<script>` tags within the `<body>` tags.

3 Add the language attribute to the `<script>` tag.

4 Set the language attribute equal to javascript.

5 Save the file as `js-skeleton.html`.

Note: This skeleton page can be used to easily create a Web page that includes JavaScript.

6 Within the `<script>` tags, add a JavaScript statement to change the background color.

7 Add a semicolon (;) to the end of the JavaScript statement.

8 Save the file as `changebg.html`.

Note: JavaScript statements placed within the `<script>` tags are executed when the file is loaded.

Apply It

Using JavaScript, you can personalize a Web page for your visitors. The following snippet of code opens a dialog box in which users can enter their names. This name is then displayed on the Web page using another JavaScript statement:

```
temp = window.prompt("What is your name?");
```

```
document.write("Welcome, " + temp + " to this Web page. I hope you enjoy your visit.");
```

To make this script work, you simply need to include it within a set of `<script>` tags and open the file within a browser.

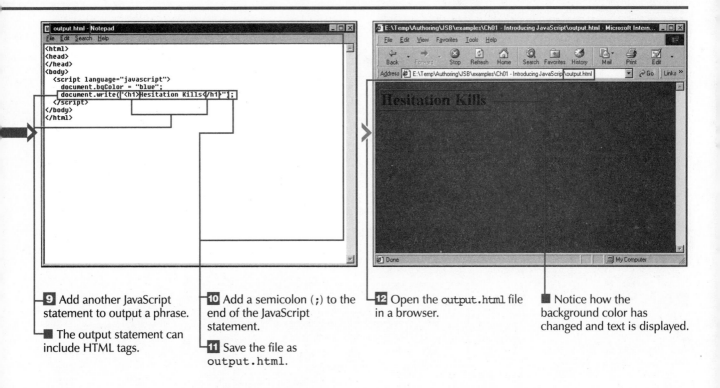

-9 Add another JavaScript statement to output a phrase.

■ The output statement can include HTML tags.

-10 Add a semicolon (;) to the end of the JavaScript statement.

11 Save the file as `output.html`.

-12 Open the `output.html` file in a browser.

■ Notice how the background color has changed and text is displayed.

LINK TO AN EXTERNAL JAVASCRIPT FILE

A nother attribute that can be used with the <script> tag is the src attribute. This attribute can be set to the URL of an external file that contains the JavaScript script.

The external file does not need to include the <script> tags, only the JavaScript statements. It also doesn't need to include the html extension. External JavaScript files typically will have a js extension.

The external JavaScript file can be anywhere on the Web and referenced using the http://

protocol keyword followed by the Web address for the external file.

For example, the statement, <script src="myfile.js"> would access the external JavaScript file named myfile.js located in the same directory as the HTML file.

This example uses the output.html file found on the book's CD-ROM (or which you may have created in the section "Embed JavaScript within an HTML Document"), but you can apply these steps to any file.

LINK TO AN EXTERNAL JAVASCRIPT FILE

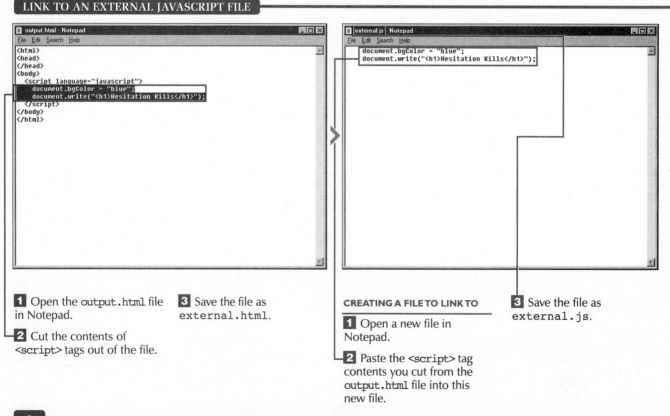

1 Open the output.html file in Notepad.

2 Cut the contents of <script> tags out of the file.

3 Save the file as external.html.

CREATING A FILE TO LINK TO

1 Open a new file in Notepad.

2 Paste the <script> tag contents you cut from the output.html file into this new file.

3 Save the file as external.js.

Extra

JavaScript is case-sensitive. If you type a JavaScript variable with a capital letter, you need to include that same capital letter when you call the variable. So the variables `hello`, `Hello`, and `HELLO` are all different. If your JavaScript statement isn't being recognized correctly, check for a misspelled keyword.

You can execute JavaScript statements multiple times by placing them within structures called *functions*. Functions are covered in Chapter 5.

Any JavaScript statements included within the `<head>` tags are executed before the remaining HTML tags. For example, if there are `<script>` tags within the `<head>` tags that contain a JavaScript statement that outputs some text, that text appears above the rest of the Web page.

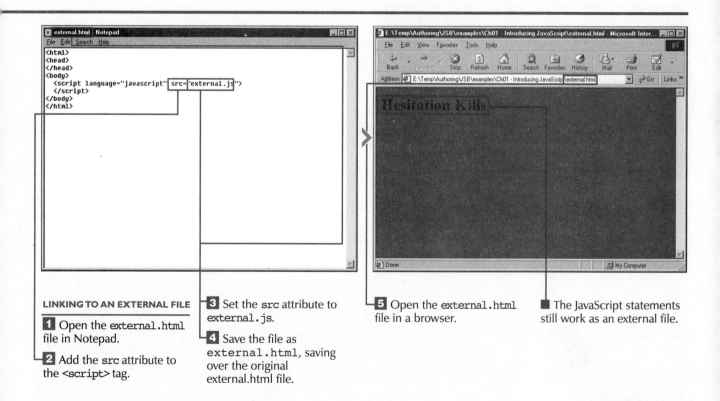

LINKING TO AN EXTERNAL FILE

1 Open the `external.html` file in Notepad.

2 Add the `src` attribute to the `<script>` tag.

3 Set the `src` attribute to `external.js`.

4 Save the file as `external.html`, saving over the original external.html file.

5 Open the `external.html` file in a browser.

■ The JavaScript statements still work as an external file.

PRESENT CONTENT TO NON-JAVASCRIPT BROWSERS

Users have the option as part of the browser configuration to disable JavaScript support. If a user has disabled JavaScript support, her browser will not display any JavaScript that you include in your Web page.

You can handle a browser that has JavaScript support disabled using the <noscript> tags. If the JavaScript cannot be processed, the content included within the <noscript> tags is displayed.

This content can explain to the users with JavaScript disabled on their browser what they would see if JavaScript were enabled.

For example, if a Web page includes the sentence "This page uses JavaScript" within <noscript> tags, this sentence will appear if JavaScript is disabled.

This example uses the output.html file found on the book's CD-ROM, but you can apply these steps to any file.

PRESENT CONTENT TO NON-JAVASCRIPT BROWSERS

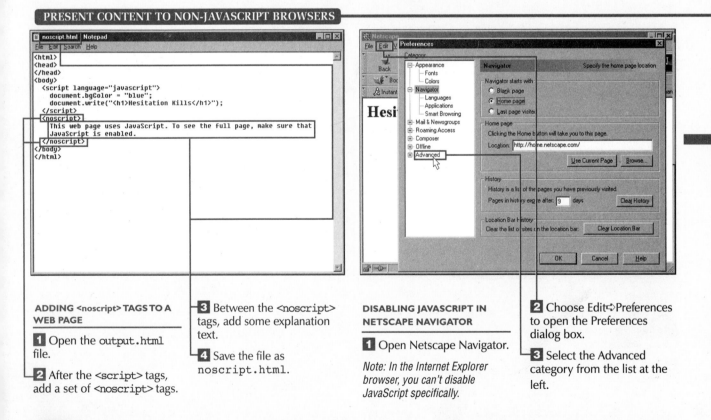

ADDING <noscript> TAGS TO A WEB PAGE

1 Open the output.html file.

2 After the <script> tags, add a set of <noscript> tags.

3 Between the <noscript> tags, add some explanation text.

4 Save the file as noscript.html.

DISABLING JAVASCRIPT IN NETSCAPE NAVIGATOR

1 Open Netscape Navigator.

Note: In the Internet Explorer browser, you can't disable JavaScript specifically.

2 Choose Edit➪Preferences to open the Preferences dialog box.

3 Select the Advanced category from the list at the left.

Extra

You cannot control a user's browser configuration, so there is no way to alter someone's configuration to enable JavaScript support. The best you can do is to tell the user how to enable it and encourage him or her to do so. You can, however, detect whether the Java programming language is enabled.

Many different Web page enhancements can be enabled or disabled using the browser preference settings. Using Netscape Navigator's Preferences dialog box, you can disable Java, JavaScript, style sheets, and cookies. Using Internet Explorer's Options dialog box, you can disable Java, ActiveX controls, scripting, and cookies.

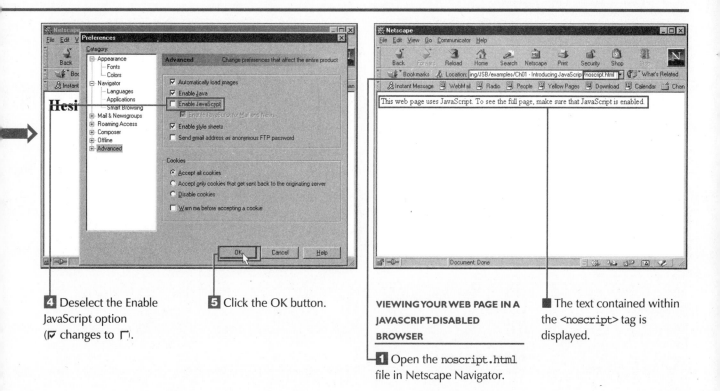

4 Deselect the Enable JavaScript option (☑ changes to ☐).

5 Click the OK button.

VIEWING YOUR WEB PAGE IN A JAVASCRIPT-DISABLED BROWSER

1 Open the noscript.html file in Netscape Navigator.

■ The text contained within the <noscript> tag is displayed.

ADD COMMENTS TO JAVASCRIPT

The JavaScript syntax can be difficult to follow if you are new to the language. One way to document what a section of code does is to include blocks of comments. These comments will be ignored by the browser and will only be visible in the actual file.

A single-line comment can be designated with two forward slashes (//). Multiple-line comments start with a forward slash and an asterisk (/*) and end with the opposite (*/). You cannot nest multiple sets of comments. All statements included within the comment symbols will be ignored.

Comments can appear anywhere within a set of <script> tags.

Besides documenting your code, you can also use comments for debugging JavaScript. Multiple-line comments can be used to quickly disable sections of your code without removing them. This ability is handy when you are trying to debug sections that aren't working properly.

This example uses the noscript.html file found on the book's CD-ROM (or which you may have created in the section "Present Content to Non-JavaScript Browsers"), but you can apply these steps to any file.

ADD COMMENTS TO JAVASCRIPT

```
<html>
<head>
</head>
<body>
  <script language="javascript">
    //The next JavaScript statement will set the page color to blue.
    document.bgcolor = "blue";
    /*The next JavaScript statement will output the HTML tags and text
      to the browser.*/
    document.write("<h1>Hesitation Kills</h1>");
  </script>
  <noscript>
    This web page uses JavaScript. To see the full page, make sure that
    JavaScript is enabled.
  </noscript>
</body>
</html>
```

1 Open the noscript.html file in Notepad.

2 Add a single-line comment in front of the first JavaScript statement.

3 Add a multiple-line comment in front of the second JavaScript statement.

4 Save the file as comments.html.

5 Open the comments.html file in a browser.

■ Notice how the comments added to the file don't appear in the browser.

Apply It

Many scripts can benefit from an explanatory header. This header can include information about the script, including the author, the date, and a description of what the script does. Such a header could be marked as a comment block like so:

```
/* Personalize Script

developed by KLM on May 16, 2000

description: The purpose of this
script  is to accept the user's name
using a prompt box, save the name in
a variable, and display the name to
the browser as part of a welcome
message. */
```

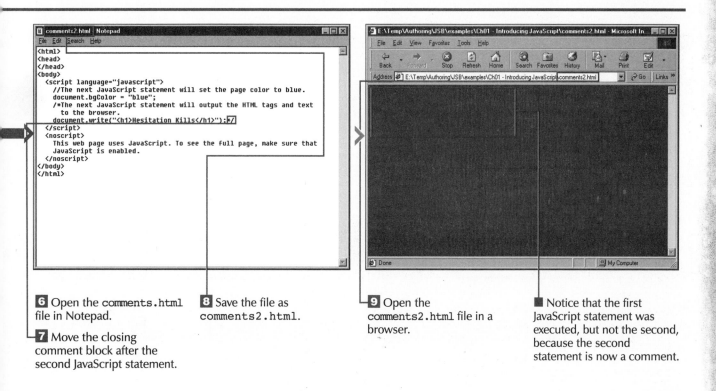

6 Open the comments.html file in Notepad.

7 Move the closing comment block after the second JavaScript statement.

8 Save the file as comments2.html.

9 Open the comments2.html file in a browser.

■ Notice that the first JavaScript statement was executed, but not the second, because the second statement is now a comment.

UNDERSTAND VARIABLE TYPES

One of the first concepts that you need to understand in JavaScript is how to work with *variables*. Variables are like a temporary holding container for values. As values change, the variable can be updated to hold the new value.

Variables can also hold *constant values.* Constant values are values that don't change. For example, you could create a variable named `hoursPerDay` and set it to `24`; within your code, you can refer to the number of hours per day using the variable `hoursPerDay`. Although simply typing the value `24` in the code would be easier, if you use a variable, the equation will have meaning when you examine it. Using variables to hold constants thus makes debugging and working with your code easier.

Variable names must meet several requirements. For example, `24` is not a good variable name because it is easily confused with a value. Variable names can include upper- and lowercase letters, numbers, and the underscore character (_). No other punctuation marks may be used. Variable names must not begin with a number and cannot include any spaces.

Variable names in JavaScript are case-sensitive. So, the variable names `Hello`, `hello`, and `HeLLo` are all different. It's a good idea to use variable names that describe the data they hold. If you consistently name variables, understanding your code when you look at it later will be easier. For example, you could consistently capitalize all constant values as a way of identifying that they will not change.

Several different types of variables exist, depending on the type of data that they hold. The various variable types can hold an assortment of numbers and words as values. Specifically, these types include the following:

- Integer numbers
- Floating-point numbers
- String
- Boolean

A good coding technique is to start the variable names with a letter that indicates the type of variable. This technique helps as you work with the code. For example, an integer variable would be named `iVar`, a floating-point variable would be `fVar`, a string variable would be `sVar`, and a Boolean variable would be `bVar`. This technique for naming variables isn't required, only suggested.

TYPES OF VARIABLES

INTEGER VARIABLES

Integer variables can hold the basic counting numbers, either positive or negative. These values can be operated on using arithmetic operators such as addition, subtraction, multiplication, and division.

Examples of integer values include 2, 345, and -34.

FLOATING-POINT VARIABLES

Floating-point variables can hold fractional numbers that include a decimal point. These variables can also be used with the standard arithmetic operators.

Examples of floating-point values include 2.5, -34.56, and 3.121.

STRING VARIABLES

String variables are simply words and sentences. These variables can hold single characters or entire paragraphs. String values are usually designated with a set of quotation marks.

Examples of string values include `"hello"`, `"abc"`, and `"This is a test"`.

BOOLEAN VARIABLES

Boolean variables are a unique variable type that can hold only the words *true* or *false*. These variables can be used to test the condition of a statement. The number `0` is also used to represent the value `false`, and `1` represents the value `true`.

DECLARE VARIABLES

JavaScript is a *loosely typed* language. This means that you don't need to explicitly declare each variable type, and different variable types can be combined without an error.

Being a loosely typed language also means that you don't need to specify the variable type when creating a new variable. All you need to do is type a variable name, and its type is automatically set based on the type of value it holds.

You can also specifically state variable names using the `var` keyword. This keyword, when placed in front of a variable name, identifies it as a variable. You can declare several variables at once by separating them with commas.

For example, `var int1, int2, str1, str2` declares four variables.

This example uses the `js-skeleton.html` file found on the book's CD-ROM, but you can apply these steps to any file.

DECLARE VARIABLES

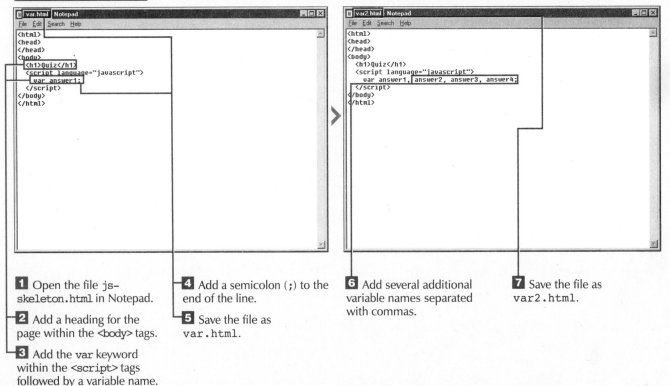

1 Open the file `js-skeleton.html` in Notepad.

2 Add a heading for the page within the <body> tags.

3 Add the `var` keyword within the <script> tags followed by a variable name.

4 Add a semicolon (;) to the end of the line.

5 Save the file as `var.html`.

6 Add several additional variable names separated with commas.

7 Save the file as `var2.html`.

ASSIGN VALUES TO VARIABLES

After a variable is declared, you can assign values to it using the equals sign (=). The value should always be placed on the right side of the equals sign with the variable name on the left.

For example, the statement `temp1 = 56;` places the value 56 within the variable named `temp1`. You can then refer to this value at any time using the `temp1` variable name.

Strings can be assigned to a variable name if they are included in quotation marks (" "). Any string without quotation marks is considered a variable name.

For example, the statement `str1 = "Hello Everybody";` places the string "Hello Everybody" in the variable `str1`.

This example uses the `var.html` and `var2.html` files found on the book's CD-ROM (or which you may have created in the section "Declare Variables"), but you can apply these steps to any file.

ASSIGN VALUES TO VARIABLES

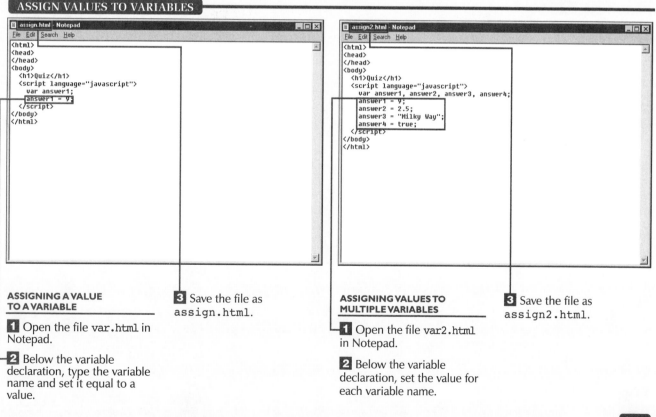

ASSIGNING A VALUE TO A VARIABLE

1 Open the file `var.html` in Notepad.

2 Below the variable declaration, type the variable name and set it equal to a value.

3 Save the file as `assign.html`.

ASSIGNING VALUES TO MULTIPLE VARIABLES

1 Open the file `var2.html` in Notepad.

2 Below the variable declaration, set the value for each variable name.

3 Save the file as `assign2.html`.

USING INTEGERS

Integers are values without a decimal point. These are typically referred to as the "counting numbers" and may be either positive or negative. Negative integer values have a minus sign (–) in front of them.

Integer values may be either decimal, hexadecimal, or octal. The difference between these types is the base of the number system. *Decimal* integers are base 10. *Hexadecimal* integers are base 16 with the numbers above 9

being represented with the letters *a–f*. *Hexadecimal* integers have a 0x in front of them. Octal integers are base 8 and include a leading 0.

For example, 24 is a decimal number, 024 is an octal number, and 0x24 is a hexadecimal number.

This example uses the js-skeleton.html file found on the book's CD-ROM, but you can apply these steps to any file.

USING INTEGERS

1 Open the js-skeleton.html file in Notepad.

2 Within the <script> tags, declare three variables with the var keyword.

3 Set each variable name to a value.

4 Use document.write statements to display the values of each variable.

5 Save the file as integer.html.

6 Open the integer.html file in a browser.

■ The variable values are displayed. Notice how each value is displayed as its decimal equivalent.

USING FLOATING-POINT NUMBERS

Floating-point values are fractional numbers that include a decimal point. These numbers can be either positive or negative.

Very large or very small numbers can be expressed in scientific notation. Scientific notation places the letter *E* within the number followed by the number of places the decimal point is moved. Positive values move the decimal to the right, and negative values move the decimal to the left.

For example, 5.14E6 represents the number 5,140,000, and 6.023E-4 represents the number 0.0006023.

This example uses the `js-skeleton.html` file found on the book's CD-ROM, but you can apply these steps to any file.

Extra

It depends on the size of a floating-point number whether it is displayed in scientific notation. Floating-point numbers that are smaller than 1.0E-7 are displayed in scientific notation, but large numbers can be as large as 1.0E20 before being displayed in scientific notation.

USING FLOATING-POINT NUMBERS

```
<html>
<head>
</head>
<body>
  <script language="javascript">
    var largeNum, veryLargeNum, smallNum, verySmallNum;
    largeNum = 123456789000000000000.0;
    veryLargeNum = 5.14e52;
    smallNum = 0.000000123;
    verySmallNum = 6.023e-23;
    document.write("This is a large number: " + largeNum + "<br>");
    document.write("This is a very large number: " + veryLargeNum + "<br>");
    document.write("This is a small number: " + smallNum + "<br>");
    document.write("This is a very small number: " + verySmallNum + "<br>");
  </script>
</body>
</html>
```

This is a large number: 1.23456789e+21
This is a very large number: 5.14e+52
This is a small number: 1.23e-7
This is a very small number: 6.023e-23

1 Open the js-skeleton.html file in Notepad.

2 Within the <script> tags, declare four variables with the var keyword.

3 Set each variable name to floating-point values, two large and two small.

4 Use document.write statements to display the values of each variable.

5 Save the file as floating-point.html.

6 Open the floating-point.html file in a browser.

■ The variable values are displayed. Notice how some of them are displayed in scientific notation.

USING BOOLEANS

Boolean values can be either `true` or `false`. In addition to the actual words, the values can be set to 0 or 1 with 0 representing `false` and 1 representing `true`.

Because Boolean values can only be `true` or `false`, they make good conditional statements. A conditional statement can be used to determine the flow of the program.

In Chapter 4, program-flow statements like `if-else` are introduced. Boolean variables work very well for these statements. For example, for a Boolean variable named `finished`, the statement `if (finished`

`== "true")` can be used to control whether one set of statements gets executed or another. You can also just use the Boolean variable name such as `if (finished)`.

This example uses the `var2.html` file found on the book's CD-ROM (or which you may have created in the section "Declare Variables"), but you can apply these steps to any file.

USING BOOLEANS

1 Open the `var2.html` file in Notepad.

2 Within the `<script>` tags, assign Boolean values to each variable.

3 Use `document.write` statements to display the values of each variable.

4 Save the file as `boolean.html`.

5 Open the `boolean.html` file in a browser.

■ The variable values are displayed.

USING STRINGS

tring values are composed of words and characters specified within a set of quotation marks.

Strings can be contained within single quotation marks (') or within double-quotation marks ("), but the beginning and ending marks must be the same.

If you want to include quotation marks within the string value, you should include the backslash symbol (\) in front of the quotation mark. This causes the quotation mark to be displayed. You can also use the backslash symbol to display backslash characters in the string.

For example, if a string is assigned to a variable like this, `str1 = "\"Hello, my name is Waldo.\""`, the quotation marks surround the string value.

When string values are displayed using the `document.write()` method, the text is displayed in the browser and is subject to the HTML display engine. This means that you can include HTML tags within your string values and they will be interpreted and used to display the text in the browser.

This example uses the `js-skeleton.html` file found on the book's CD-ROM, but you can apply these steps to any file.

USING STRINGS

```
<html>
<head>
</head>
<body>
  <script language="javascript">
  var str1, str2;
  str1 = "Why did the chicken cross the road?<br>";
  str2 = 'Because there weren\'t any connecting flights.<br>';
  document.write(str1);
  document.write(str2);
  </script>
</body>
</html>
```

Why did the chicken cross the road?
Because there weren't any connecting flights.

1 Open the js-skeleton.html file in Notepad.

2 Within the <script> tags, declare two variables with the var keyword.

3 Set each variable name to a string value.

4 Use document.write statements to display the values of each variable.

5 Save the file as string.html.

6 Open the string.html file in a browser.

■ The string values are displayed.

DETERMINE VARIABLE TYPE

Variables are often combined with one another. For example, if you include an equation within your code, two variables are combined to produce a result. If you try to combine two variables that are different types, you may run into trouble. In cases like this, you may want to determine the variables' type.

JavaScript includes a keyword that you can use to check a variable's type — typeof. When the typeof keyword is placed in front of a variable name, the variable type is returned as a string.

When the typeof keyword is placed in front of a variable, it returns number for integer and

floating-point variables, string for string variables, boolean for Boolean variables, and undefined if the variable type cannot be determined.

For example, if the variable int1 is assigned to 24, the statement typeof int1; would return number.

This example uses the assign2.html and var2.html files found on the book's CD-ROM (or which you may have created in the sections "Assign Values to Variables" and "Declare Variables"), but you can apply these steps to any file.

DETERMINE VARIABLE TYPE

```
typeof.html - Notepad
File Edit Search Help
<html>
<head>
</head>
<body>
  <h1>Quiz</h1>
  <script language="javascript">
  var answer1, answer2, answer3, answer4;
  answer1 = 9;
  answer2 = 2.5;
  answer3 = "Milky Way";
  answer4 = true;
  document.write(answer1 + " is of type: " + typeof answer1 + "<br>");
  document.write(answer2 + " is of type: " + typeof answer2 + "<br>");
  document.write(answer3 + " is of type: " + typeof answer3 + "<br>");
  document.write(answer4 + " is of type: " + typeof answer4 + "<br>");
  </script>
</body>
</html>
```

E:\Temp\Authoring\JSB\examples\Ch02 - Using Variables and Arrays\typeof.html - Microsoft Int...
File Edit View Favorites Tools Help
Back Forward Stop Refresh Home Search Favorites History Mail Print Edit
Address E:\Temp\Authoring\JSB\examples\Ch02 - Using Variables and Arrays\typeof.html

Quiz

9 is of type: number
2.5 is of type: number
Milky Way is of type: string
true is of type: boolean

Done — My Computer

1 Open the assign2.html file in Notepad.

2 Use document.write statements to display the values of each variable.

3 Add the typeof keyword to each document.write statement followed by the variable name.

4 Save the file as typeof.html.

5 Open the typeof.html file in a browser.

■ The variable type for each variable is displayed.

Extra

The `typeof` keyword can also be used to identify other types of elements: objects, forms, and functions. Each form, function, and object has a name. Using the `typeof` keyword with these names returns the element's type.

If the `undefined` value is returned as a result of the `typeof` keyword, the variable doesn't exist or hasn't been defined yet. If you misspell the variable name, it isn't recognized and the `undefined` value is returned. Another case in which the `undefined` value is returned is if you use `typeof` before the variable gets assigned a value: If the `typeof` keyword appears in the script before the variable or function is encountered, the `typeof` keyword returns `undefined`.

DETERMINE UNASSIGNED VARIABLES

```
typeof2.html - Notepad
File  Edit  Search  Help
<html>
<head>
</head>
<body>
  <h1>Quiz</h1>
  <script language="javascript">
    var answer1, answer2, answer3, answer4;
    document.write(answer1 + " is of type: " + typeof answer1 + "<br>");
    document.write(answer2 + " is of type: " + typeof answer2 + "<br>");
    document.write(answer3 + " is of type: " + typeof answer3 + "<br>");
    document.write(answer4 + " is of type: " + typeof answer4 + "<br>");
  </script>
</body>
</html>
```

E:\Temp\Authoring\JSB\examples\Ch02 - Using Variables and Arrays\typeof2.html - Microsoft I...

File Edit View Favorites Tools Help

Back Forward Stop Refresh Home Search Favorites History Mail Print Edit

Address E:\Temp\Authoring\JSB\examples\Ch02 - Using Variables and Arrays\typeof2.html

Quiz

undefined is of type: undefined
undefined is of type: undefined
undefined is of type: undefined
undefined is of type: undefined

Done   My Computer

1 Open the `var2.html` file in Notepad.

2 Use `document.write` statements to display the type of each unassigned variable.

3 Save the file as `typeof2.html`.

4 Open the file `typeof2.html` in a browser.

■ The variable type for each unassigned variable is displayed as undefined.

CONVERT STRINGS TO NUMBERS

Before you can perform arithmetic operations between numbers, you have to make sure that you are dealing with number variable types and not strings. If a number is included within quotes when it is assigned to a variable, it is a string and not a number, which will cause problems if you try to add this number to another number.

JavaScript includes a couple of functions that can be used to strip the numbers off the front of a string and convert them to a number variable type.

Strings that begin with numbers can be converted into a number variable type using `parseInt()` for integers and `parseFloat()` for floating-point numbers. The variable name that holds the string should be placed within the parentheses.

For example, to convert the string "256" in the variable named `temp` to a number, you use the `parseInt(temp);` statement.

This example uses the `js-skeleton.html` file found on the book's CD-ROM, but you can apply these steps to any file.

CONVERT STRINGS WITH INTEGERS TO NUMBERS

parseint.html - Notepad

```
<html>
<head>
</head>
<body>
    <script language="javascript">
    var str1 = "31 days in January";
    var int1 = parseInt(str1);
    document.write(str1 + " is of type: " + typeof str1 + "<br>");
    document.write(int1 + " is of type: " + typeof int1 + "<br>");
    </script>
</body>
</html>
```

E:\Temp\Authoring\JSB\examples\Ch02 - Using Variables and Arrays\parseint.html - Microsoft I...

Address: E:\Temp\Authoring\JSB\examples\Ch02 - Using Variables and Arrays\parseint.html

31 days in January is of type: string
31 is of type: number

■1 Open the js-skeleton.html file in Notepad.

■2 Add two new variables and assign the first one to be a string that starts with a number.

■3 Use the `parseInt()` function to convert the string to a number.

■4 Use `document.write` statements to display the values and type of each variable.

■5 Save the file as parseint.html.

■6 Open the file parseint.html in a browser.

■ The variable type for each variable is displayed.

Extra

If the variable starts with a character that isn't a number, the `parseInt()` function returns `NaN`, which stands for "not a number."

JavaScript includes a simple method that can determine if a variable is a number. The `isNaN()` function returns `true` if the variable is "not a number" or `false` if it is.

A string value can be assigned to a variable and later an integer value assigned to the same variable without causing an error: Because JavaScript is loosely scripted, you can assign different values to a variable at any time without an error.

CONVERT STRINGS WITH FLOATING POINT VALUES TO NUMBERS

```
parsefloat.html - Notepad
File  Edit  Search  Help
<html>
<head>
</head>
<body>
  <script language="javascript">
    var str1 = "6.23E-23";
    var float1 = parseFloat(str1);
    document.write(str1 + " is of type: " + typeof str1 + "<br>");
    document.write(float1 + " is of type: " + typeof float1 + "<br>");
  </script>
</body>
</html>
```

```
E:\Temp\Authoring\JSB\examples\Ch02 - Using Variables and Arrays\parsefloat.html - Microsof...
File  Edit  View  Favorites  Tools  Help
Back    Forward    Stop    Refresh    Home    Search    Favorites    History    Mail    Print    Edit
Address  E:\Temp\Authoring\JSB\examples\Ch02 - Using Variables and Arrays\parsefloat.html    Go    Links

6.23E-23 is of type: string
6.23e-23 is of type: number

Done                                                          My Computer
```

■ Open the js-skeleton.html file in Notepad.

2 Add two new variables and assign the first one to be a string that starts with a floating-point number.

3 Use the `parseFloat()` function to convert the string to a number.

4 Use `document.write` statements to display the values and type of each variable.

5 Save the file as `parsefloat.html`.

6 Open `parsefloat.html` in a browser.

■ The variable type for each variable is displayed.

CONVERT NUMBERS TO STRINGS

In Chapter 9, many string-specific methods are covered, such as formatting strings and working with substrings. If these methods are used with a variable that contains a number instead of a string, they will result in an error. If you convert a variable containing numbers to a string, however, these methods will work.

Numbers can be easily converted to strings by adding quotation marks or a space in front of the number. For example, if a variable named temp1 holds the value 36, the statement `""` + temp1; would automatically convert temp to a string.

Another way to convert numbers to strings is with the `toString()` method. To use this method, you simply need to attach the method name to the end of the variable name with a period in between. For example, to convert a variable named temp2 holding the value 36 to a string, you can use the statement `temp2.toString();`.

This example uses the `js-skeleton.html` file found on the book's CD-ROM, but you can apply these steps to any file.

ADD A SPACE BEFORE THE NUMBER

```
tostring.html - Notepad
File  Edit  Search  Help
<html>
<head>
</head>
<body>
  <script language="javascript">
    var int1 = 256;
    var str1 = "" + int1;
    document.write(int1 + " is of type: " + typeof int1 + "<br>");
    document.write(str1 + " is of type: " + typeof str1 + "<br>");
  </script>
</body>
</html>
```

```
256 is of type: number
256 is of type: string
```

1 Open the js-skeleton.html file in Notepad.

2 Add two new variables and assign the first one to be a number.

3 Convert the second variable to a string by adding it to "".

4 Use document.write statements to display the values and type of each variable.

5 Save the file as tostring.html.

6 Open tostring.html in a browser.

■ The variable type for each variable is displayed.

Extra

If the toString() method is used with a variable that already holds a string value, nothing happens and the resulting variable is a string.

Variables can be changed at any time between strings and numbers, so you can convert variables from a number to a string and back several times. But remember that some string information may be truncated using the parseInt() and parseFloat() functions.

Converting a number to a string by adding quote marks in front of it is a quick trick, but the more correct way to convert a number to a string is to use the toString() method. Using this method makes it easy to spot exactly what you are doing, and it is good code practice.

USING THE TOSTRING() METHOD

```
tostring2.html - Notepad
File Edit Search Help
<html>
<head>
</head>
<body>
  <script language="javascript">
    var int1 = 256;
    var str1 = int1.toString();
    document.write(int1 + " is of type: " + typeof int1 + "<br>");
    document.write(str1 + " is of type: " + typeof str1 + "<br>");
  </script>
</body>
</html>
```

```
E:\Temp\Authoring\JSB\examples\Ch02 - Using Variables and Arrays\tostring2.html - Microsoft ...
File Edit View Favorites Tools Help
Back  Forward  Stop  Refresh  Home  Search  Favorites  History  Mail  Print  Edit
Address E:\Temp\Authoring\JSB\examples\Ch02 - Using Variables and Arrays\tostring2.html    Go  Links

256 is of type number
256 is of type string

Done                                    My Computer
```

1 Open the js-skeleton.html file in Notepad.

2 Add two new variables and assign the first one to be a number.

3 Change the second variable to a string by using the toString() method.

4 Use document.write statements to display the values and type of each variable.

5 Save the file as tostring2.html.

6 Open tostring2.html in a browser.

■ The variable type for each variable is displayed.

27

DECLARE AN ARRAY

Several variables can be grouped together as a numbered index called an *array*. All variables within the array are referenced with the same name, but have a different index value. The index number is placed after the array name in square brackets ([]).

Arrays can be created by assigning a variable name to new Array() where the number of elements in the array are included within the parentheses.

After an array is created, you can reference individual elements of the array using the array name followed by the index number in square brackets. Array index values always start with 0.

For example, array1 = new Array(10) would create an array that can hold ten values. The first element would be array1[0] and the final element of the array would be array1[9].

This example uses the js-skeleton.html file found on the book's CD-ROM, but you can apply these steps to any file.

CREATE AN ARRAY OF STRING VARIABLES

1 Open the js-skeleton.html file in Notepad.

2 Add a new variable name and assign it to new Array() with the number of elements in the array within the parentheses.

3 Assign each array element to a string.

4 Use a document.write statement to display the value of each array element.

5 Save the file as array.html.

6 Open array.html in a browser.

■ A string made from all the individual array elements is displayed.

Extra

All the elements of a JavaScript array don't have to contain the same variable type. The elements of an array can hold several different types of variables. For example, the first element in an array could be an integer, the second element could be a string, and the third element could be a floating-point number. Each array element is independent of the other elements. However, if you try to multiply array elements of different types, an error occurs.

JavaScript supports two-dimensional arrays. You can create a *two-dimensional array* by creating an array of an array. The way this works is to create a single one-dimensional array and then to create an array of the existing array. It can be confusing when you try to refer to an array of an array, but for the right application, it is worth the effort.

CREATE AN ARRAY OF INTEGER VARIABLES

array2.htm - Notepad

File Edit Search Help

```
<html>
<head>
</head>
<body>
  <script language="javascript">
    primeNum = new Array(5);
    primeNum[0] = 1;
    primeNum[1] = 3;
    primeNum[2] = 5;
    primeNum[3] = 7;
    primeNum[4] = 11;
    document.write("Prime Numbers: " + primeNum[0] + " " + primeNum[1] + " "
+ primeNum[2] + " " + primeNum[3] + " " + primeNum[4]);
  </script>
</body>
</html>
```

E:\Temp\Authoring\JSB\examples\Ch02 - Using Variables and Arrays\array2.html - Microsoft Int...

File Edit View Favorites Tools Help

Back Forward Stop Refresh Home Search Favorites History Mail Print Edit

Address E:\Temp\Authoring\JSB\examples\Ch02 - Using Variables and Arrays\array2.htm

Prime Numbers: 1 3 5 7 11

Done   My Computer

1 Open the js-skeleton.html file in Notepad.

2 Add a new variable name and assign it to new Array() with the number of elements in the array within the parentheses.

3 Assign each array element to an integer.

4 Use a document.write statement to display the value of each array element.

5 Save the file as array2.html.

6 Open array2.html in a browser.

■ The value contained within each array element is displayed.

29

DETERMINE THE NUMBER OF ELEMENTS OF AN ARRAY

I f an array is created and filled with elements as the script is executed, you may lose track of the number of elements contained within the array. Knowing the number of elements contained within the array tells you how often you need to loop through the array in order to process all the data in the array.

An array is an object. Objects include properties that describe them and methods, which can execute a built-in function specific to the object. Chapter 7 covers objects in more detail.

The `array` object includes a property named `length` that can be used to return the number of elements in an array. The `length` property is a statement just like a variable. It is created by placing the `length` property name with a period after the array name. For example, if an array named `array1` is declared, the length of the property can be returned using the `array1.length` statement.

This example uses the `array.html` and `js-skeleton.html` files found on the book's CD-ROM, but you can apply these steps to any file.

DETERMINE THE LENGTH OF A PREDEFINED ARRAY

```
length.htm - Notepad
<html>
<head>
</head>
<body>
  <script language="javascript">
    array1 = new Array(5);
    array1[0] = "I challenge ";
    array1[1] = "you ";
    array1[2] = "to engage in ";
    array1[3] = "random acts ";
    array1[4] = "of kindness.";
    document.write(array1[0],array1[1],array1[2],array1[3],array1[4] +
"<br/>");
    document.write("This array includes " + array1.length + " elements.");
  </script>
</body>
</html>
```

D:\JSB\examples\Ch02 - Using Variables and Arrays\length.html - Microsoft Internet Explorer

I challenge you to engage in random acts of kindness.
This array includes 5 elements.

1 Open the `array.html` file in Notepad.

2 Add + "<br/>" `document.write` statement to add a line break.

3 Add a new `document.write` statement to display the length of the array.

4 Save the file as `length.html`.

5 Open `length.html` in a browser.

■ The browser displays the number of elements in the array.

Extra

What happens if the array elements are filled intermittently depends on whether the array size is specified. If the array size is specified, the `length` property always returns the specified size. This is the number of places of memory that has been set aside for the array. If the size isn't specified, the `length` property is determined by the array element with the greatest index value. For example, if only the second and fourth elements of an array are filled, the `length` property will identify four elements in the array even if the first and third elements contain no data.

The `length` property is a read-only property, which means that it can return information about the object, but it cannot be used to set the object's property. The `length` property, therefore, cannot be used to set an array's size.

DETERMINE THE NUMBER OF ELEMENTS IN AN ARRAY

```
length2.html - Notepad
File  Edit  Search  Help
<html>
<head>
</head>
<body>
    <script language="javascript">
    array1 = new Array();
    array1[0] = "bark";
    array1[1] = "apple";
    array1[2] = "nebula";
    document.write(array1[0],array1[1],array1[2] + "<br/>");
    document.write("This array includes " + array1.length + " elements.");
    </script>
</body>
</html>
```

```
D:\JSB\examples\Ch02 - Using Variables and Arrays\length2.html - Microsoft Internet Explorer -...
File  Edit  View  Favorites  Tools  Help
Back   Forward   Stop   Refresh   Home   Search   Favorites   History   Mail   Print   Links
Address  D:\JSB\examples\Ch02 - Using Variables and Arrays\length2.html           Go

barkapplenebula
This array includes 3 elements.

Done                                                    My Computer
```

1 Open the `js-skeleton.html` file in Notepad.

2 Add a new variable name and assign it to `new Array()` without specifying the number of elements in the array.

3 Assign several array elements a value.

4 Use `document.write` statements to display the array values and the number of array elements.

5 Save the file as `length2.html`.

6 Open `length2.html` in a browser.

■ The number of array elements is displayed.

CONVERT AN ARRAY INTO A STRING

Arrays can be large and can contain many different elements. To display all the elements of an array, you may find it easiest to convert the array to a string.

The `array` object includes a method that converts the array elements to a string. This method is `join()`. The `join()` method accepts a single string as a parameter. This string is inserted between each separate array element as it is converted to a string. The default separator is a comma (`,`), but you can use a different separator if you specify one. For example, if you have an array of numbers called `array1`, the statement `str1 = array1.join(" ")` places a space between each array element (instead of a comma). The variable `str1` will then contain a string of numbers with a space placed between each element.

This example uses the `js-skeleton.html` file found on the book's CD-ROM, but you can apply these steps to any file.

CONVERT AN ARRAY TO A STRING

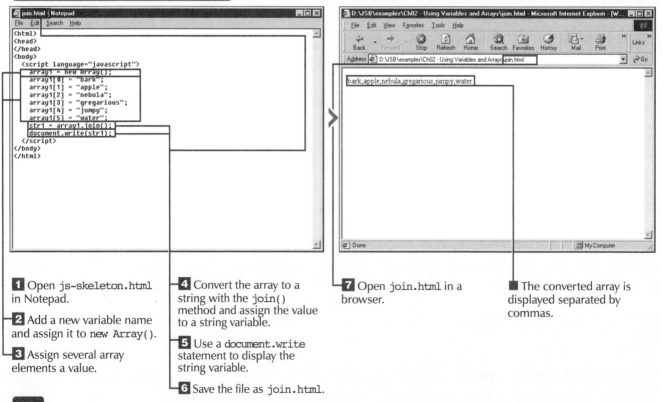

1 Open `js-skeleton.html` in Notepad.

2 Add a new variable name and assign it to `new Array()`.

3 Assign several array elements a value.

4 Convert the array to a string with the `join()` method and assign the value to a string variable.

5 Use a `document.write` statement to display the string variable.

6 Save the file as `join.html`.

7 Open `join.html` in a browser.

■ The converted array is displayed separated by commas.

Apply It

Large arrays can be difficult to search through to find specific pieces of data. An easier way to search through an array is to convert the entire array to a single string and then use the `indexOf()` method to locate the specific data:.

```
Example:

array1 = new Array("hello",
"123", "senior", "blank",
"fixed");

str1 = array1.join(" ");

beginChar = str1.indexOf("123");
```

These statements declare an array of elements, convert the array of elements into a string called `str1`, and then set the variable `beginChar` equal to the position in the string where the value `"123"` starts. Using these statements, you can locate specific elements within the array. After you locate these elements, you can parse out the data by using other `string` object methods. Chapter 9 covers `string` object methods in detail.

SPECIFY A UNIQUE SEPARATOR

```
join2.html - Notepad
File Edit Search Help
<html>
<head>
</head>
<body>
  <script language="javascript">
    array1 = new Array();
    array1[0] = "bark";
    array1[1] = "apple";
    array1[2] = "nebula";
    array1[3] = "gregarious";
    array1[4] = "jumpy";
    array1[5] = "water";
    str1 = array1.join(" ");
    document.write(str1);
  </script>
</body>
</html>
```

D:\JSB\examples\Ch02 - Using Variables and Arrays\join2.html - Microsoft Internet Explorer

Address: D:\JSB\examples\Ch02 - Using Variables and Arrays\join2.html

bark apple nebula gregarious jumpy water

1 Open the `join.html` file in Notepad.

2 Add a string with a space as a parameter to the `join()` method.

Note: In Step 2, you are specifying to use a space as a separator rather than the default comma, so a space will appear in between each array element.

3 Save the file as `join2.html`.

4 Open `join2.html` in a browser.

■ The converted array is displayed separated by spaces.

SORT AN ARRAY

An array full of elements can be converted to a string using the `join()` method, as shown in the section "Convert an Array into a String." The `array` object also includes another method that sorts the array elements in ascending alphabetical order before converting them into strings — `sort()`.

For example, if you have an array of words named `array1`, you can sort the words and convert them to a string using the `str1 = array1.sort()` statement.

When the `sort()` method is used on an array of numbers, the numbers are sorted alphabetically instead of in numerical order. For example, an array containing 1, 2, 10, 12 would be sorted as 1, 10, 12, 2.

This example uses the `join.html` file found on the book's CD-ROM (or which you may have created in the section "Convert an Array into a String"), but you can apply these steps to any file.

SORT AN ARRAY OF WORDS

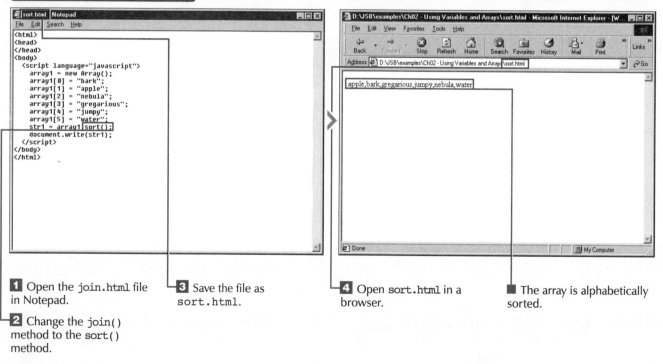

1 Open the `join.html` file in Notepad.

2 Change the `join()` method to the `sort()` method.

3 Save the file as `sort.html`.

4 Open `sort.html` in a browser.

■ The array is alphabetically sorted.

Apply It

The sort() method can accept a function name as a parameter. The function name can contain an alternative way to sort the array. This parameter can be used to sort an array of numbers numerically instead of alphabetically. The statements for this would look like this:

```
function numSort(var1, var2) {

    return var1 - var2;

}

array1 = new Array("1", "2",
"12", "34", "72");

str1 = array1.sort(numSort);
```

When the sort() method is executed, the function numSort is called. This function accepts two parameters and returns the difference between them. This difference is used by the sort() method to sort the numbers in numerical order. As the sort() method traverses the array elements, the numSort function is called as often as needed to complete the sorting.

SORT AN ARRAY OF NUMBERS

```
sort2.html - Notepad
File  Edit  Search  Help
<html>
<head>
</head>
<body>
  <script language="javascript">
    array1 = new Array();
    array1[0] = "1";
    array1[1] = "10";
    array1[2] = "160";
    array1[3] = "101";
    array1[4] = "2";
    array1[5] = "23";
    str1 = array1.sort();
    document.write(str1);
  </script>
</body>
</html>
```

D:\JSB\examples\Ch02 - Using Variables and Arrays\sort2.html - Microsoft Internet Explorer - [...
File Edit View Favorites Tools Help

Back Forward Stop Refresh Home Search Favorites History Mail Print   Links

Address D:\JSB\examples\Ch02 - Using Variables and Arrays\sort2.html

1,10,101,160,2,23

Done   My Computer

1 Open the sort.html file in Notepad.

2 Change the array elements from strings to numbers.

3 Save the file as sort2.html.

4 Open sort2.html in a browser.

■ The array is sorted, but not in numerical order.

USING ARITHMETIC OPERATORS

Expressions are used to compose mathematical equations. These equations can compute a desired result, which can then be displayed in a browser.

Expressions are created with variables or literals on either side of an operator. Literals can be numerical or string values.

The easiest expressions to create use arithmetic operators. The four standard arithmetic operators are addition (+), subtraction (–), multiplication (*), and division (/). These operators only work if the variables on both sides of the operator are numbers. However, the addition operator can also be used to combine strings.

The subtraction operator can be used as a negation operator if it is placed in front of a variable or number. For example, `temp1 = -var1;` makes the value of `var1` negative and places the result in `temp1`.

Another less popular arithmetic operator is the *modulus operator* (%). This operator returns the value of the remainder after dividing two numbers. For example, `11%5` would return a value of 1, because 5 goes into 11 two times with a remainder of 1.

This example uses the `js-skeleton.html` file found on the book's CD-ROM, but you can apply these steps to any file.

USING ARITHMETIC OPERATORS

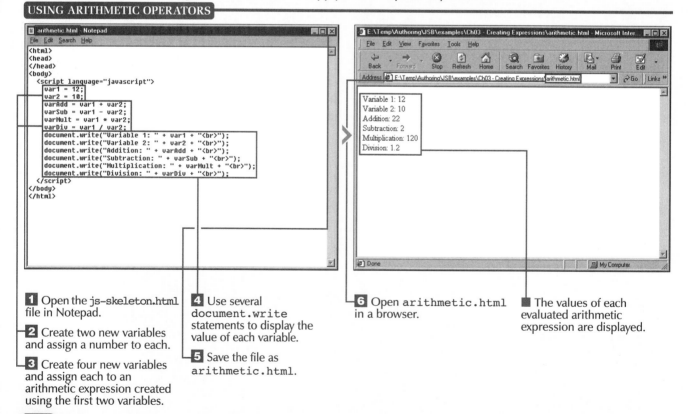

1 Open the js-skeleton.html file in Notepad.

2 Create two new variables and assign a number to each.

3 Create four new variables and assign each to an arithmetic expression created using the first two variables.

4 Use several document.write statements to display the value of each variable.

5 Save the file as arithmetic.html.

6 Open arithmetic.html in a browser.

■ The values of each evaluated arithmetic expression are displayed.

Extra

The addition operator can be used to combine strings, but all other arithmetic operators return a NaN value if they are used on strings. NaN stands for "not a number." If the string is a number and it doesn't include any letters, JavaScript automatically converts the string to a number and evaluates the expression. See Chapter 9 for more details on using strings.

You can define a factorial as subtracting one from the current value and multiplying it times the result. For example, 3 factorial would be $3 \times 2 \times 1$ for a result of 6. A function to compute factorials would look like this:

```
function factorial(num) {
    for (j=num;j>0;j—)
        result *= num;
    return result
}
```

This function uses several expressions to evaluate the factorial result. The result is then returned.

USING THE MODULUS OPERATOR

```
<html>
<head>
</head>
<body>
    <script language="javascript">
        var1 = 12;
        var2 = 10;
        varAdd = var1 + var2;
        varSub = var1 – var2;
        varMult = var1 * var2;
        varDiv = var1 / var2;
        varMod = var1 % var2;
        document.write("Variable 1: " + var1 + "<br>");
        document.write("Variable 2: " + var2 + "<br>");
        document.write("Addition: " + varAdd + "<br>");
        document.write("Subtraction: " + varSub + "<br>");
        document.write("Multiplication: " + varMult + "<br>");
        document.write("Division: " + varDiv + "<br>");
        document.write("Modulus: " + varMod + "<br>");
    </script>
</body>
</html>
```

Variable 1: 12
Variable 2: 10
Addition: 22
Subtraction: 2
Multiplication: 120
Division: 1.2
Modulus: 2

1 Open the arithmetic.html file in Notepad.

2 Create a new variable and assign it to a modulus expression using the first two variables.

3 Use a document.write statement to display the value of the modulus expression.

4 Save the file as modulus.html.

5 Open the file modulus.html in a browser.

■ The value of the modulus expression is displayed.

INCREMENT AND DECREMENT VARIABLES

One of the simplest expressions to create is one that increments or decrements a variable. Incrementing expressions are useful as counters and for loops.

Variables can be incremented by adding 1 with the variable and assigning it to the same variable like this, var = var + 1. JavaScript, however, offers an easier way to increment values with two plus symbols (++) attached to the variable.

For example, var++ automatically increases the value of the variable named var when evaluated.

Variables can in a like manner be decremented using two minus signs (--). This character set causes the variable to be decreased by 1. For example, var-- automatically reduces the value of var by 1.

The increment and decrement operators are both *unary operators,* which means that they require only a single operand instead of two like the arithmetic operators.

This example uses the js-skeleton.html file found on the book's CD-ROM, but you can apply these steps to any file.

INCREMENT VARIABLES

1 Open js-skeleton.html in Notepad.

2 Create a new variable and assign it a number.

3 Use a document.write statement to display the value of the variable.

4 Increment the variable with the ++ symbols.

5 Add another document.write statement to again display the value of each variable.

6 Save the file as inc.html.

7 Open inc.html in a browser.

■ The values of each variable are displayed before and after the increment and decrement expressions.

Extra

The increment or decrement operator doesn't always have to follow the variable: The increment or decrement operator can come before or after the variable, but subtle differences distinguish the two when used with an assignment operator (=). If the increment or decrement operator comes before the variable, like `var1 = ++var2`, `var2` gets incremented before the value is assigned to `var1`. If, however, the operator comes after the variable, the value of `var2` gets assigned to `var1` before it is incremented or decremented.

You can use the similar expression `x = x + 1` instead of the simpler `x++`. The increment operator is used often enough, however, to make it worth having.

DECREMENT VARIABLES

```
<html>
<head>
</head>
<body>
  <script language="javascript">
    days = 1;
    weeks = 7;
    document.write("Values before: " + days + " and " + weeks + "<br>");
    days++;
    weeks--;
    document.write("Values after: " + days + " and " + weeks + "<br>");
  </script>
</body>
</html>
```

Values before: 1 and 7
Values after: 2 and 6

1 Open the `inc.html` file in Notepad.

2 Create another variable and assign it a number.

3 Add a `document.write` statement to display the value of each variable.

4 Decrement the variable with the -- symbols.

5 Add another `document.write` statement to again display the value of the variables.

6 Save the file as `dec.html`.

7 Open `dec.html` in a browser.

■ The values of each variable are displayed before and after the increment and decrement expressions.

CREATE COMPARISON EXPRESSIONS

*C*omparison expressions are used to compare the values of two variables. When evaluated, comparison expressions result in a Boolean value of either true or false.

These statements are typically used to control the program flow and are covered in more detail in Chapter 4. For example, an if statement uses comparison expressions to decide whether to execute certain statements.

The *comparison operator* is designated with two equals signs (==). It is used to determine if two values are equal and is different from the assignment symbol (=). Using a single equals

sign in a comparison expression is a common error in JavaScript.

Another common comparison operator compares if two variables are not equal. This operator is specified with an exclamation point in front of an equals sign (!=).

You can also check to see if two variables are greater than (>), less than (<), greater than or equal to (>=), or less than or equal to (<=) each other.

This example uses the js-skeleton.html file found on the book's CD-ROM, but you can apply these steps to any file.

CREATE COMPARISON EXPRESSIONS

1 Open the js-skeleton.html file in Notepad.

2 Create a new variable and assign it a number.

3 Create a comparison expression as part of an if statement. Within the if

statement, assign another variable a value.

4 Use document.write statements to display the value of each variable.

5 Save the file as comp.html.

6 Open the file comp.html in a browser.

■ The values of each variable are displayed.

Extra

Although it is relatively easy to determine the results of a comparison expression when numbers are used, comparison operators can also use strings. When comparing strings to be equal such as (`"happy birthday" == "Happy Birthday"`), the result would be false because JavaScript is case sensitive.

The less than and greater than operators can also be used with strings. When strings are compared, their ASCII values are compared. ASCII values associate a number to each character on the keyboard. The computer can recognize these numbers and use them to display the proper characters on the screen. The comparison results in A being less than a and a being less than b, because the ASCII value for A is less than the ASCII value for a.

```
comp2.html - Notepad
File  Edit  Search  Help
<html>
<head>
</head>
<body>
  <script language="javascript">
    daysOfMonth = 31;
    if (daysOfMonth == 28)
      month = "February";
    if (daysOfMonth == 30)
      month = "April or June or September or November";
    if (daysOfMonth > 30)
      month = "January or March or May or July or August or October or
December";
    document.write("Days of Month: " + daysOfMonth + "<br>");
    document.write("Month: " + month + "<br>");
  </script>
</body>
</html>
```

```
D:\JSB\examples\Ch03 - Creating Expressions\comp2.html - Microsoft Internet Explorer
File  Edit  View  Favorites  Tools  Help
Address  D:\JSB\examples\Ch03 - Creating Expressions\comp2.html

Days of Month: 31
Month: January or March or May or July or August or October or December

Done                                              My Computer
```

7 Open `comp.html` in Notepad.

8 Reset the variable's value.

9 Create a comparison expression like Step 3's.

10 Create another comparison expression using the greater than operator within an `if` statement. Within the `if` statement, assign another variable a value.

11 Use `document.write` statements to display the value of each variable.

12 Save the file as `comp2.html`.

13 Open `comp2.html` in a browser.

■ The values of each variable are displayed.

CREATE LOGICAL EXPRESSIONS

A nother type of operator is a *logical operator*. Logical operators can be used to combine several different comparison expressions together into a single complex statement. They also result in a Boolean value and are often used to control program flow.

The logical operators include and, which is expressed as two ampersand symbols (&&); or, which is expressed as two bar symbols (||); and not, expressed as an exclamation point (!).

The and operator produces a true value if both sides of the expression are true. The or operator produces a true value if either side of the expression is true. The not operator simply reverses the Boolean value.

These logical operators when used should appear in between statements and should be surrounded with parentheses.

This example uses the comp.html file found on the book's CD-ROM (or which you may have created in the section "Create Comparison Expressions"), but you can apply these steps to any file.

CREATE LOGICAL EXPRESSIONS

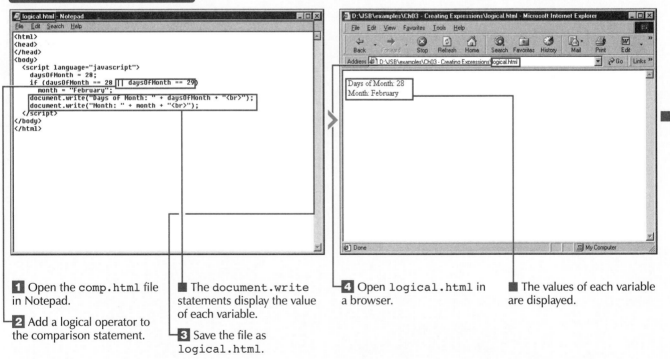

1 Open the comp.html file in Notepad.

2 Add a logical operator to the comparison statement.

■ The document.write statements display the value of each variable.

3 Save the file as logical.html.

4 Open logical.html in a browser.

■ The values of each variable are displayed.

Extra

To get a better idea of all the variations of using the logical operators, consider the following examples. First, the and operator:

```
true && true = true

true && false = false

false && true = false

false && false = false
```

For the or operator, the following apply:

```
true || true = true

true || false = true

false || true = true

false || false = false
```

For the not operator, only two possibilities exist:

```
!true = false

!false = true
```

Logical operators evaluate the expression on each side of the logical operator first and then evaluate the logical operator. For example, the statement (var1 > 17 && var1 < 25) combines the two statements in comparing whether the variable is greater than 17 and less than 25. If the value of var1 equals 18, the result of this expression is true.

```html
<html>
<head>
</head>
<body>
  <script language="javascript">
    daysOfMonth = 29;
    Year = 2000;
    if (daysOfMonth == 28 || daysOfMonth == 29)
      month = "February";
    if (daysOfMonth == 29 && (Year % 4) == 0)
      LeapYear = true;
    document.write("Days of Month: " + daysOfMonth + "<br>");
    document.write("Month: " + month + "<br>");
    document.write("Year: " + Year + "<br>");
    document.write("Leap Year: " + LeapYear + "<br>");
  </script>
</body>
</html>
```

Days of Month: 29
Month: February
Year: 2000
Leap Year: true

5 Open the logical.html file in Notepad.

6 Create another logical expression as part of an if statement.

7 Add document.write statements to display the value of the variables.

8 Save the file as logical2.html.

9 Open the file logical2.html in a browser.

■ The values of each variable are displayed.

43

USING CONDITIONAL OPERATORS

A *conditional operator* is a single operator used as a shortcut for a single if-else statement. if-else statements are covered in Chapter 4. This operator consists of a question mark (?) and a colon (:).

A conditional statement appears to the left of the question mark. If the conditional statement is true, the expression to the immediate left of the question mark is evaluated. Following the first expression comes the colon symbol and another expression. If the conditional statement is false, JavaScript evaluates the statement that follows the colon.

For example, the statement (var1 == 23) ? (str2 = 'yes') : (str2 = 'no') would compare the value of var1. If this value equals 23, the variable str2 is assigned the value of yes; if the value does not equal 23, str2 would be assigned no.

This example uses the js-skeleton.html file found on the book's CD-ROM, but you can apply these steps to any file.

USING CONDITIONAL OPERATORS

1 Open the js-skeleton.html file in Notepad.

2 Create new variables and assign them values.

3 Use a conditional expression to determine the value of a variable.

4 Use a document.write statement to display the value of each variable.

5 Save the file as conditional.html.

6 Open the file conditional.html in a browser.

■ The browser displays the values of each variable.

Apply It

The value of the conditional expression is best seen when compared with the structure that it replaces. Consider the following code:

```
if (condition1 == true) {
   expression1;
}
else {
   expression2;
}
```

This is a simple `if-else` structure that evaluates `expression1` if `condition1` is true or `expression2` if `condition1` is false. This same structure can be replaced with a single conditional statement that looks like this:

```
(condition1 == true) ? expression1 :
expression2;
```

Some examples of a conditional expression include the following:

```
(flipCoin) ? result="heads" :
result="tails";

(today=birthday) ?
document.write("Happy Birthday") :
document.write("Happy Un-birthday");
```

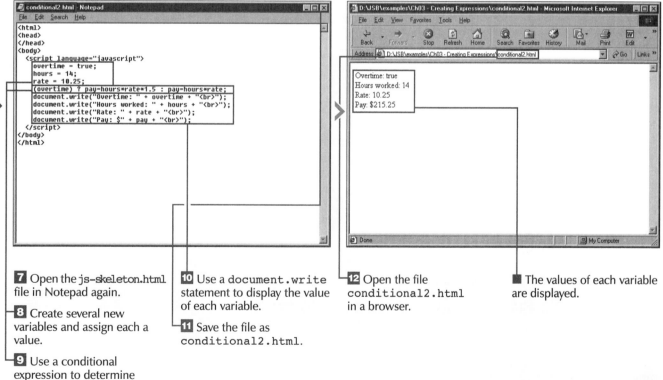

7 Open the `js-skeleton.html` file in Notepad again.

8 Create several new variables and assign each a value.

9 Use a conditional expression to determine which expression to evaluate.

10 Use a `document.write` statement to display the value of each variable.

11 Save the file as `conditional2.html`.

12 Open the file `conditional2.html` in a browser.

■ The values of each variable are displayed.

UNDERSTAND PRECEDENCE

JavaScript evaluates operators in a specific order. This order is known as *operator precedence*. The operators with the highest precedence get evaluated first.

Parentheses have the highest precedence. If you are ever in doubt of which expression is to be evaluated first, include the separate expressions within parentheses.

If the operators have the same level of precedence, such as an expression full of addition operators, JavaScript evaluates the operators from left to right.

Extra

The order of operator precedence after parentheses is as follows:

1. Unary operators: ++, --, -, !

2. Arithmetic operators: *, /, %, +, -

3. Comparison operators: >, <, >=, <=

4. Logical operators: &&, ||

5. Conditional operator: ?:

6. Assignment operator: =

UNDERSTAND PRECEDENCE

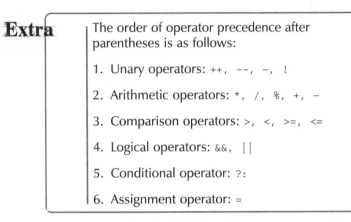

1 Open the js-skeleton.html file from the CD-ROM in Notepad.

2 Create several variables and assign each an expression with the same type of operators.

3 Add pairs of parentheses to the expressions in different places.

4 Use document.write statements to display the results of each expression.

5 Save the file as precedence.html.

6 Open precedence.html in a browser.

■ Notice how the values of each expression are different.

EVALUATE STRING EXPRESSIONS

S ometimes expressions are contained within a
string, such as when enabling the user to input to
an expression into a form field. Using the `eval()`
function, you can instruct JavaScript to evaluate the
string as an expression.

For example, if a string variable called `str1` was
assigned an expression such as `128 + 62`, displaying
this variable value would be "`128 + 62`". On the
other hand, if you were to display `eval(str1)`, the
expression would be evaluated and the value of `190`
would be displayed.

This example uses the `js-skeleton.html` file found
on the book's CD-ROM, but you can apply these steps
to any file.

Extra

You can use the `eval()` function to
evaluate JavaScript commands in a
roundabout way: When the `eval()`
function is called, the JavaScript
interpreter attempts to evaluate any
string that is passed to it; you can
save a JavaScript statement within
a string and evaluate it using the
`eval()` function.

EVALUATE STRING EXPRESSIONS

```html
<html>
<head>
</head>
<body>
  <script language="javascript">
    hoursPerYear = "365 * 24";
    document.write("To compute the number of hours in a year, you can use
this expression: " + hoursPerYear + "<br>");
    document.write("The result of this expression is: " +
eval(hoursPerYear));
  </script>
</body>
</html>
```

To compute the number of hours in a year, you can use this expression: 365 * 24
The result of this expression is: 8760

1 Open the `js-skeleton.html`
file in Notepad.

2 Create a new variable and
assign it an expression as a
string in quotation marks.

3 Use a `document.write`
statement to display the value
of the string variable.

4 Use another
`document.write`
statement and the `eval()`
keyword to evaluate and
display the result of the
string variable.

5 Save the file as
`eval.html`.

6 Open the file `eval.html`
in a browser.

■ The string variable is
shown before and after it
has been evaluated.

IDENTIFY NUMBERS

JavaScript includes a unique method that can be used to identify variables as numbers. This functionality is useful when you accept input from the user and want to verify that the values entered are actually numbers. Trying to evaluate a numerical expression with a string value causes an error.

The method to verify if a variable is a number actually checks to see if it is *not a number*. This method is `isNaN()`, which accepts a single parameter that is checked. If the variable sent to the method is a number, the method returns a `false` value; if the variable is not a number, a `true` value is returned.

For example, if a statement is defined as `var1 = 23`, the expression `isNaN(var1)` returns a `false` value because the value of `var1` *is* a number (23).

This example uses the `js-skeleton.html` file found on the book's CD-ROM, but you can apply these steps to any file.

IDENTIFY NUMBERS

```
<html>
<head>
</head>
<body>
  <script language="javascript">
    var1 = 24;
    (isNaN(var1))?document.write("The variable, " + var1 + " is not a
number.<br/>"):document.write("The variable, " + var1 + " is a number.<br/>"
);
  </script>
</body>
</html>
```

The variable, 24 is a number.

1 Open the js-skeleton.html file in Notepad.

2 Create a new variable and assign it a numeric value.

3 Add a conditional expression based on the isNaN method.

4 Include some document.write statements to display the results of the conditional statement.

5 Save the file as isNaN.html.

6 Open the file isNaN.html in a browser.

■ The browser determines that the variable is a number.

Apply It

One of the best ways to use the `isNaN()` method is to validate data entered into a form. For example, if you accept numerical values in a form field that you are using to compute an equation, you can cause an alert box to appear if the user enters some input that is not a number. The code for this looks like this:

```
<form name="form1">

   Enter the circle radius.<input
type="text" name="text1"
onchange="(isNaN(this.value))?window.
alert('This is not a number. Please
enter a numerical value.'):document.
form1.text2.value = (document.form1.
text1.value*document.form1.text1.value*
Math.PI)"/>
```

```
   Area: <input type="text" name="text2"/>
</form>
```

This form includes two text fields. The first text field is where the user enters the radius of a circle. The onchange event executes the conditional statement when a number is entered and the focus of the text field is lost. The conditional statement checks the `isNaN()` method to see whether the text entered is a number. If it is, the area of the circle is computed. If not, an alert dialog box is displayed.

---

isNaN2.html - Notepad
File Edit Search Help
```
<html>
<head>
</head>
<body>
  <script language="javascript">
    var1 = "apple";
    (isNaN(var1))?document.write("The variable, " + var1 + " is not a
number.<br/>"):document.write("The variable, " + var1 + " is a number.<br/>"
);
  </script>
</body>
</html>
```

D:\JSB\examples\Ch03 - Creating Expressions\isNaN2.html - Microsoft Internet Explorer
File Edit View Favorites Tools Help
Back Forward Stop Refresh Home Search Favorites History Mail Print Links
Address D:\JSB\examples\Ch03 - Creating Expressions\isNaN2.html Go

The variable, apple is not a number

Done — My Computer

7 Open the `isNaN.html` file in Notepad again.

8 Change the variable to a string.

9 Save the file as `isNaN2.html`.

10 Open the file `isNaN.html` in a browser.

■ The browser detects that this variable is not a number.

USING IF-ELSE STATEMENTS

As you write scripts, you may sometimes want to execute certain statements depending on a condition. For example, if a user submits a form with no data, you will want to respond differently than if he or she submitted the form correctly. One way to control this type of program flow is with if-else statements.

The syntax of an if statement includes the if keyword followed by a conditional statement within parentheses. If only a single statement needs to be executed, it can be positioned directly after the conditional statement and should end with a semicolon. If several statements need to be executed, they can be contained within a set of brackets.

An alternative statement is positioned below the if statement in an else statement. The else statement can also hold a set of brackets containing several JavaScript statements.

If the if condition statement is false, the statements in the else statement are executed.

A single if statement can be followed by several else if statements, but the final else statement should not include the if keyword.

This example uses the js-skeleton.html file found on the book's CD-ROM, but you can apply these steps to any file.

USING IF-ELSE

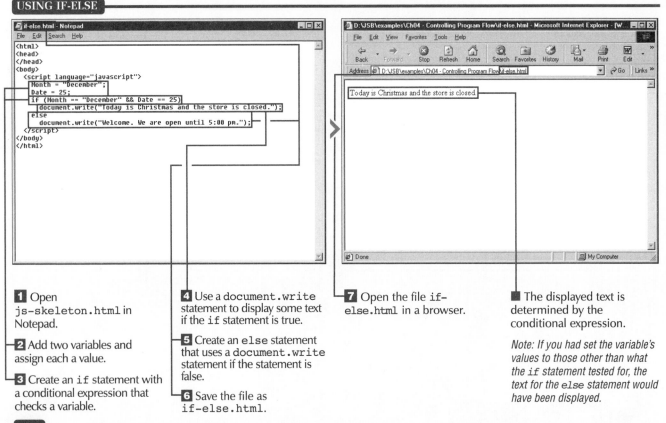

1 Open js-skeleton.html in Notepad.

2 Add two variables and assign each a value.

3 Create an if statement with a conditional expression that checks a variable.

4 Use a document.write statement to display some text if the if statement is true.

5 Create an else statement that uses a document.write statement if the statement is false.

6 Save the file as if-else.html.

7 Open the file if-else.html in a browser.

■ The displayed text is determined by the conditional expression.

Note: If you had set the variable's values to those other than what the if statement tested for, the text for the else statement would have been displayed.

Apply It

if loops can be nested one within another. This enables you to drill down from general conditions to more specific ones. Each level of a nested if-else structure could contain some statements. Using this structure, you can pinpoint the exact criteria for your statements. For example, look how this code works:

```
function coolCar() {
  if (car == "Mustang")
    if (year == 1965)
      if (parts == "original")
        document.write("cool car!");
      else
        document.write("at least it runs.");
}
```

This simple function compares successive different attributes of a car. If each criteria is met, the cool car! statement is displayed. If any of the criteria isn't met, an alternative message is displayed.

USING MULTIPLE ELSE STATEMENTS

1 Open if-else.html in Notepad.

2 Change the values of the variables.

3 In between the if and else statements, add two else if statements with different conditional expressions.

4 Add statements to be executed under the else if statements.

Note: The final else statement should not include the if keyword.

5 Save the file as elseif.html.

6 Open the file elseif.html in a browser.

■ The displayed text is determined by the conditional expression.

USING FOR LOOPS

A nother common program flow method is used to execute a statement or statements a given number of times. This can be efficiently done using a `for` loop.

A `for` statement consists of three distinct parts within parentheses that are separated by semicolons. The first part defines the loop's initial condition, the second part defines the loop's terminating condition, and the final part defines how the loop is incremented.

The `for` loop begins at the defined initial condition and continually executes the statement or statements that follow the `for`

statement until the termination condition is met. The `for` loop variable is incremented each time through the loop.

For example, the statement `for (i=1;i<10;i++)` begins with the loop variable `i` set equal to 1 and loops through the statements that follow nine times before exiting the loop.

This example uses the `js-skeleton.html` file found on the book's CD-ROM, but you can apply these steps to any file.

USING FOR LOOPS

1 Open `js-skeleton.html` in Notepad.

2 Add a `for` loop that starts at 1 and counts to 10.

Note: The three parts of this example's `for` loop are as follows: `count=1` defines the loop's initial condition to be 1; `count<=10` sets the loop's

terminating condition as 10; and `count++` determines that the variable is incremented by 1.

3 Use a `document.write` statement to display the value of the variable.

4 Save the file as `forloop.html`.

5 Open `forloop.html` in a browser.

■ The value at each step in the loop is displayed.

Apply It

Although the example in this section increments the `loop` variable, you can just as easily cause the `loop` variable to decrement. For example, consider the following loop:

```
function countdown(start) {
  for (j=1start;j>0;j--)
    document.write(j + "<br/>");
}
```

This function counts down from the number passed in as a parameter. The loop begins at the start value and decreases by one each time through the loop until the loop value is no longer greater than 0.

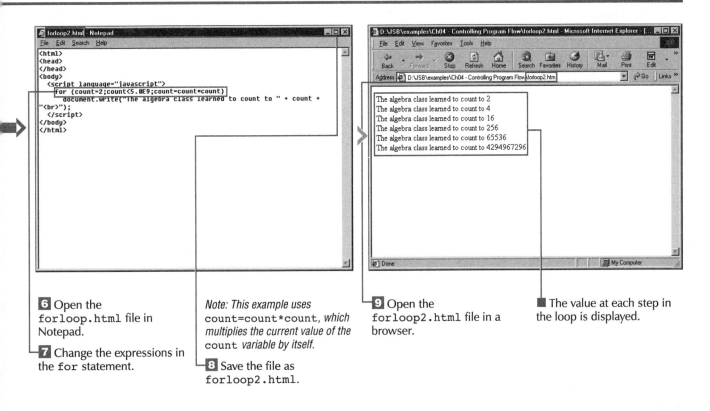

6 Open the forloop.html file in Notepad.

7 Change the expressions in the for statement.

Note: This example uses count=count*count, *which multiplies the current value of the* count *variable by itself.*

8 Save the file as forloop2.html.

9 Open the forloop2.html file in a browser.

■ The value at each step in the loop is displayed.

USING WHILE LOOPS

Another type of loop used in JavaScript is the while loop. This loop is different from the for loop because it doesn't count to an end result. It simply continues to loop through the statements contained within the brackets until a conditional expression evaluates to false. This loop includes only a conditional expression after the while keyword.

When using a while loop, you need to be sure that the conditional statement will eventually become false or the loop will continue indefinitely. You should also make sure that all variables in the conditional statement are defined.

For example, the statement while (var1 <= 100) executes the statements that follow until the variable, var1, is greater than 100. If the statements within the loop never change the value of var1, then the loop will continue indefinitely.

The while loop can also execute multiple statements by including statements within brackets.

This example uses the forloop.html and forloop2.html files found on the book's CD-ROM (or which you may have created in the section "Using for Loops"), but you can apply these steps to any file.

USING WHILE LOOPS

1 Open the forloop.html file in Notepad.

2 Add a count variable and assign it a value.

3 Replace the for loop with a while loop.

4 Add a count variable incrementing the statement within the loop.

5 Save the file as while.html.

6 Open while.html in a browser.

■ The values of the loop variable are displayed.

Extra

There are many ways to think about how to construct your loops; there will be times when you want to use a `while` loop and others when you want to use a `for` loop. The two different ways of looping are similar, but the `for` loop requires all the information about the loop to be part of the `for` statement. The `while` loop can use variables that have been declared elsewhere.

If a `while` loop doesn't include brackets, only the first statement that follows the `while` statement will be executed. If multiple statements need to be executed, all statements should be included within brackets.

To exit a loop that appears to be looping indefinitely, besides using the conditional statement as part of the `while` loop, you can use the `break` statement. The section "Break Loops" discusses this in detail.

```html
<html>
<head>
</head>
<body>
  <script language="javascript">
    count = 2;
    while (count < 5.0E9) {
       document.write("The algebra class learned to count to " + count +
"<br>");
       count = count * count;
    }
  </script>
</body>
</html>
```

The algebra class learned to count to 2
The algebra class learned to count to 4
The algebra class learned to count to 16
The algebra class learned to count to 256
The algebra class learned to count to 65536
The algebra class learned to count to 4294967296

Open the `forloop2.html` file in Notepad.

8 Add a `count` variable and assign it a value.

9 Replace the `for` loop with a `while` loop.

10 Add a `count` incrementing statement within the loop.

11 Save the file as `while2.html`.

12 Open `while2.html` in a browser.

■ The `count` variable values are displayed as the loop progresses.

BREAK LOOPS

Sometimes you can get stuck in a loop. This scenario is called an *infinite loop*. To break out of an infinite loop, you can use the break keyword.

When JavaScript encounters the break keyword within a loop, it automatically terminates the loop and executes the first statement that comes after the loop.

For example, if a while loop included a conditional expression that was always true, such as while (true), you could break out of this loop with the break statement.

This example uses the while.html file found on the book's CD-ROM (or which you may have created in the section "Using while Loops"), but you can apply these steps to any file.

Extra

After you break out of a loop, you cannot return to it. The break statement exits the loop and doesn't enable you to return to it. All variables remain in the same state they are in when the loop is broken.

BREAK LOOPS

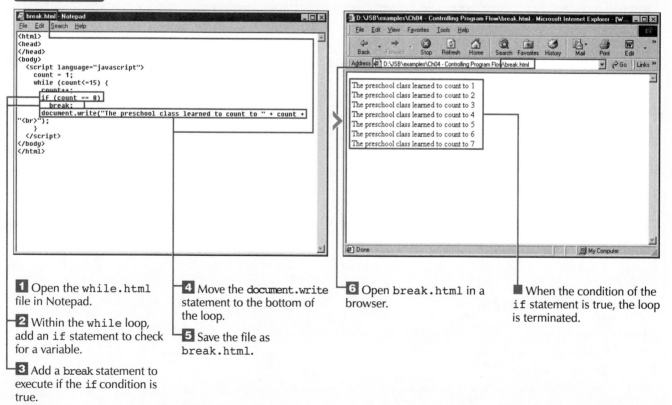

1 Open the while.html file in Notepad.

2 Within the while loop, add an if statement to check for a variable.

3 Add a break statement to execute if the if condition is true.

4 Move the document.write statement to the bottom of the loop.

5 Save the file as break.html.

6 Open break.html in a browser.

■ When the condition of the if statement is true, the loop is terminated.

CONTINUE LOOPS

Another keyword that works with loops is the `continue` statement. This statement stops the execution of a loop and returns to the top of the loop as if all the statements had been executed. Any statements that follow the `continue` statement will not be executed for this time through the loop.

This enables you to check for special exceptions within the loop and skip them without interrupting the normal flow of the loop.

For example, if a `while` loop were to continue until `var1 == 100`, you could skip the

execution of the number 50 with the statement `if (var1 == 50) continue;`.

This example uses the `break.html` file found on the book's CD-ROM (or which you may have created in the section "Break Loops"), but you can apply these steps to any file.

Extra

A single loop can include both `break` and `continue` statements, but after a `break` statement is executed, the loop is finished.

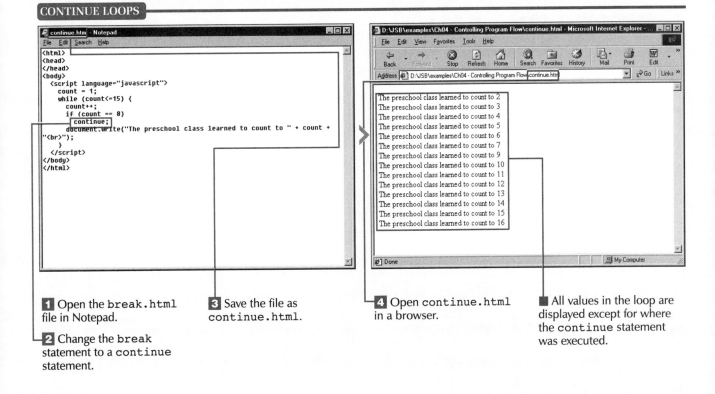

CONTINUE LOOPS

1 Open the `break.html` file in Notepad.

2 Change the `break` statement to a `continue` statement.

3 Save the file as `continue.html`.

4 Open `continue.html` in a browser.

■ All values in the loop are displayed except for where the `continue` statement was executed.

USING JAVASCRIPT TIMERS

JavaScript can be used to set up timers that let certain scripts be executed at different times. These can be useful for timing different actions on the Web page.

The function that makes timers possible is the `window.setTimeout()` function. This function accepts two parameters. The first parameter is a JavaScript statement to execute. This can be a single statement, such as `document.bgcolor = 'blue'`, or the name of a function that is defined elsewhere in the Web page. The statement to execute can even be several statements separated with semicolons. The statements that make up this

first parameter need to be enclosed within quotation marks.

The second parameter accepted by the `window.setTimeout()` function is the `time` value to wait before the JavaScript statement is executed. This value is measured in milliseconds. For example, a value of `5000` would wait 5 seconds and a value of `10000` would wait 10 seconds.

This example uses the `js-skeleton.html` file found on the book's CD-ROM, but you can apply these steps to any file.

USING JAVASCRIPT TIMERS

1 Open `js-skeleton.html`.

2 Add a function that uses a `document.write()` statement to display a heading and an image.

3 Add onload to the <body> tag and set it equal to `window.setTimeout()`.

4 Add the function name as the first parameter of `setTimeout()` and a time value, in milliseconds, as the second parameter.

5 Add a single heading to the <body> tags.

6 Save the file as `timeout.html`.

7 Open the `timeout.html` file in a browser.

■ The <body> tags' heading is displayed in the browser.

Apply It

Chapter 11 covers the `Math` object. This object includes a method that is used to create random numbers between 0 and 1. Using this method, you can create a script that lets you play musical chairs by randomly selecting a timeout. The code for this looks like this:

```
<form name="form1">

  <input type="button" name="button1"
value="Get Ready"
onclick="stopMusic()"/>

  <input type="text" name="text1"
value="music is playing"/>

</form>
<script language="javascript">

  function stopMusic() {
```

```
    seat = Math.floor(Math.random() *
10000);

    stop =
window.setTimeout("document.form1.text1.va
lue = 'music stopped'",seat);

}
</script>
```

The code creates a form with a button and a text box. When a user clicks the button, the `stopMusic()` function is called. This function randomly selects a number that is used for the `setTimeout()` method. The text box is updated when the time expires to inform the users that the music has stopped.

8 Wait for the designated time value.

■ The script `function` is executed after the timeout value is reached, displaying `function`'s heading and image.

9 Open the `timeout.html` file again in a browser.

10 Click the Stop button before the timeout value is reached.

■ The timeout is not stopped, and the image is again displayed.

Note: The timeout can only be cleared using the `clearTimeout()` method, which is discussed in the section "Clear Timeouts and Intervals" later in this chapter.

SET REGULARLY TIMED INTERVALS

etting timeouts results in a one-time execution of a statement or function. If you want to set multiple timeouts, you can include the setTimeout() method within a for loop, or you can use another method that can set up regularly repeating timeouts: setInterval().

The setInterval() method can be used to execute a statement, function, or group of statements at regular intervals repeatedly. The setInterval() method accepts two parameters, just like the setTimeout() methods. The first parameter is the statement to execute, and the second parameter is the

time in milliseconds until the statement is executed. You must enclose the first parameter within quotation marks.

Timeouts created with the setInterval() method continue indefinitely unless the clearInterval() method is called. The section "Clear Timeouts and Intervals," later in this chapter, covers this method in detail.

This example uses the js-skeleton.html file found on the book's CD-ROM, but you can apply these steps to any file.

SET REGULARLY TIMED INTERVALS

1 Open js-skeleton.html in Notepad.

2 Add a window.setInterval() method.

3 Add a form with two text boxes.

4 Set the first parameter of setInterval() to update the second text box with the contents of the first text box.

5 Set the second parameter of setInterval() to a time value.

6 Save the file as setInterval.html.

7 Open setInterval.html in a browser.

■ Two text boxes are displayed.

Apply It

Chapter 10 covers the `Date` object. This object includes a method called `getLocaleString()` that gets the current locale's time. Using this method and the `setInterval()` method, you can create a clock with the following code:

```
<form name="form1">

  <input type="text" name="text1"/>

</form>
<script language="javascript">

  stop = window.setInterval("time = new
Date();document.form1.text1.value =
time.toLocaleString()",1000);

</script>
```

The code creates a form with a single text box. `Interval()` is then set to respond every second. At each interval, the time object is created and the `toLocaleString()` method is displayed in the text box. The time due to the `setInterval()` method is updated every second.

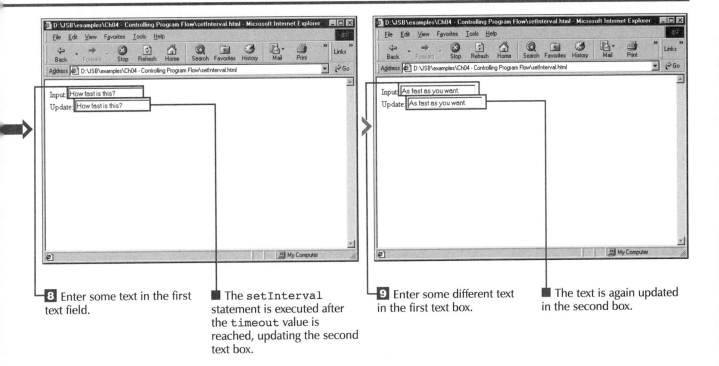

8 Enter some text in the first text field.

■ The `setInterval` statement is executed after the `timeout` value is reached, updating the second text box.

9 Enter some different text in the first text box.

■ The text is again updated in the second box.

CLEAR TIMEOUTS AND INTERVALS

In the section "Using JavaScript Timers," I show that the Stop button on the browser does not end a timeout. Timeouts can only be cleared internally using the `clearTimeout()` method. This method is part of the `window` object and can be referenced in the current window as `window.clearTimeout()`.

To use the `clearTimeout()` method, you need to name the timeout when it is set. You can name a timeout by assigning the `setTimeout()` method to a variable name. This variable name can then be used as a parameter to the `clearTimeout()` method to terminate the timeout.

For example, if a timeout is assigned to a variable like `timer1 = setTimeout(x++, 1000)`, the timeout can be canceled at any time with the `clearTimeout(timer1)` statement.

You can use a similar method for clearing interval timeouts created with the `setInterval()` method. This method is `clearInterval()`.

This example uses the `setInterval.html` file found on the book's CD-ROM, but you can apply these steps to any file.

CLEAR TIMEOUTS AND INTERVALS

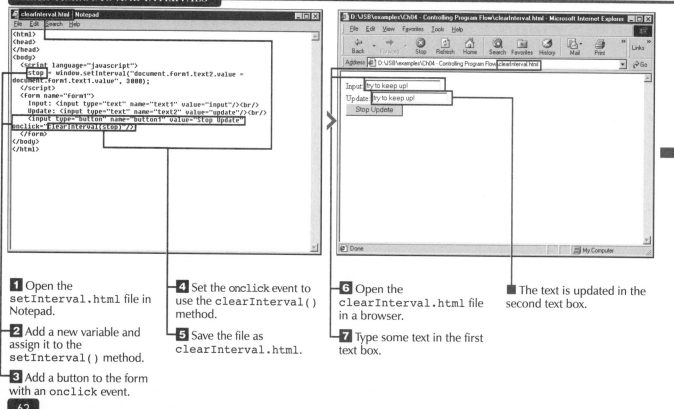

1 Open the `setInterval.html` file in Notepad.

2 Add a new variable and assign it to the `setInterval()` method.

3 Add a button to the form with an `onclick` event.

4 Set the `onclick` event to use the `clearInterval()` method.

5 Save the file as `clearInterval.html`.

6 Open the `clearInterval.html` file in a browser.

7 Type some text in the first text box.

■ The text is updated in the second text box.

Apply It

The clock example created in the section "Set Regularly Timed Intervals" can be modified to include a button that stops the clock. The following code adds the Stop button:

```
<form name="form1">

    <input type="text" name="text1"/>

    <input type="button" name="button1"
value="Stop"
onclick="window.clearInterval(stop)"/>

    </form>

    <script language="javascript">

    stop = window.setInterval("time =
new Date();document.form1.text1.value =
time.toLocaleString()",1000);

    </script>
```

In this code, a button is added to the form with an onclick event. The onclick event is assigned to clear the interval with the clearInterval() method. The parameter to the clearInterval() method is the variable name that was assigned to the setInterval() method.

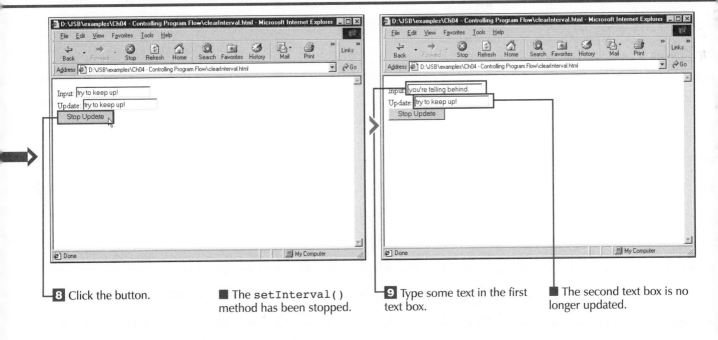

8 Click the button.

■ The setInterval() method has been stopped.

9 Type some text in the first text box.

■ The second text box is no longer updated.

DECLARE A FUNCTION

You can group sections of code together into a structure called a *function*. You can call and access a function at any time. You can send parameters to functions, and functions can return values.

You declare functions with the `function` keyword followed by the function name. Parentheses always immediately follow the function name. Parameters for the function are contained within these parentheses, but parameters are not required.

For example, the statement, `function hello()` would declare a function named `hello`.

All JavaScript statements within the function should be contained within braces after the function declaration.

The function statements will not be executed until the function is called.

Function names have the same limitations and follow the same requirements as variables. They must begin with a letter, they must not contain any spaces, and they cannot use any special characters like `+`, `*`, `/`, `&`, `%`, `$`, `#`, `@`, or `!`. Also, remember that function names are case-sensitive.

This example uses the `js-skeleton.html` file found on the book's CD-ROM, but you can apply these steps to any file.

DECLARE A FUNCTION

```
<html>
<head>
</head>
<body>
   <script language="javascript">
   function quote() {
      document.write("You should always listen, but sometimes you should
only listen.");
   }
   </script>
</body>
</html>
```

1 Open the file `js-skeleton.html` in Notepad.

2 Create a new function definition with the function keyword and a name.

3 Add a JavaScript statement within braces after the function declaration.

4 Save the file as `function.html`.

5 Open `function.html` in your browser.

■ The function statements are not executed because they haven't been called.

Note: By grouping statements within a function, you can execute the statements in the function as many times as needed.

CALL A FUNCTION

After you declare a function, you can execute it at any time from anywhere within the document by listing the function name.

You need to include parentheses when calling a function whether or not the function has parameters.

For example, if a function is defined as function hello(), then you can execute this function with the statement hello();.

The function call can come before or after the function declaration.

This example uses the function.html file found on the book's CD-ROM (or which you may have created in the section "Declare a Function"), but you can apply these steps to any file.

Extra

If you use the javascript: keyword, you can call a function from an HTML link by using the href attribute of an HTML <a> tag. The section "Call a Function from an HTML Link," later in this chapter, shows how to do this.

CALL A FUNCTION

```
<html>
<head>
</head>
<body>
  <script language="javascript">
    function quote() {
      document.write("You should always listen, but sometimes you should
only listen.");
    }
    quote();
  </script>
</body>
</html>
```

You should always listen, but sometimes you should only listen.

1 Open the file function.html in Notepad.

2 Add a function call after the function statement.

3 Save the file as function-call.html.

4 Open function-call.html in a browser.

■ The function statements are executed, and the results appear on the screen.

Note: When the function name is referenced, the statements within the function are executed. Functions can be called many times within a single file.

65

UNDERSTAND GLOBAL AND LOCAL VARIABLES

Any variables declared with the var keyword within a function will be local to the function that they appear in. These local variables will only be understood within the function and are not recognized in any JavaScript statements outside of the function.

For example, if a variable named myVar1 is declared within a function using the var keyword, then within the function the variable can be used, but if it is referenced outside of the function, then the value will be unknown.

Variables that are implicitly declared without the var keyword in a function will be global. Variables declared outside of functions (even if they are declared using the var keyword) are also global. Global variables can be used anywhere within the current document including both inside and outside of functions.

This example uses the js-skeleton.html file found on the book's CD-ROM, but you can apply these steps to any file.

GLOBAL VARIABLES

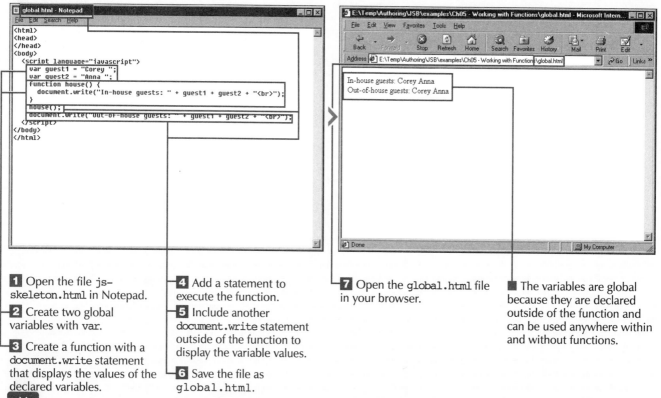

1 Open the file js-skeleton.html in Notepad.

2 Create two global variables with var.

3 Create a function with a document.write statement that displays the values of the declared variables.

4 Add a statement to execute the function.

5 Include another document.write statement outside of the function to display the variable values.

6 Save the file as global.html.

7 Open the global.html file in your browser.

■ The variables are global because they are declared outside of the function and can be used anywhere within and without functions.

Extra

A convenient way to keep track of global and local variables is to adopt specific coding conventions that have a naming standard that helps to keep the scope of a variable straight. For example, if you place a lowercase *g* on the front of every global variable, as in gVar1, then you can identify a global variable by just looking at the variable name.

One reason to use local variables is that you want to build functions that can be easily reused. By using local variables, you can be guaranteed that regardless of where the function is copied, it will not conflict with a global variable that shares the same variable name.

It's a good idea to use the var keyword outside of functions. Any variables that are declared without the var keyword are global. Any variables declared outside of a function are also global. Using the var keyword will make it obvious to anyone looking at your code that you are declaring a variable.

LOCAL VARIABLES

```
local.html - Notepad
File  Edit  Search  Help
<html>
<head>
</head>
<body>
  <script language="javascript">
    function house() {
      var guest1 = "Corey ";
      var guest2 = "Anna ";
      document.write("In-house guests: " + guest1 + guest2 + "<br>");
    }
    house();
    document.write("Out-of-house guests: " + guest1 + guest2 + "<br>");
  </script>
</body>
</html>
```

In-house guests: Corey Anna

Internet Explorer

Problems with this Web page might prevent it from being displayed properly or functioning properly. In the future, you can display this message by double-clicking the warning icon displayed in the status bar.

☑ Always display this message when a page contains errors.

OK   Hide Details <<

Line: 12
Char: 5
Error: 'guest1' is undefined
Code: 0
URL: file://E:\Temp\Authoring\JSB\examples\Ch05 - Working with

■1 Open the file global.html in Notepad.

■2 Move the two variable declarations within the function.

Note: This makes the variables local to the function because they are declared with the var keyword and are now within the function.

■3 Save the file as local.html.

■4 Open local.html in your browser.

■ A dialog box appears stating that the page has errors.

■5 Click the Show/Hide Details button to see the errors.

■ Notice that the local variables are undefined when used in the document.write statement outside of the function.

PASS PARAMETERS TO A FUNCTION

I f you want to execute a function using different variable values, you can pass these as parameters to a function.

Parameters can be passed into a function within the parentheses that follow the function name. Several variables can be passed if you separate them with commas.

The calling statement should include the values, and the function definition should include the variable name. You can then use these variable names within the function. The number of values in the function call should

match the number of variables in the function definition.

For example, if a function is defined as `function sum(a, b, c)`, then the function call `sum(16, 34, 98)` would place the value of 16 in the variable named `a`, 34 in the variable named `b` and 98 in the variable named `c`.

This example uses the `js-skeleton.html` file found on the book's CD-ROM, but you can apply these steps to any file.

PASS A SINGLE PARAMETER

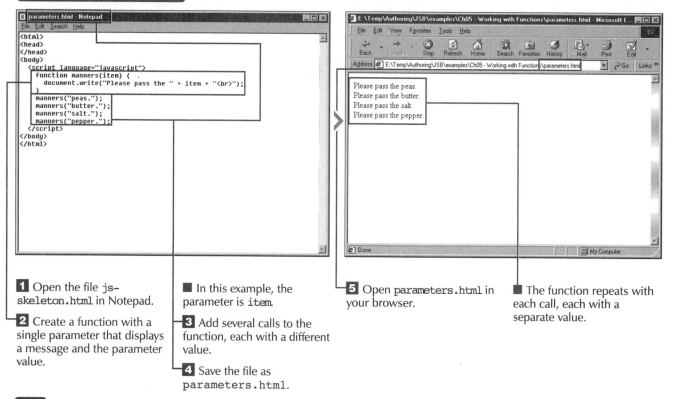

1 Open the file js-skeleton.html in Notepad.

2 Create a function with a single parameter that displays a message and the parameter value.

■ In this example, the parameter is `item`.

3 Add several calls to the function, each with a different value.

4 Save the file as parameters.html.

5 Open parameters.html in your browser.

■ The function repeats with each call, each with a separate value.

Extra

Parameters that are passed to a function are local to the function. If a parameter variable is used outside of the function, it will generate an error.

If a function call doesn't include any parameters, the function name still needs an empty set of parentheses. These parentheses help identify the name as a function.

There is no limit to the number of parameters that can be passed to a function, so you can pass as many parameters to a function as you need.

When you call a function, the parameter that is passed can be a variable or a value. If a variable is passed, then the value of the variable at the time the function is called is sent to the function.

PASS SEVERAL PARAMETERS

```
<html>
<head>
</head>
<body>
  <script language="javascript">
    function average(var1, var2, var3) {
      ave = (var1 + var2 + var3) / 3;
      document.write("The average of  " + var1 + " " + var2 + " " + var3 + "
equals " + ave + "<br>");
    }
    average(34, 56, 78);
  </script>
</body>
</html>
```

The average of 34 56 78 equals 56

1 Open the file js-skeleton.html in Notepad.

2 Create a function with several parameters that computes and displays a value.

3 Add a call to the function.

4 Save the file as parameters2.html.

5 Open the parameters2.html file in your browser.

■ The computed value is determined by the values passed to the function.

RETURN VALUES FROM A FUNCTION

You can return values from a function by using the `return` keyword. This allows the function to determine a resulting value and send that value back to the main program.

For example, if you create a function that computes a sum and the sum value is stored in a variable named `total`, then the statement `return total` would send the value of `total` back to where the function was called.

Because a value is being passed back to the function call, the function call needs to be a

statement that uses the returned value. For example, `var1 = func1()` would place the returned value from the `func1()` function into a variable named `var1`.

The type of data returned from a function could be a string, number, or any other value.

This example uses the `js-skeleton.html` file found on the book's CD-ROM, but you can apply these steps to any file.

RETURN VALUES FROM A FUNCTION

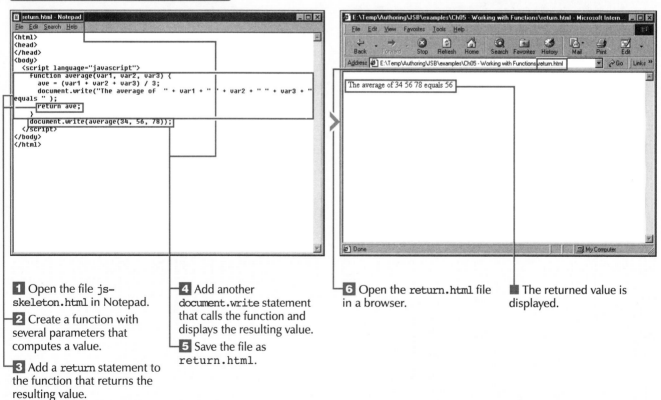

1 Open the file js-skeleton.html in Notepad.

2 Create a function with several parameters that computes a value.

3 Add a return statement to the function that returns the resulting value.

4 Add another document.write statement that calls the function and displays the resulting value.

5 Save the file as return.html.

6 Open the return.html file in a browser.

■ The returned value is displayed.

Apply It

A good example of a function that returns a value is one that accepts parameters, computes a result of an equation, and returns the resulting value. For example, a function that computes and returns the computed area of a box, given width, height, and depth parameters, looks like this:

```
function computeArea(width, height,
depth) {

   area = width * height * depth;

   return area;

}
```

If this function is included in a Web page file, you could call the function with the following statement:

```
computeArea(3, 4, 5);
```

The function result is returned directly to the function call and can be used within a statement such as this:

```
document.write("The area of the box with
the dimensions: " + width + ", " + height
+ ", " + depth + " equals " +
computeArea(3, 4, 5));
```

RETURN HTML VALUES

```
<html>
<head>
</head>
<body>
   <script language="javascript">
   function underline(str1) {
      ustr = "<u>"+str1+"</u>";
      return ustr;
   }
   document.write(underline("Beware of dogs and hot dogs."));
   </script>
</body>
</html>
```

Beware of dogs and hot dogs.

■1 Open the file js-skeleton.html in Notepad.

■2 Add a function that accepts a single string parameter.

■3 Surround the string parameter with a set of HTML tags and set it equal to a return variable.

■4 Return the modified string with the return keyword.

■5 Use a document.write statement to display the returned string.

■6 Save the file as return2.html.

■7 Open the return2.html file in your browser.

■ The string passed to a function is returned formatted.

Note: Functions that return desired results can be included within statements.

CALL A FUNCTION FROM AN HTML LINK

Functions can be called by referencing the function name as a JavaScript statement. You can also call a JavaScript function by referencing the function name within an HTML link. This is done using the javascript keyword followed by a colon and the function name.

For example, if a link is defined using the <a> tag and the href attribute is set to javascript: hello(), then the hello() function would be called when you click the link.

You can also use this format to call a function from the browser's Address field. If you type in **javascript:** and the function name, the function will be executed.

This example uses the function.html file found on the book's CD-ROM (or which you may have created in the section "Declare a Function"), but you can apply these steps to any file.

CALL A FUNCTION FROM AN HTML LINK

```
<html>
<head>
</head>
<body>
  <script language="javascript">
    function quote() {
        document.write("You should always listen, but sometimes you should
only listen.");
    }
  </script>
  <a href="javascript:quote()">see a quote</a>
  <a href="javascript:document.write('Hesitation can kill.')">see another
quote</a>
</body>
</html>
```

see a quote see another quote

1 Open the file function.html in Notepad.

2 Outside of the <script> tags, add two <a> tags and include some link text.

3 Add the href attribute to each set of <a> tags.

4 Set the first href attribute equal to javascript: and the function name.

5 Set the second href attribute equal to javascript: and a JavaScript statement.

6 Save the file as href.html.

7 Open the href.html file in your browser.

■ Two links are displayed.

8 Click the first link.

Apply It

Another place within an HTML page where a function call can be placed is within the action attribute of a `<form>` tag. For example,

```
function hello() {

    document.write("Hello and Welcome");

}

. . .

<form action="javascript:hello()">

 <input type="submit" value="Display
Welcome"/>

</form>
```

The HTML form displays a submit button labeled "Display Welcome" in the browser. Clicking this button executes the `hello()` function, which displays a welcome message.

■ The function executes and the quote is displayed.

Note: Clicking the HTML link calls the function that displays a quote.

9 Click the **Back** button on your browser.

10 Click the second link.

■ Clicking this second link executes another JavaScript statement, which displays another quote.

USING JAVASCRIPT EVENTS

J avaScript events are bits of code that link users actions with the scripts that need to be executed. These actions can be clicking the mouse, pressing a keyboard key, selecting or changing form elements, or even loading and unloading a Web page.

You can position JavaScript events within HTML tags just like the other attributes. You can set them equal to a small line of JavaScript code or to the name of a JavaScript function declared elsewhere in the Web page.

For example, the onclick event can be added as an attribute to the <button> tag and set equal to the function named blink, like this:

```
<button onclick="blink();"/>
```

This tag will not only display a button on the Web page, but after you click this button, the blink() JavaScript function will also be executed.

There are a number of different events that you can use within a Web page, and the places where you can use them are different for each event. Some of the more common JavaScript events are covered in this chapter, including mouse events, keyboard events, and selection events.

MOUSE EVENTS

Mouse events fire when the user clicks or moves the mouse. If the user clicks the mouse button once, the onclick event fires. If the user clicks the mouse button twice, ondblclick event is fired.

For more precise details, you can use the onmousedown event to signal when the mouse button is pressed down and the onmouseup event when a mouse button is released.

The onmouseover event detects when the mouse cursor moves over the top of an element. The onmouseout event detects when the mouse cursor moves off an element.

KEYBOARD EVENTS

The `onkeypress` event can be used to detect when a key on the keyboard is pressed. The specific key that was pressed can be found in the `window.event.keycode` object.

Similar to the mouse button clicks, the `onkeydown` event detects after the key is first pressed and held down, and the `onkeyup` event fires after the pressed key is released.

SELECTION EVENTS

When an element is highlighted in the browser, it is said to have *focus*. The `onfocus` event is used to signal when an element has the focus. Pressing the Tab key can change this focus. When an element loses the focus, the `onblur` event fires.

When you select an element, the `onselect` event is fired.

MISCELLANEOUS EVENTS

Another common event used with form elements is the `onchange` event. This event fires whenever the data of the form element is changed.

The `onload` event is used to detect when a Web page has completely finished loading. Similarly, the `onunload` event is fired when a Web page is unloaded. This happens when you leave the current page or when you click the browser's Refresh button.

When you cancel a Web page that is loading into your browser, then the `onabort` event is called.

Two form buttons have specific functions — `submit` and `reset`. These same functions can be detected using the `onsubmit` and `onreset` events.

DETECT A MOUSE CLICK

One of the keys to interacting with the user is to detect mouse clicks. When a user clicks the Web page, he or she usually expects something to happen. Buttons and links are prime targets for a clicking mouse, but form elements, including radio and check box buttons, can also be clicked with the mouse.

A single mouse click can be detected using the onclick event. This event can then trigger an effect using JavaScript.

The onclick event is typically added to form buttons such as submit and reset buttons,

created using the <input/> and/or <button> tags. You can also use the onclick event within the <a> tag.

The onclick event is one of the *intrinsic* events that is recognized by almost every Web element. Intrinsic events are a set of common events that you can use with a majority of the standard HTML tags.

This example uses the skeleton.html file found on the book's CD-ROM, but you can apply these steps to any file.

DETECT A MOUSE CLICK

1 Open the file skeleton.html in Notepad.

2 Add <form> and <input/> tags between the <body> tags.

3 Add the name attribute to the <form> tag and set it to form1.

4 Add the type, name, and value attributes to the <input/> tag.

5 Set the type attribute to button, the name attribute to button1, and the value attribute to the button face text.

6 Add the onclick JavaScript event to the <input/> tag.

7 Set the onclick event equal to a JavaScript statement that changes the button text.

8 Save the file as onclick.html.

Extra

The onclick event detects when the mouse button is clicked and released. The action of clicking and releasing the mouse button can be detected individually using the onmousedown and onmouseup events. The user could press the mouse and not release it. In this case, the onclick event would not detect this action, but the onmousedown event would.

The onmousedown and onmouseup events are very similar to the onclick function. They are also intrinsic events that you can use with almost every HTML tag.

There is a separate event for detecting double-clicks: The onclick event detects a single click, but the ondblclick event detects double-clicks. This event is covered in the next section, "Detect a Double-Click."

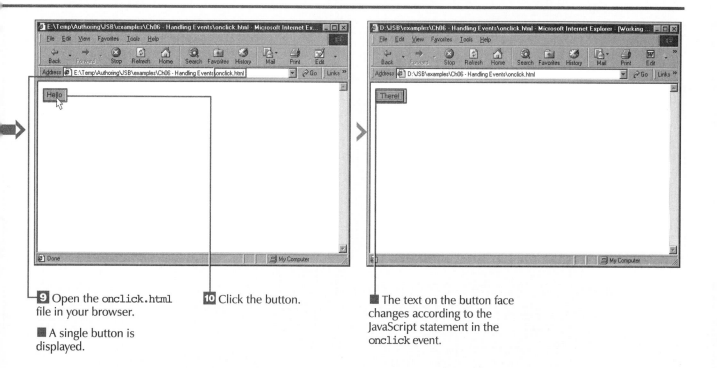

9 Open the onclick.html file in your browser.

■ A single button is displayed.

10 Click the button.

■ The text on the button face changes according to the JavaScript statement in the onclick event.

DETECT A DOUBLE-CLICK

Double-clicking is very similar to single-clicking except that the user clicks twice rapidly instead of once on the mouse button.

Double-clicks can be detected using the `ondblclick` event. You can add this event to all the same elements as the `onclick` event, including the `<input/>`, `<button>`, and `<a>` tags.

The `ondblclick` event is also an intrinsic event. This means that you can use it with almost any Web element.

You can use double-clicks to add a dual function to a button. If you set the `onclick` event to process one set of commands and the `ondblclick` event to process a second set of commands, then you can use single interface elements, like a button, to accomplish twice as much work.

This example uses the `onclick.html` file found on the book's CD-ROM (or which you may have created in the section "Detect a Mouse Click"), but you can apply these steps to any file.

DETECT A DOUBLE-CLICK

1 Open the file `onclick.html` in Notepad.

2 After the `onclick` event, add the `ondblclick` event.

3 Set the `ondblclick` event equal to a JavaScript statement to change the button text.

4 Save the file as `ondblclick.html`.

5 Open the `ondblclick.html` file in your browser.

■ A single button is displayed.

6 Click the button.

Extra

If the `ondblclick` event is fired, the `onclick` event fires as well, because the `onclick` event is fired any time the mouse is clicked — even when the `ondblclick` event is fired.

A single tag can include multiple events. These events are processed in the order that they are listed. For example, if a tag includes both `onclick` and `ondblclick` events, then both will be processed any time the element is clicked twice rapidly.

Intrinsic events are a set of events that can be added to almost every Web element. The list of intrinsic events includes `onclick`, `ondblclick`, `onmousedown`, `onmouseup`, `onmouseover`, `onmousemove`, `onmouseout`, `onkeypress`, `onkeydown`, and `onkeyup`.

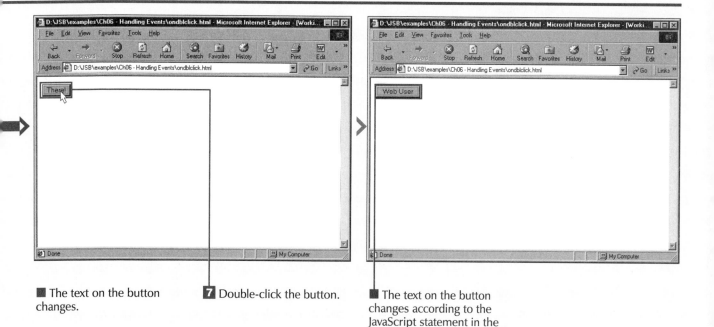

■ The text on the button changes.

7 Double-click the button.

■ The text on the button changes according to the JavaScript statement in the `ondblclick` event.

CREATE ROLLOVER BUTTONS

Rollover buttons are useful in helping the user to navigate through a Web page. When the mouse cursor moves over the top of a rollover button, the button changes its appearance. In JavaScript, you accomplish this by replacing the original image with a new image.

You can create rollover buttons by using the onmouseover and onmouseout events. The onmouseover event is set to display a new image in place of the original, and the onmouseout event is set to display the original image.

Using the onmouseover and onmouseout events causes the new image to display when the mouse cursor is over the top of the button and the original image to display after the mouse cursor leaves the button.

You can use the onmouseover and onmouseout events with hypertext links, image maps, and images.

This example uses the skeleton.html file found on the book's CD-ROM, but you can apply these steps to any file.

CREATE ROLLOVER BUTTONS

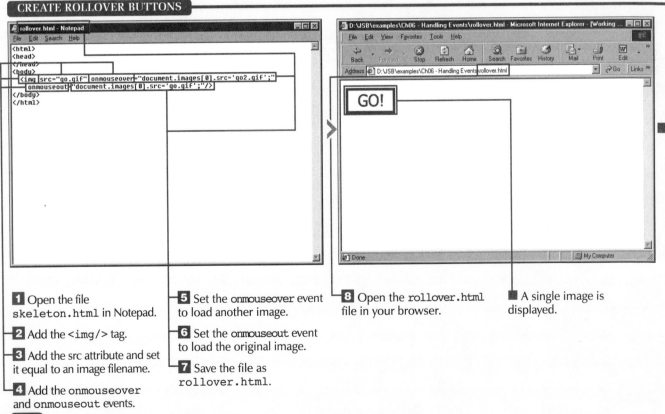

1 Open the file skeleton.html in Notepad.

2 Add the <img/> tag.

3 Add the src attribute and set it equal to an image filename.

4 Add the onmouseover and onmouseout events.

5 Set the onmouseover event to load another image.

6 Set the onmouseout event to load the original image.

7 Save the file as rollover.html.

8 Open the rollover.html file in your browser.

■ A single image is displayed.

Extra

Events don't always need to call a JavaScript function. You can set JavaScript events equal to any valid JavaScript code. This code could be a single line of JavaScript, multiple lines of JavaScript, or a call to a function that is defined within a set of <script> tags. Within the event, each line of JavaScript must end with a semicolon (;) including function calls.

The onmousemove event triggers whenever the mouse moves. This means that when the onmouseover or the onmouseout events fire, the onmousemove event also fires. This event can be useful for detecting when a user is using the computer.

The <p> tag can accept the onmouseover and onmouseout events. Using this tag, you can execute JavaScript statements when the mouse rolls over normal text.

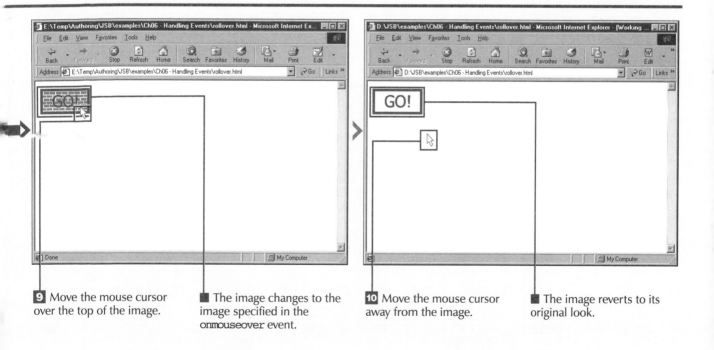

9 Move the mouse cursor over the top of the image.

■ The image changes to the image specified in the onmouseover event.

10 Move the mouse cursor away from the image.

■ The image reverts to its original look.

DETECT A KEY PRESS

You can enter text into a text field or textarea element using the keyboard, but there may be times when you want to detect a single key press, such as a key to start a certain function.

When a keystroke on the keyboard is pressed, it can be detected using the onkeypress event. The actual key that was pressed is identified using the window.event.keyCode object.

Using the onkeypress event, you can check for the key that was pressed and react accordingly.

The onkeypress event is an intrinsic event, so you can use it with most Web elements.

With the onkeypress events, you can assign all your interface elements a quick selection key. This enables users to navigate your interface using just the keyboard. It also makes your site accessible for people with disabilities.

This example uses the skeleton.html file found on the book's CD-ROM, but you can apply these steps to any file.

DETECT A KEY PRESS

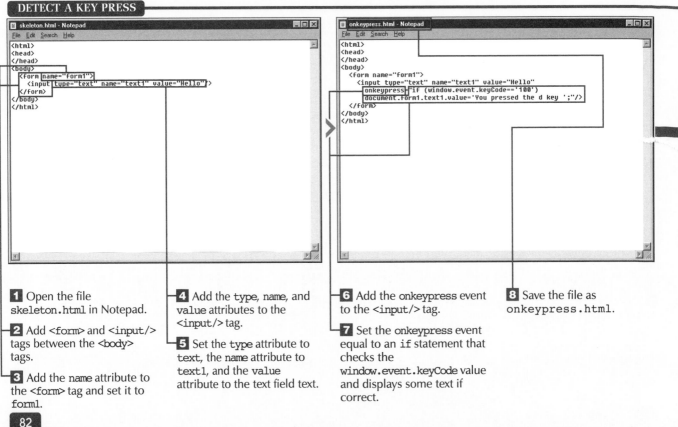

1 Open the file skeleton.html in Notepad.

2 Add <form> and <input/> tags between the <body> tags.

3 Add the name attribute to the <form> tag and set it to form1.

4 Add the type, name, and value attributes to the <input/> tag.

5 Set the type attribute to text, the name attribute to text1, and the value attribute to the text field text.

6 Add the onkeypress event to the <input/> tag.

7 Set the onkeypress event equal to an if statement that checks the window.event.keyCode value and displays some text if correct.

8 Save the file as onkeypress.html.

Extra

The onkeydown and onkeyup events are very similar to the onmousedown and onmouseup events. It is possible that the user could press a keyboard key and not release it. In this case, the onkeydown event would detect this action, but the onkeypress event would not until the keyboard key was finally released.

The onkeydown and onkeyup events will always be fired whenever the onkeypress event is fired, but the onkeydown event will be detected before the onkeyup event.

If the onkeypress event is added to two or more elements, the event will only be detected if the element has focus. You can change the focus of elements by using the Tab key.

9 Open the onkeypress.html file in your browser.

■ A single text field is displayed.

10 Click in the text field to give it the focus.

11 Press the **D** key on the keyboard.

■ The text updates to what you set it to in the onkeypress event.

SET FOCUS

ocus determines which `form` element will be affected if the keyboard keys are pressed. For example, if a button has the focus and you press the Enter key, it would respond just as if you had clicked the button with the mouse cursor.

Using HTML, you can set the tab order of `form` elements. Using the Tab key, you can move the focus between different `form` elements.

As the focus moves, you can detect if an element has the focus by using the `onfocus`

event. Using the `onblur` event, you can set an action to occur when an element loses focus.

You can use the `onfocus` and `onblur` events with the `<select>`, `<input/>`, and `<textarea>` tags, as well as with `framesets`.

This example uses the `onkeypress.html` file found on the book's CD-ROM (or which you may have created in the section "Detect a Key Press"), but you can apply these steps to any file.

SET FOCUS

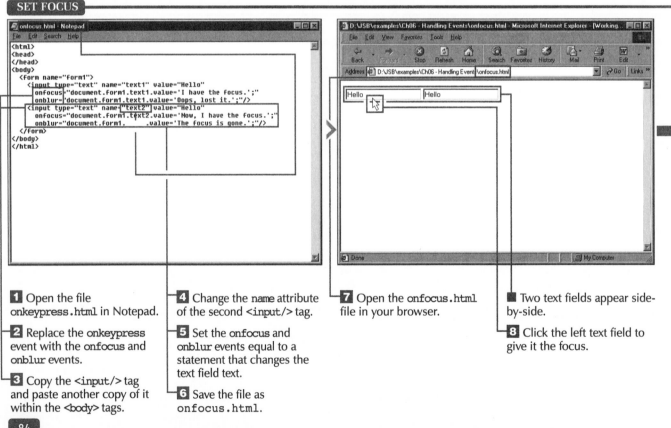

1 Open the file onkeypress.html in Notepad.

2 Replace the onkeypress event with the onfocus and onblur events.

3 Copy the <input/> tag and paste another copy of it within the <body> tags.

4 Change the name attribute of the second <input/> tag.

5 Set the onfocus and onblur events equal to a statement that changes the text field text.

6 Save the file as onfocus.html.

7 Open the onfocus.html file in your browser.

■ Two text fields appear side-by-side.

8 Click the left text field to give it the focus.

Extra

You can use the `onselect` event with text fields and `textarea` elements to detect when a section of text is selected. After you know that text is highlighted, you can work with the selected section and replace, delete, or change it.

There are two events that can detect when a form is reset and submitted: `onreset` and `onsubmit`. The `onreset` event happens when a reset button is clicked, and the `onsubmit` event happens when a submit button is clicked. Using these events, you can override the default HTML action that happens when these buttons are used.

One example of a situation in which you would need to know if an element has focus is when you are trying to detect a keypress, because the `onkeypress` event will only work for the element that has focus.

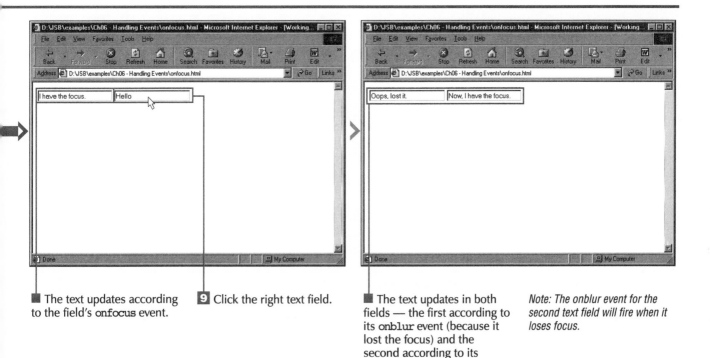

■ The text updates according to the field's **onfocus** event.

9 Click the right text field.

■ The text updates in both fields — the first according to its **onblur** event (because it lost the focus) and the second according to its **onfocus** event (because it gained the focus).

Note: The onblur event for the second text field will fire when it loses focus.

DETECT A PULL-DOWN MENU SELECTION

The selection list element is a common way to offer a list of choices to the user. You can create selection lists within a form by using the `<select>` tag. You can create each separate list item by using the `<option>` tags within the `<select>` tags. Using the `onchange` event, you can detect when a list item is selected.

The `onchange` event can detect when a form element changes. The `onchange` event can be used with the `<select>`, `<input/>`, and `<textarea>` tags.

When you use the `onchange` event with the text field and textarea elements, it detects when the text within these fields changes. By using this event, you can detect if the text was updated. Required fields can be checked to see if they have been filled out before the form is submitted.

This example uses the `skeleton.html` file found on the book's CD-ROM, but you can apply these steps to any file.

DETECT A PULL-DOWN MENU SELECTION

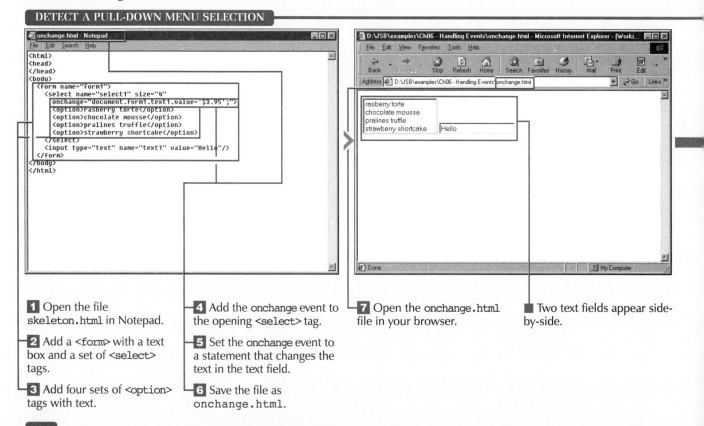

1 Open the file skeleton.html in Notepad.

2 Add a `<form>` with a text box and a set of `<select>` tags.

3 Add four sets of `<option>` tags with text.

4 Add the onchange event to the opening `<select>` tag.

5 Set the onchange event to a statement that changes the text in the text field.

6 Save the file as onchange.html.

7 Open the onchange.html file in your browser.

■ Two text fields appear side-by-side.

Apply It

The onchange event is very useful for validating forms because it fires anytime a form element is changed. For example, if a text field is created that asks the user to input an integer value between 0 and 9, you can create a function that validates the value that is entered into the text field. Such a function looks like this:

```
function intCheck(val) {
  if (val < 0 || val > 9)
    document.alert("This value
is out of range. Please enter an
integer value between 0 and
9.");
}
```

```
. . .
<form name="form1">
  <input type="text" name="text1"
value="1"
onchange="intCheck(this.value)"/>
</form>
```

When the text field is changed, the function is called. The value for this text field is passed as a parameter. This parameter is checked to see if it is less than 0 or greater than 9. If it is, an alert dialog box is displayed with a message.

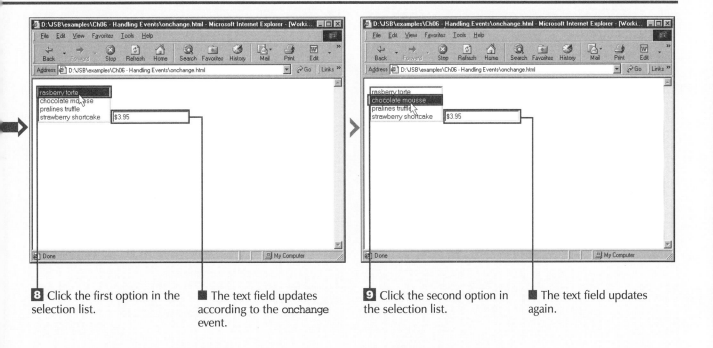

8 Click the first option in the selection list.

■ The text field updates according to the onchange event.

9 Click the second option in the selection list.

■ The text field updates again.

CREATE PAGE LOADING AND UNLOADING MESSAGES

A s Web pages get more complex, they may take longer to load. This can be confusing to the user who isn't quite sure if the page has fully loaded or not.

Using the onload event, you can notify the user when the page has completely finished loading. This event is usually placed within the <body> tag.

The onload event is useful to ensure that all the graphics have been downloaded from the server before executing a script on the page.

A similar event to onload is onunload. This event happens when the current page is left or when the page is reset using a browser's Refresh button.

You can use the onunload event to set any default values or provide a message to users before they leave the current page.

This example uses the skeleton.html file found on the book's CD-ROM, but you can apply these steps to any file.

CREATE PAGE LOADING AND UNLOADING MESSAGES

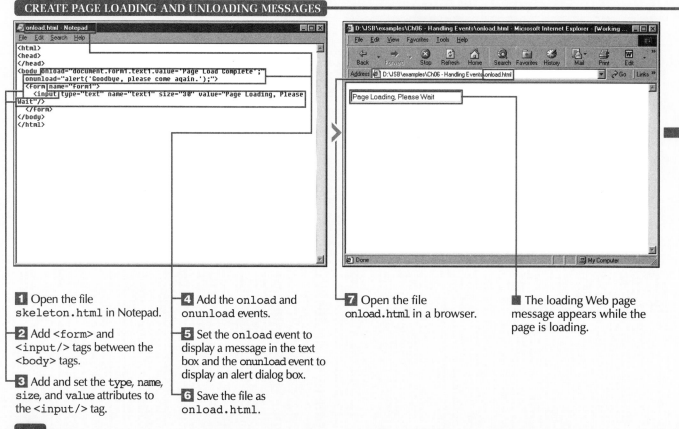

1 Open the file skeleton.html in Notepad.

2 Add <form> and <input/> tags between the <body> tags.

3 Add and set the type, name, size, and value attributes to the <input/> tag.

4 Add the onload and onunload events.

5 Set the onload event to display a message in the text box and the onunload event to display an alert dialog box.

6 Save the file as onload.html.

7 Open the file onload.html in a browser.

■ The loading Web page message appears while the page is loading.

Extra

Any time a Web page is loading in a browser, the user can cancel the page by clicking the Stop browser button. This action can be detected using the `onabort` event. This provides a useful way to inform the user what has happened if all the elements haven't loaded.

The `onerror` event lets you detect when an error loading elements occurs. If the browser experiences trouble loading an image or a page, then the `onerror` event fires. Using this event, you can present a message to the user that is easy to understand.

It's not always a good idea to display alert dialog boxes before the user leaves a Web page. Many users will not appreciate having to click in an alert dialog box before they can leave your Web page. This technique should be used with caution.

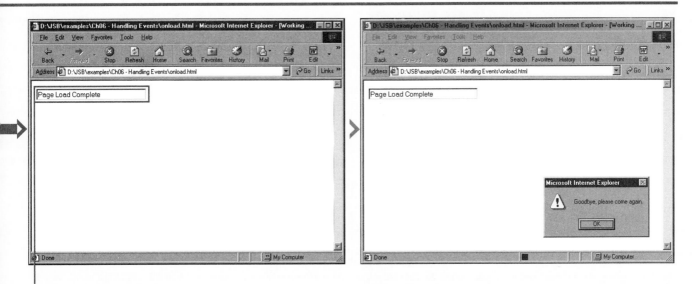

■ After the Web page has finished loading, the message updates.

■ Load a separate Web page in your browser.

■ An alert box appears with a message.

UNDERSTAND OBJECTS, PROPERTIES, AND METHODS

To unleash the power of JavaScript, you need to understand the concept of *objects*. An object is an abstract container that holds data. This data can be a single number or a complex data structure.

In JavaScript, you can create your own objects, or you can use predefined objects, such as `string`, `frame`, `image`, `date`, and `textarea`.

Objects can have *properties* that can provide information about them. For example, the `document` object includes properties that hold the background color and title of the page. Properties can be referenced

by placing a period between the object and property name, as in `document.title`.

Objects can also have *methods,* which are functions specific to the object that perform a task. For example, the `document` object has a method named `write()` that displays the value of the variable or string contained within the parentheses. Methods are referenced just like properties, such as `document.write()`.

This example uses the `js-skeleton.html` file found on the book's CD-ROM, but you can apply these steps to any file.

UNDERSTAND OBJECTS, PROPERTIES, AND METHODS

1 Open the Notepad file.

2 Add an attribute to the `<body>` tag that sets the background color.

3 Within the `<script>` tags, add the `document.write()` method to display some text.

4 Within the parentheses of the `document.write()` method, add the `document.bgColor` property.

5 Save the file as `object.html`.

6 Open the file `object.html` in a browser.

■ The `document` object's method displays the object's property value.

Extra

Here's how you can tell the difference between a property and a method: An object property reference ends with a single variable name, but a method always ends with a set of parentheses. So any object reference that includes a set of parentheses is a method. The parentheses may or may not contain a set of parameter values. Either way, the parentheses are required.

Almost all the preset objects include properties and methods. Objects you create, however, will not necessarily have properties and methods. Creating objects is covered later in this chapter in the section "Create New Objects."

Although several objects have common properties and methods, most are unique to the object. No specific properties or methods are common for all objects.

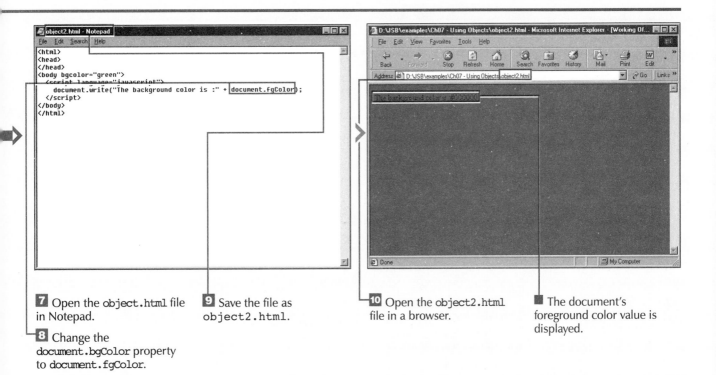

7 Open the object.html file in Notepad.

8 Change the document.bgColor property to document.fgColor.

9 Save the file as object2.html.

10 Open the object2.html file in a browser.

■ The document's foreground color value is displayed.

USING WEB PAGE ELEMENT OBJECTS

The complete collection of JavaScript objects that refer to Web page elements is called the *Document Object Model* (DOM).

The parent object (the top object that contains a subobject) of the Document Object Model is the `window` object. This object includes everything that deals with the browser window, such as the location of the Web pages and the *history*, which is a list of the previously visited pages.

The `window` object also includes the `document` object. The `document` object includes all the elements that make up the Web page, such as links, images, and forms.

The `form` object includes many different objects representing the various elements that can be placed on a form such as `text`, `textarea`, `password`, `button`, `radio`, `checkbox`, `select`, and `combo`.

As the DOM is traversed, objects are referred to as subobjects of their parent. For example, a radio button on a form is referred to as `window.document.form.radio`.

This example uses the `js-skeleton.html` file found on the book's CD-ROM, but you can apply these steps to any file.

USING WEB PAGE ELEMENT OBJECTS

1 Open the Notepad file.

2 Add a form with a `textarea` element under the `<script>` tags.

3 Add buttons to the form using `<input/>` tags.

4 Add the `onclick` event to each `<input/>` tag.

5 Set the `onclick` event for the first button to use a method.

6 Set the `onclick` event for the second button to use a property.

7 Save the file as `ta_object.html`.

8 Open `ta_object.html` in a browser.

■ The `textarea` element is displayed with two buttons.

9 Click the first button.

Extra

All Web page elements are included within the `window` parent object. This parent object is assumed and doesn't need to be included along with objects that are part of the `document` object. For example, a radio button object can be referred to as `document.form.radio` instead of `window.document.form.radio`.

The `window` object needs to be referred to for any object used outside of the current document. This includes the `location` and `history` objects; the `history` object is covered later in this chapter in the section "Using the `history` Object." For example, to refer to the `history` object, you need to use the `window.history` notation.

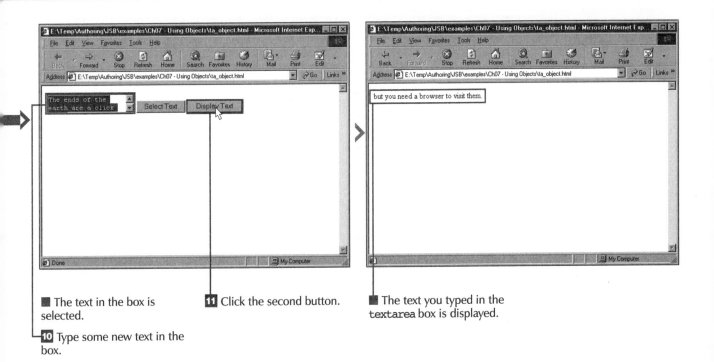

■ The text in the box is selected.

10 Type some new text in the box.

11 Click the second button.

■ The text you typed in the `textarea` box is displayed.

USING SUBOBJECTS

Objects can be nested in a hierarchy. Objects that are contained within another object are referred to as *subobjects*.

These subobjects are linked to the parent object (see the section "Using Web Page Element Objects") with a period (.). Subobjects can also contain additional subobjects, thereby providing more and more detail as the object definition is traversed.

For example, if a Web page includes a form named `form1`, and the form includes a text field named `text1`, the value of the text field

can be identified as `window.document.form1.text1.value`. Here, `document` is the parent, and `form` is a subobject. `form` also serves as the parent to the text field (its subobject).

Object properties and methods can also be referenced using the period (.). For example, `document.bgColor` is the background color property for a Web page, and the method `document.write("hello")` writes the word *hello* to the Web page.

This example uses the `js-skeleton.html` file found on the book's CD-ROM, but you can apply these steps to any file.

CHANGE A TEXT FIELD

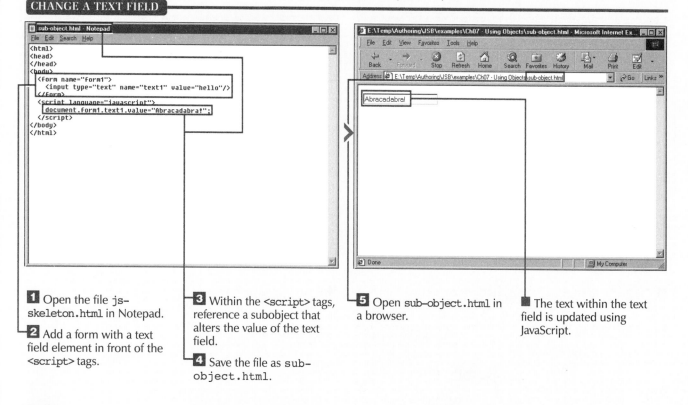

1 Open the file `js-skeleton.html` in Notepad.

2 Add a form with a text field element in front of the `<script>` tags.

3 Within the `<script>` tags, reference a subobject that alters the value of the text field.

4 Save the file as `sub-object.html`.

5 Open `sub-object.html` in a browser.

■ The text within the text field is updated using JavaScript.

Extra

When referencing subobjects, the reference should always end with either an object property or a method. If the reference doesn't conclude with a property or a method, the object is undetermined.

A reference to a subobject can be used within a JavaScript statement just like a variable.

You can't include a space in a subobject name. You can, however, use the underscore character to separate terms in a name. The JavaScript syntax uses periods to connect subobjects to their parents. If a space is used in the subobject name, the parent will be unidentified.

CHECK A RADIO BUTTON

```
sub-object2.html - Notepad
File  Edit  Search  Help
<html>
<head>
</head>
<body>
<form name="form1">
  <input type="radio" name="radio1"/>true
  <input type="radio" name="radio2"/>false
</form>
<script language="javascript">
  document.form1.radio1.checked=true;
</script>
</body>
</html>
```

E:\Temp\Authoring\JSB\examples\Ch07 - Using Objects\sub-object2.html - Microsoft Internet E...

File Edit View Favorites Tools Help

Back Forward Stop Refresh Home Search Favorites History Mail Print Edit

Address E:\Temp\Authoring\JSB\examples\Ch07 - Using Objects\sub-object2.html   Go   Links

(•) true ( ) false

Done   My Computer

1 Open the file js-skeleton.html in Notepad.

2 Add a form with two radio button elements in front of the <script> tags.

3 Within the <script> tags, reference a subobject that displays a check mark in one of the radio buttons.

4 Save the file as sub-object2.html.

5 Open the file sub-object2.html in a browser.

■ One of the radio buttons is checked (⦿) using JavaScript.

USING PREDEFINED OBJECTS

JavaScript's predefined objects include useful objects for working with dates and mathematical functions, as well as objects for interacting with all the various elements of a Web page.

Many predefined objects, such as form, button, and frame, let you work with actual Web page elements. These objects are discussed in the earlier section "Using Web Page Element Objects." Other predefined objects, such as String, Date, and Math, let you work with different types of data.

Each of these objects has properties and methods that can be used to get information about the object or to perform a certain task. These objects, their properties, and their methods are covered in more detail in Chapters 10–14.

This example uses the js-skeleton.html file found on the book's CD-ROM, but you can apply these steps to any file.

USING THE STRING OBJECT

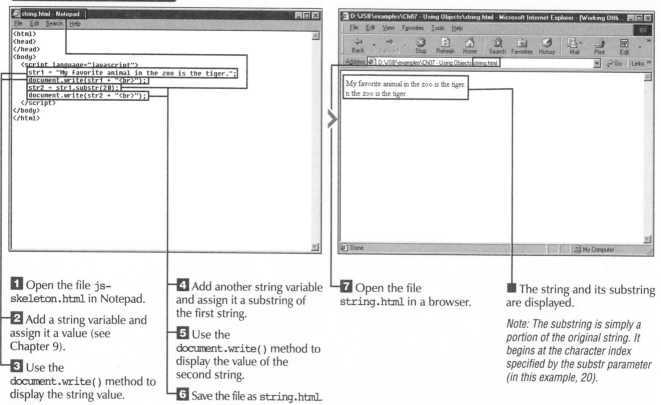

1 Open the file js-skeleton.html in Notepad.

2 Add a string variable and assign it a value (see Chapter 9).

3 Use the document.write() method to display the string value.

4 Add another string variable and assign it a substring of the first string.

5 Use the document.write() method to display the value of the second string.

6 Save the file as string.html.

7 Open the file string.html in a browser.

■ The string and its substring are displayed.

Note: The substring is simply a portion of the original string. It begins at the character index specified by the substr parameter (in this example, 20).

Extra

Many of JavaScript's predefined objects, their properties, and their methods are covered in Chapters 9–11. These objects include `Array`, `Date`, `Math`, and `String`. The `Array` object is used to create and manipulate an array of variables. The `Date` object is used to create and manipulate dates and times. The `Math` object is used to represent mathematical constants such as logarithms and mathematical expressions. The `String` object enables you to work with strings.

An example of each of these objects is

```
MyArray = new Array(20);
MyDate = new Date(20);
Area = Math.PI * Math.pow(radius, 2);
MyString = "Welcome to here.";
```

A predefined object exists for almost every Web page element, including browser history, anchors, links, plug-ins, check boxes, and reset buttons. Many are accessible using general browser objects. Chapters 12 and 14 discuss these in detail.

USING THE MATH OBJECT

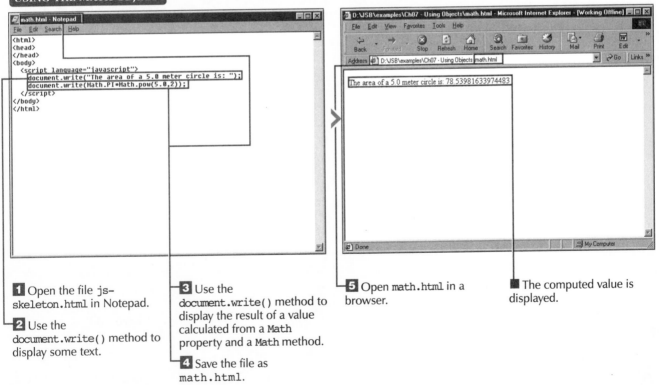

1 Open the file js-skeleton.html in Notepad.

2 Use the document.write() method to display some text.

3 Use the document.write() method to display the result of a value calculated from a `Math` property and a `Math` method.

4 Save the file as math.html.

5 Open math.html in a browser.

■ The computed value is displayed.

CREATE NEW OBJECTS

Some objects, like the string object, are created implicitly whenever a string is declared. For example, if you assign a string to a variable such as str1 = "Hello, everyone", you can access the properties and methods of this object by referring to the variable name, such as str1.length.

Other objects, such as the Date object, need to be created using the new keyword and a function constructor. For example, to create a new Date object named myDate, you would

set the variable name equal to the new keyword and the constructor function for the Date object like this: myDate = new Date().

The new keyword, when used with the Object() constructor, can be used to create user-defined objects.

This example uses the js-skeleton.html file found on the book's CD-ROM, but you can apply these steps to any file.

1 Open the file js-skeleton.html in Notepad.

2 Add a variable and assign it a new Date object.

Note: This new Date object allows you to retrieve the current date using the toLocaleString() method (see Chapter 10).

3 Use the document.write() method to display the values of the current date and month.

4 Save the file as new.html.

5 Open the new.html file in a browser.

■ The current date and month are displayed.

You can create custom objects by using a function to define the object. Variables within these functions become object properties, and the names of other functions become the object methods.

For example,

```
function helloObject(var1, var2, var3)
{
    helloObject.name = var1;
    helloObject.birthdate = var2;
```

```
    helloObject.age = var3;
    helloObject.welcome = printObject;
}
function printObject(name) {
    document.write("Welcome " + name);
}
```

creates a new object named `helloObject` that has `name`, `birthdate`, and `age` as properties and `welcome()` as a method.

```
new2.html - Notepad
File  Edit  Search  Help
<html>
<head>
</head>
<body>
   <script language="javascript">
     today = new Date();
     document.write("Today is day number " + today.getDate() + " of month " +
(today.getMonth()+1));
     document.write("   The current time is " + today.toLocaleString());
   </script>
</body>
</html>
```

```
E:\Temp\Authoring\JSB\examples\Ch07 - Using Objects\new2.html - Microsoft Internet Explorer
File  Edit  View  Favorites  Tools  Help
Back  Forward  Stop  Refresh  Home  Search  Favorites  History  Mail  Print  Edit
Address  E:\Temp\Authoring\JSB\examples\Ch07 - Using Objects\new2.html        Go   Links
```

Today is day number 15 of month 6 The current time is 06/15/2000 14:24:10

6 Open the new.html file in Notepad.

7 Add another document.write statement to display the current time.

8 Save the file as new2.html.

9 Open the file new2.html in a browser.

■ The current time is also displayed.

REFER TO THE CURRENT OBJECT

As you work with subobjects (see the section "Using Subobjects"), you will find that it is cumbersome to reference the entire object tree every time you want to use an object. JavaScript includes a keyword that can be used to reference the current object.

The keyword to reference the current object is this. The this keyword can be placed in place of the object's parent but can only be used within the current function.

For example, if you are using variables passed to a function, such as function

hello(str1), you can use the this keyword to refer to these variables, such as this.name = str1.

Another place you can use the this keyword is to refer to the current Web element. For example, if you pass the text field value of a form to a function, you can refer to the value within the event handler as this.value.

This example uses the js-skeleton.html file found on the book's CD-ROM, but you can apply these steps to any file.

IDENTIFY OBJECT PROPERTIES

1 Open the file js-skeleton.html in Notepad.

2 Create a function with parameters.

3 Create a property for each parameter and assign it the parameter's value.

4 Using the new keyword, create another object.

5 Using document.write statements, display the object's property values.

6 Save the file as this.html.

7 Open this.html in a browser.

■ The values of the object instance are displayed.

Apply It

The `this` keyword can also be used as a parameter that is passed to a function. For example, suppose you have a function like the following:

```
function makeBold(text1) {
    document.write("<b>" + text1 +
"</b>");
}
```

Then, you could call this function from an event within an HTML element like so:

```
<form name="form1">
    <input type="text" name="text1"
onclick="makeBold(this.value)"
</form>
```

This `onclick` event would pass the value of the current element to the function. In this case, the value of the text field would be passed.

REFER TO THE CURRENT WEB PAGE ELEMENT

```
<html>
<head>
</head>
<body>
    <script language="javascript">
    </script>
    <form name="form1">
        <input type="text" name="text1" value="The ends of the earth are a click
away." onclick="this.select()"/>
    </form>
</body>
</html>
```

1 Open the js-skeleton.html file in Notepad.

2 Add a form with a text field to the page.

3 Add the onclick event to the text field.

4 Set the onclick event equal to the this.select() method.

5 Save the file as this2.html.

6 Open this2.html in a browser.

7 Click the text field.

■ The text in the text field is selected.

VIEW OBJECT PROPERTIES

When working with an object, knowing all the object properties that the object supports is quite helpful. Having a JavaScript reference handy can help with this, but you can also use JavaScript to list an object's properties.

A special version of the `for` loop can be used to look into the object and view all its properties. This `for` loop includes the `in` keyword and the object name.

For example, the statement `for (prop in window)` loops through all the properties in

the `window` object. You can then include a `document.write` statement with the `for` loop to display the properties. You can also use the `window[prop]` statement to display the values of the property.

These statements can only be used on objects that have been defined. If an object doesn't exist, no properties are displayed.

This example uses the `js-skeleton.html` file found on the book's CD-ROM, but you can apply these steps to any file.

VIEW OBJECT PROPERTIES

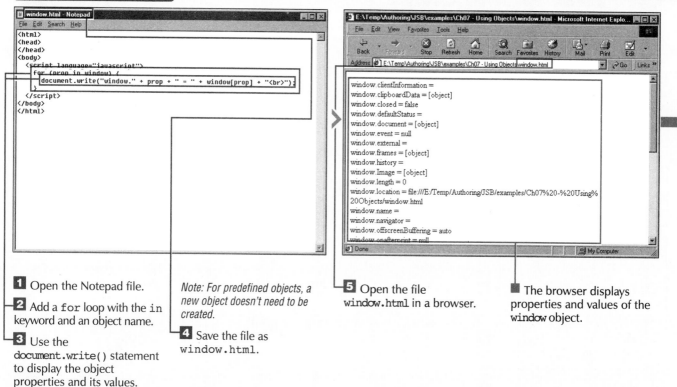

1 Open the Notepad file.

2 Add a for loop with the in keyword and an object name.

3 Use the `document.write()` statement to display the object properties and its values.

Note: For predefined objects, a new object doesn't need to be created.

4 Save the file as `window.html`.

5 Open the file `window.html` in a browser.

■ The browser displays properties and values of the `window` object.

To make this object property viewer routine more usable, you can include it as part of a function and pass the object name to it. The completed function looks something like this:

```
function displayObjectProperties(obj) {
  objName = obj + "";
  for (prop in obj) {
  document.write(objName + "." + prop +
" = " + obj[prop] + "<br>");
    }
```

This function can then be called with an object name, and the properties and their values will be displayed. The statement to call this function looks like this:

```
displayObjectProperties(window);
```

location.html - Notepad

```
<html>
<head>
</head>
<body>
  <script language="javascript">
    for (prop in location) {
      document.write("location." + prop + " = " + location[prop] + "<br>");
    }
  </script>
</body>
</html>
```

E:\Temp\Authoring\JSB\examples\Ch07 - Using Objects\location.html - Microsoft Internet Expl...

Address E:\Temp\Authoring\JSB\examples\Ch07 - Using Objects\location.html

```
location.hash =
location.host =
location.hostname =
location.href = file:///E:/Temp/Authoring/JSB/examples/Ch07%20-%20Using%
20Objects/location.html
location.pathname = /E:\Temp\Authoring\JSB\examples\Ch07 - Using Objects\location.html
location.port =
location.protocol = file:
location.search =
```

6 Open the window.html file in Notepad.

7 Change the object in the for loop.

8 Save the file as location.html.

9 Open the file location.html in a browser.

■ The properties for the new object are displayed.

USING THE ARRAY OBJECT

I n Chapter 2, you find out about arrays and how to create an array of variables. After an array is created, you can work with the `Array` object.

The `Array` object has a property called `length` that returns the length of the given array. For example, if you create a new array with the statement `array1 = new Array(30)`, the `array1.length` property is equal to 30.

The `Array` object also includes several methods that can be used to manipulate the array elements. The `join()` method combines all array elements into a single string,

separating each element with a user-defined value passed as a parameter. For example, for an array named `array1`, the statement `array1.join(" and ")` produces a string of all array elements with the word *and* in between each element.

You can also sort all the elements of an array using the `sort()` method. The `reverse()` method reverses the order of all array elements.

This example uses the `js-skeleton.html` file found on the book's CD-ROM, but you can apply these steps to any file.

USING THE ARRAY OBJECT

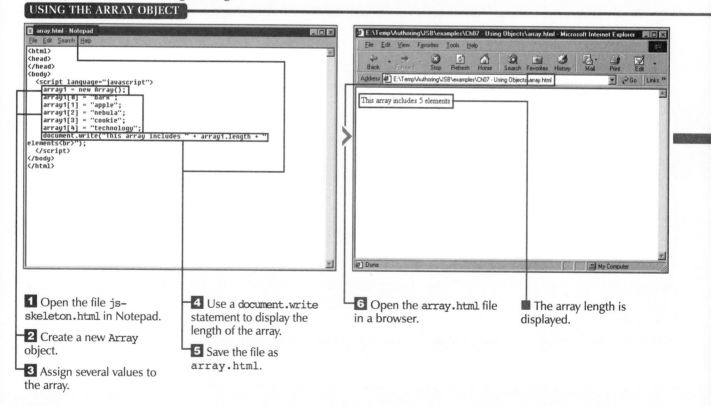

1 Open the file js-skeleton.html in Notepad.

2 Create a new Array object.

3 Assign several values to the array.

4 Use a document.write statement to display the length of the array.

5 Save the file as array.html.

6 Open the array.html file in a browser.

■ The array length is displayed.

Apply It

In addition to the methods described in this section, the `Array` object includes another method called `slice()`. This method can be used to take a subsection of an existing array and extract it to create a new array. The `slice()` method takes two parameters. The first parameter is the index of the first array element to include in the new array, and the second parameter is the last array element to include in the new array. A statement that uses the `slice()` method would look like this:

```
array1 = new Array(5);
array1[0] = "Thomas";
array1[1] = "Dave";
array1[2] = "Sue";
```

```
array1[3] = "Adam";
array1[4] = "Richard";
array2 = array1.slice(1,2);
```

These statements create an array named `array1` that holds five elements. A new array, named `array2`, is created that holds two elements — Dave and Sue.

```
array2.html - Notepad
File  Edit  Search  Help
<html>
<head>
</head>
<body>
  <script language="javascript">
    array1 = new Array(10);
    array1[0] = "bark";
    array1[1] = "apple";
    array1[2] = "nebula";
    array1[3] = "cookie";
    array1[4] = "technology";
    document.write("This array includes " + array1.length + "
elements<br>");
    document.write("Joined Array: " + array1.join(" ") + "<br>");
    document.write("Sorted Array: " + array1.sort() + "<br>");
  </script>
</body>
</html>
```

```
E:\Temp\Authoring\JSB\examples\Ch07 - Using Objects\array2.html - Microsoft Internet Explorer
File  Edit  View  Favorites  Tools  Help
Back   Forward   Stop   Refresh   Home   Search  Favorites  History   Mail   Print   Edit
Address  E:\Temp\Authoring\JSB\examples\Ch07 - Using Objects\array2.html                    Go   Links

This array includes 10 elements
Joined Array: bark apple nebula cookie technology
Sorted Array: apple,bark,cookie,nebula,technology,,,,,

Done                                                               My Computer
```

7 Open the `array.html` file in Notepad.

8 Add another `document.write` statement that uses the `join()` method to display the contents of the array.

9 Add another `document.write` statement that uses the `sort()` method to sort and display the array.

10 Save the file as `array2.html`.

11 Open the `array2.html` file in a browser.

Note: The array is defined to hold 10 elements, but only 5 of them are filled, so extra commas show the empty array slots.

■ The `join()` method lists the contents of the array in their original order. The `sort()` method displays a sorted list of the array elements.

■ The array length is now returned as 10 instead of 5.

USING THE IMAGE OBJECT

The image object exists for any Web page that includes at least one image. Web page elements such as images, forms, applets, and links are included in an array and can be referred to using an index that matches its position in the Web page file.

For example, if a Web page has two images, you can refer to the first one as document.images[0] and the second one as document.images[1]. Remember that array indexes always start at 0.

Using the index, you can find out information about the image, such as its border width, its dimensions, its name, source, and spacing attributes. There aren't any methods for the image object, but you can change the properties of the images dynamically.

This example uses the js-skeleton.html file found on the book's CD-ROM, but you can apply these steps to any file.

USING THE IMAGE OBJECT

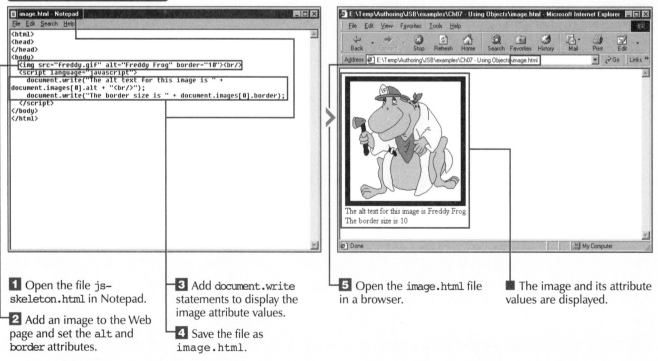

1 Open the file js-skeleton.html in Notepad.

2 Add an image to the Web page and set the alt and border attributes.

3 Add document.write statements to display the image attribute values.

4 Save the file as image.html.

5 Open the image.html file in a browser.

■ The image and its attribute values are displayed.

PRELOAD IMAGES

Using a new image object, you can preload an image into memory while the page initially loads. After the image is preloaded, JavaScript can reference the image object and display it immediately.

To create a new image object, you need to specify an image name and use the new keyword — for example, myImage = newImage().

After creating a new image object, you can set its attributes using the image object properties, such as myImage.src = "house.gif", myImage.border = "20", and myImage.hspace = "10".

This example uses the js-skeleton.html file found on the book's CD-ROM, but you can apply these steps to any file.

PRELOAD IMAGES

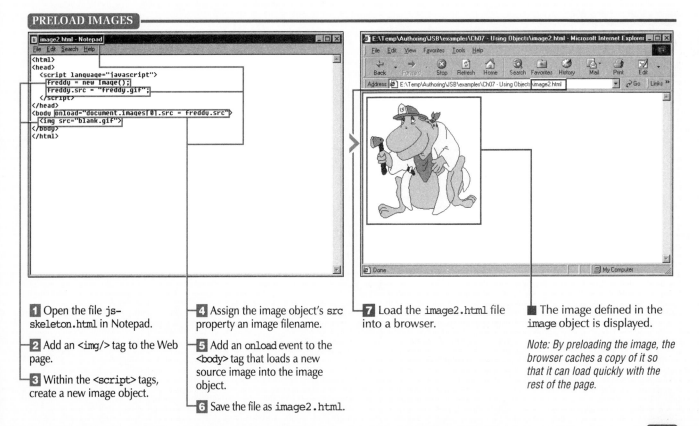

1 Open the file js-skeleton.html in Notepad.

2 Add an <img/> tag to the Web page.

3 Within the <script> tags, create a new image object.

4 Assign the image object's src property an image filename.

5 Add an onload event to the <body> tag that loads a new source image into the image object.

6 Save the file as image2.html.

7 Load the image2.html file into a browser.

■ The image defined in the image object is displayed.

Note: By preloading the image, the browser caches a copy of it so that it can load quickly with the rest of the page.

CHANGE IMAGES

Many of the `image` object properties are the same as the attributes of the `<img/>` tag — such as `border`, `width`, `hspace`, and `src`. When these properties are changed in a JavaScript statement, the image on the Web page is changed dynamically. These properties enable you to change an image's attributes dynamically using JavaScript.

In addition to the image attributes, setting the image's `src` attribute to a new value can change the actual image that is loaded in a

Web page. Before changing images, you should preload the new image so that the image is immediately available to be displayed (see the section "Preload Images").

For example, the first image on the Web page can be referenced as `document.images[0]`, so if you set `document.images[0].src` to a new image, the image on the page will change.

This example uses the `js-skeleton.html` file found on the book's CD-ROM, but you can apply these steps to any file.

CHANGE IMAGES

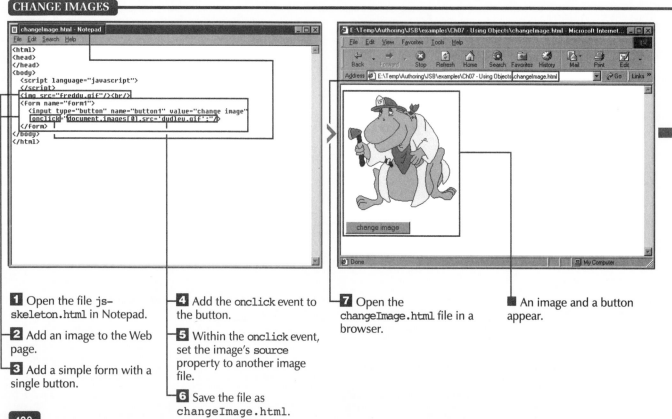

1 Open the file `js-skeleton.html` in Notepad.

2 Add an image to the Web page.

3 Add a simple form with a single button.

4 Add the `onclick` event to the button.

5 Within the `onclick` event, set the image's **source** property to another image file.

6 Save the file as `changeImage.html`.

7 Open the `changeImage.html` file in a browser.

■ An image and a button appear.

Apply It

Another property of the `image` object is the `complete` property. This property is a Boolean value that is `false` until an image is completely loaded. When completely loaded, the `complete` property is set to `true`. Using this value, you can check to see if an image is loaded before changing it. For example, if you have an image loaded that will change, you can check the `complete` property before allowing the image to change. The JavaScript statements for checking whether an image is fully loaded look something like this:

```
function changeImage() {

  if (document.images[0].complete)

    document.images[0].src =
"newImage.gif";

}
```

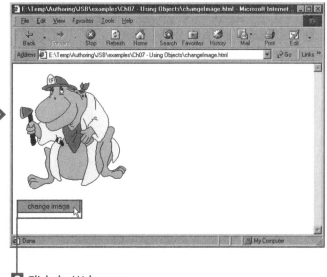

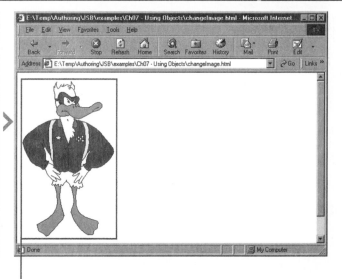

8 Click the Web page button.

■ The new image appears.

USING THE LINK AND ANCHOR OBJECTS

J ust like the image object, the link and anchor objects are included in an array for reference using JavaScript. The order that the link appears on the page is the index for the array. Links and anchors are counted independent of one another.

For example, if a page has two anchors and three links, the first anchor is referenced as document.anchors[0] and the first link would be referenced as document.links[0].

The link object includes href and target properties that can be used to dynamically

change the link. The anchor object includes a name property that can dynamically change the anchor name.

Other link properties are used to describe the link components. The host property includes the domain name, the protocol property lists the protocol, such as http:, and the pathname property lists the path of the URL in UNC (Uniform Naming Convention) format.

This example uses the js-skeleton.html file found on the book's CD-ROM, but you can apply these steps to any file.

USING THE LINK AND ANCHOR OBJECTS

1 Open the file js-skeleton.html in Notepad.

2 Add several links and anchors above the <script> tags.

3 Within the <script> tags, add document.write statements to display the length of the links and anchors arrays.

4 Save the file as links.html.

5 Open the links.html file in a browser.

■ The links and number of links are displayed.

Extra

Links can be decomposed into their various components by using the properties of the link object. The protocol property lists the protocol for the URL, which can be something like http: or ftp:. The hostname property includes the domain name, and the pathname property includes the path to the Web file. The port property lists the port value for the Web page, and the host property includes the hostname and port values together. The final piece of a URL is the anchor name, which can be obtained from the hash property. A complete URL can be generated from the following:

```
myLink.protocol + myLink.hostname +
myLink.pathname + myLink.port +
myLink.hash
```

The anchor object doesn't include all the same properties as the link object: The anchor object includes only a single property — name.

---

links2.html - Notepad

File Edit Search Help

```
<html>
<head>
</head>
<body>
  <a name="anchor1">Anchor #1<br/>
  <a href="www.animabets.com">Animabets.com</a><br/>
  <a href="www.microsoft.com">Microsoft.com</a><br/>
  <a href="www.cnn.com">CNN News</a><br/>
  <a name="anchor2">Anchor #2<br/>
  <script language="javascript">
    document.write("This web page has " + document.links.length + "
links.<br/>");
    document.write("This web page has " + document.anchors.length + "
anchors.<br/>");
    document.write("Link #1 protocol: " + document.links[0].protocol +
"<br/>");
    document.write("Link #1 pathname: " + document.links[0].pathname +
"<br/>");
    document.write("Link #1 href: " + document.links[0].href + "<br/>");
  </script>
</body>
</html>
```

E:\Temp\Authoring\JSB\examples\Ch07 - Using Objects\links2.html - Microsoft Internet Explorer

File Edit View Favorites Tools Help

Back Forward Stop Refresh Home Search Favorites History Mail Print Edit

Address E:\Temp\Authoring\JSB\examples\Ch07 - Using Objects\links2.html   Go   Links

Anchor #1
Animabets.com
Microsoft.com
CNN News
Anchor #2
This web page has 3 links.
This web page has 2 anchors.
Link #1 protocol: file:
Link #1 pathname: E:\Temp\Authoring\JSB\examples\Ch07%20-%20Using%20Objects\www.animabets.com
Link #1 href: file:///E:/Temp/Authoring/JSB/examples/Ch07%20-%20Using%20Objects/www.animabets.com

Done   My Computer

■6 Open the links.html file in Notepad.

■7 Add several document.write statements to display information about one of the links.

■8 Save the file as links2.html.

■9 Open the links2.html file in a browser.

■ The link information is displayed.

CHANGE LINKS

Many objects contain all the various elements on a Web page. For example, the `link` object holds all the links included on the Web page.

Individual links can be located by specifying the index value for the link. These index values are numbered sequentially from the top of the page to the bottom, starting at 0 for the first link.

The index value is specified within square brackets immediately after the link's object name. For example, the first link on the page can be referred to as `document.links[0]`.

The `link` object shares many of the same properties as the `location` object, including `host`, `hostname`, `href`, `pathname`, `port`, and `protocol`.

This example uses the `js-skeleton.html` file found on the book's CD-ROM, but you can apply these steps to any file.

CHANGE LINKS

1 Open the `js-skeleton.html` file.

2 Add a link to a Web page.

3 Add a form with a single button.

4 Add `onclick` to the button and set the event to change the `href` property of the link.

Note: Changing the `href` property in Step 4 is what actually changes the link.

5 Save the file as `changeLink.html`.

6 Open the `changeLink.html` file in a browser.

■ A single link and a button are displayed.

Apply It

You can create a random link generator by creating several links, placing them in an array, and then randomly selecting a link and changing a generic link with the random one. The code for this would look like this:

```
function randomLink() {
    randomLink = new Array();
    randomLink[0] = "www.animabets.com";
    randomLink[1] = "www.microsoft.com";
    randomLink[2] = "www.cnn.com";
    randNo = Math.floor(randomLink.length
* Math.random());
    document.links[0].href =
randomLink[randNo];
}
```

In this example, I included the `Math.floor()` method because it rounds down to the closest integer.

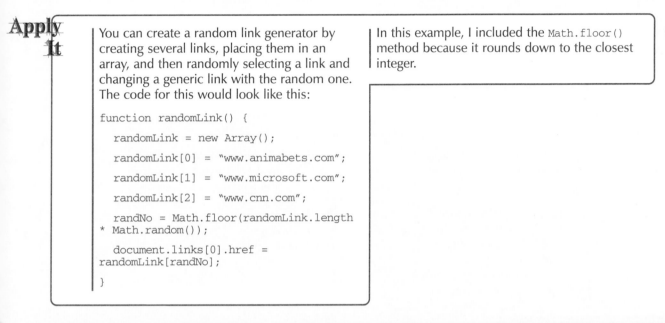

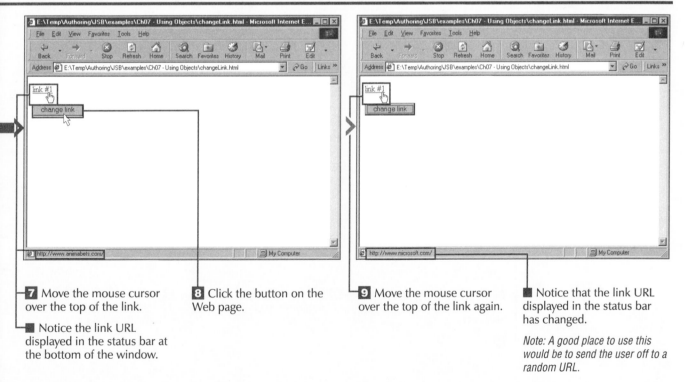

7 Move the mouse cursor over the top of the link.

■ Notice the link URL displayed in the status bar at the bottom of the window.

8 Click the button on the Web page.

9 Move the mouse cursor over the top of the link again.

■ Notice that the link URL displayed in the status bar has changed.

Note: A good place to use this would be to send the user off to a random URL.

USING THE HISTORY OBJECT

The `history` object enables you to duplicate the browser's Forward and Back buttons to move between viewed Web pages.

You can use the `history` object's `length` property to view the length of the current history list saved by the browser.

The `history` object includes several methods. The `back()` method can cause the previously loaded Web page to appear in the browser. The `forward()` method displays the next page in the browser. (To go forward, the user must have first gone back to previous pages.)

The `go()` method accepts a number parameter, which can be positive or negative, and moves you forward or backward in the History list.

For example, the statement `document.history.go(-2)` displays the Web page that is two pages back in the History list.

This example uses the `js-skeleton.html` file found on the book's CD-ROM, but you can apply these steps to any file.

USING THE HISTORY OBJECT

1 Open the file js–skeleton.html in Notepad.

2 Add a form with a single button.

3 Add the onclick event to the button.

4 Set the onclick event to move back two pages in the history list.

5 Save the file as history.html.

6 Open the history.html file in a browser.

7 Click the arrow ( ) to the right of the Back button to view the history list.

Extra

The `history.go()` method can be used to reload the current page. If the index is set to 0, then the current page is the one in the history list that is loaded. This has the same effect as a page refresh. The code looks like this:

```
document.history(0);
```

You can set the number of places to go back in the history list using a user-inputted value from a form element such as a selection list or a text field. The code to do this would look like this:

```
document.history(document.form1.text1.
value);
```

You can prevent a user from going back with the Back button by using the `window.location.replace()` method. This method enables you to replace the current history list entry with a URL that is passed as a parameter.

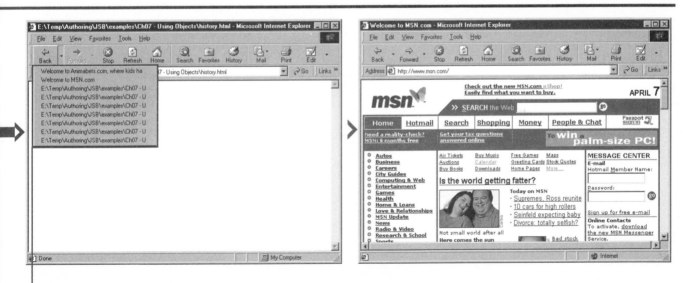

■ The history list is displayed in a drop-down list.

8 Click anywhere in the browser window to make the list disappear.

9 Click the button.

■ The Web page back two places is loaded in the browser.

USING THE WINDOW AND DOCUMENT OBJECTS

JavaScript includes two parent objects that are used to control the appearance and look of a browser window. These two objects are the window and document objects.

The window object is the top-level parent for all objects and includes the document, location, and history objects as sub-objects. window also includes properties and methods for controlling the external look of a browser window. I describe several of these in this chapter, but you can find many more throughout the remaining chapters.

The document object allows access to the various HTML elements that make up a Web page. One of the document object methods is write(), which is used to output text and HTML to the browser window.

For example, the JavaScript statement document.write('hello', name) prints the word *hello* in bold letters in the browser followed by the value of the JavaScript variable name.

USING THE WINDOW AND DOCUMENT OBJECTS

```
write.html - Notepad
File  Edit  Search  Help
<html>
<head>
</head>
<body>
  <script language="javascript">
    document.write('<h1>Welcome to the Here and Now</h1>');
    document.write('<p>For all you that have been elsewhere, ');
    document.write('past and present, this is your official ');
    document.write('salutation welcoming you to wherever you are.</p>');
  </script>
</body>
</html>
```

E:\Temp\Authoring\JSB\examples\Ch08 - Working with Windows\write.html - Microsoft Internet...

Address E:\Temp\Authoring\JSB\examples\Ch08 - Working with Windows\write.html

Welcome to the Here and Now

For all you that have been elsewhere, past and present, this is your official salutation welcoming you to wherever you are.

■1 Open the CD file js-skeleton.html in Notepad.

■2 Add several document.write() statements.

■3 Within the parentheses of the document.write()

statements, add HTML code within single quote marks.

Note: You can find specifics on HTML in Appendix A, or for more comprehensive coverage try Teach Yourself Visually HTML.

■4 Save the file as write.html.

■5 Open the write.html file in a browser.

■ The HTML code is displayed within the browser.

Extra

In addition to the `document.write()` method which has already been used and explained, JavaScript includes another similar method, `document.writeln()`. This method also displays the passed parameter in the browser window, except it includes a new line character at the end of the line. For example, the statements

```
document.writeln("Hello ");

document.writeln("and welcome ");

document.writeln("to my page.");
```

include a new line character at the end of each line. Because the browser interprets the text as HTML, the new line characters are interpreted as white space, causing the text to run together.

If the statement is written with the `window` object in front of it, it will still work fine. For example, `window.document.write()` works the same as `document.write()`.

```
write2.html | Notepad
File Edit Search Help
<html>
<head>
</head>
<body>
  <script language="javascript">
    document.write('<h1>Welcome to the Here and Now</h1>');
    document.write('<p>For all you that have been elsewhere, ');
    document.write('past and present, this is your official ');
    document.write('salutation welcoming you to wherever you are.</p>');
    planet = 17;
    document.write('From planet no. ', planet);
  </script>
</body>
</html>
```

E:\Temp\Authoring\JSB\examples\Ch08 - Working with Windows\write2.html - Microsoft Intern...

File   Edit   View   Favorites   Tools   Help

Back   Forward   Stop   Refresh   Home   Search   Favorites   History   Mail   Print   Edit

Address   E:\Temp\Authoring\JSB\examples\Ch08 - Working with Windows\write2.html   Go   Links

Welcome to the Here and Now

For all you that have been elsewhere, past and present, this is your official salutation welcoming you to wherever you are.

From planet no. 17

My Computer

ADD A VARIABLE

1 Open the `write.html` file in Notepad.

2 Add a variable definition and set it equal to a value.

3 Beneath the variable definition, add another `document.write()` statement to display the variable value.

4 Save the file as `write2.html`.

5 Open the `write2.html` file in a browser.

■ The text along with the variable value is displayed.

DISPLAY TEXT ON A BROWSER'S STATUS BAR

The browser window status bar is the space at the bottom of the window between the document and the edge of the window. This area is used to display useful information to the user, such as the link address when the mouse cursor is moved over a link.

Using the window.status property, you can set the text that is displayed in the status bar. To do this, you simply need to set the window.status property equal to a line of text. This text can also include JavaScript statements.

For example, the statement window.status="hello and welcome" displays "hello and welcome" in the status bar of the current window.

If window.status is used to display text in the status bar and then the mouse cursor is moved over a link, the text displays the link's location.

This example uses the skeleton.html file found on the book's CD-ROM, but you can apply these steps to any file.

DISPLAY TEXT ON A BROWSER'S STATUS BAR

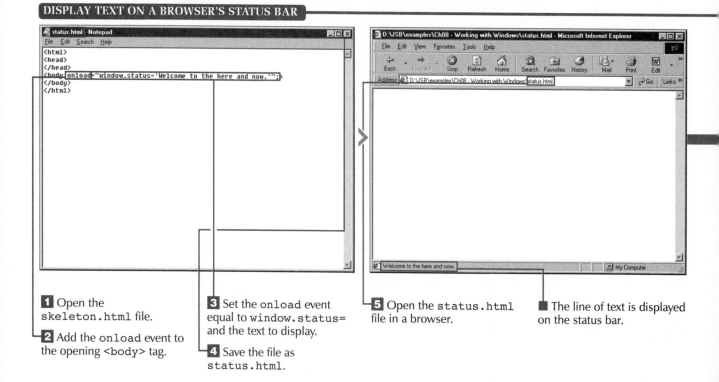

1 Open the skeleton.html file.

2 Add the onload event to the opening <body> tag.

3 Set the onload event equal to window.status= and the text to display.

4 Save the file as status.html.

5 Open the status.html file in a browser.

■ The line of text is displayed on the status bar.

Extra

If the text string displayed in the browser status bar is longer than the browser window, the browser truncates and displays as much of the text string that it can.

The text on the status bar can be changed in response to an event using the `window.status` property, but you can also set the default text that should appear on the status bar when no events are detected using the `window.defaultStatus` property. For example, setting

```
window.defaultStatus =¯ "Processing"
```

displays "Processing" as the default text that appears anytime no events are happening.

---

status2.html - Notepad

File Edit Search Help

```
<html>
<head>
</head>
<body onload="window.status='Welcome to the here and now.'";>
<a href="www.animabets.com">Animabets.com</a>
</body>
</html>
```

D:\JSB\examples\Ch08 - Working with Windows\status2.html - Microsoft Internet Explorer

File Edit View Favorites Tools Help

Back · Forward · Stop · Refresh · Home · Search · Favorites · History · Mail · Print · Edit

Address D:\JSB\examples\Ch08 - Working with Windows\status2.html

Animabets.com

file:///D:/JSB/examples/Ch08 - Working with Windows/www.animabets.com · My Computer

6 Open the `status.html` file in Notepad.

7 Add a link to a Web page.

8 Save the file as `status2.html`.

9 Open the `status2.html` file in a browser.

10 Move the mouse cursor over the top of the link text.

■ The status bar text is replaced with the link reference.

Note: Link addresses are displayed by the browser by default and cannot be overwritten with other text.

CHANGE BACKGROUND COLORS

The background color can be set using the bgcolor attribute of the `<body>` tag in standard HTML, but JavaScript enables you to dynamically change the background color.

The document.bgColor object property holds the current color of the background, or if you assign this object a color, you can set the background color.

For example, if you set the document. bgColor property to blue, the background color becomes blue when the document is displayed.

Color values can be either browser-recognized color names like red, blue, or orange, or colors can be represented as RGB hexadecimal numbers. RGB hexadecimal numbers include the number sign (#) followed by the hexadecimal values of red, green, and blue ranging from 00 to FF.

For example, red is represented as #FF0000, blue is #0000FF, and purple is #FF00FF.

This example uses the js-skeleton.html file found on the book's CD-ROM, but you can apply these steps to any file.

CHANGE BACKGROUND COLORS

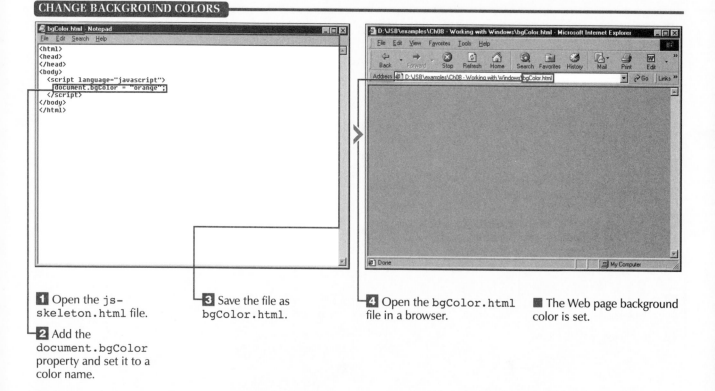

1 Open the js-skeleton.html file.

2 Add the document.bgColor property and set it to a color name.

3 Save the file as bgColor.html.

4 Open the bgColor.html file in a browser.

■ The Web page background color is set.

Extra

JavaScript is case-sensitive. That means that the exact capitalization needs to be used, including the C in bgColor. If you were to use the document.bgcolor property with a lowercase c, the browser would return an object not recognized error. This can be a tricky error to debug, especially because HTML is not case-sensitive.

A statement like

```
document.bgColor = "#80FFCC"
```

sets the background color when this statement is executed, but you can change the background color at any time using an event. For example,

```
onclick = "document.bgColor =
document.form1.text1.value"
```

dynamically sets the background color to the value taken from a text field whenever the event is triggered.

LIST THE BACKGROUND COLOR

```
<html>
<head>
</head>
<body bgcolor="green">
  <script language="javascript">
    document.write("The background color for this page is " +
document.bgColor);
  </script>
</body>
</html>
```

The background color for this page is #008000

1 Open the js-skeleton.html file.

2 Add the bgcolor attribute to the <body> tag and set it equal to a color.

3 Add a document.write statement within the <script> tags that displays the document.bgColor property value.

4 Save the file as bgColor2.html.

5 Open the bgColor2.html file in a browser.

■ The background color value is displayed.

CHANGE TEXT AND LINK COLORS

The document object also includes properties for setting the foreground text color and the link colors. In HTML, you can set these colors using the text, link, alink, and vlink attributes of the <body> tag. Using JavaScript, however, you can dynamically change these colors as the user interacts with the page.

The object property for the foreground text color is document.fgColor. This property sets the color of the text for the Web page. Care should be taken to ensure that this color is different from the background color; otherwise, the text will not be readable.

The object property for the link color is document.linkColor. This sets the color of the links whether applied to text or images. You can also set the active link color and the visited link color with document.alinkColor and document.vlinkColor, respectively.

This example uses the bgColor.html file found on the book's CD-ROM (or which you may have created in the section "Change Background Colors"), but you can apply these steps to any file.

SET THE FOREGROUND COLOR

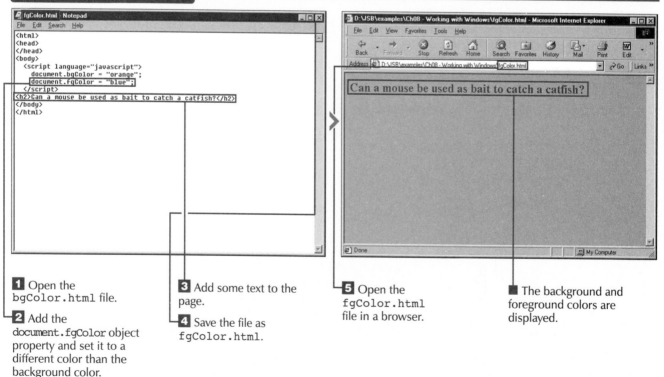

■1 Open the bgColor.html file.

■2 Add the document.fgColor object property and set it to a different color than the background color.

■3 Add some text to the page.

■4 Save the file as fgColor.html.

■5 Open the fgColor.html file in a browser.

■ The background and foreground colors are displayed.

Apply It

The document.fgColor property holds the value of the text color. This property can be used to display the current text color or to set the current text color with a statement like

```
document.fgColor = "#80FFCC"
```

You can also dynamically set the text and link colors using the value from a form text field. For example,

```
onclick = "document.fgColor =
document.form1.text1.value"
```

dynamically sets the text color to the value taken from a text field. Because this statement is executed as part of an event, the user could input a different color value in the text field and trigger the onclick event to update the text color.

A color management function could be written like this:

```
function colors(background, textCol,
linkCol, vlinkCol) {
    document.bgColor = background;
    document.fgColor = textCol;
    document.linkColor = linkCol;
    document.vlinkColor = vlinkCol;
}
```

Calling this function with specified colors sets the color scheme for the Web page. For example, the statement colors("black", "red", "orange", "purple") sets the colors.

SET THE LINK COLOR

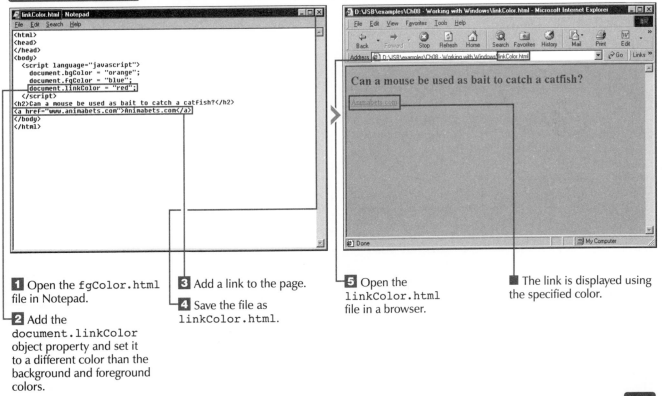

1 Open the fgColor.html file in Notepad.

2 Add the document.linkColor object property and set it to a different color than the background and foreground colors.

3 Add a link to the page.

4 Save the file as linkColor.html.

5 Open the linkColor.html file in a browser.

■ The link is displayed using the specified color.

CHANGE THE DOCUMENT TITLE

The document title appears in the title bar for the current window. It is typically set using the `<title>` tag, which appears within a Web page's `<head>` tags. JavaScript includes a document object property that lets you control the title more than you can using `<title>` tags: `document.title`.

The `document.title` property holds the current document title, or it can be set to a new value that appears when the page is loaded.

For example, to set the title of a document to "Welcome to Joe's," you could set a `name` variable equal to `Joe's` and then set the

`document.title` property equal to `"Welcome to " + name`, which would dynamically generate the title for the current document.

The document title is different from the window name. Each Web page can have a title that appears in the window title bar. Each window can have a name, which is used by JavaScript to identify the window. The window name isn't displayed within the browser and is mainly used internally.

This example uses the `js-skeleton.html` file found on the book's CD-ROM, but you can apply these steps to any file.

CHANGE THE DOCUMENT TITLE

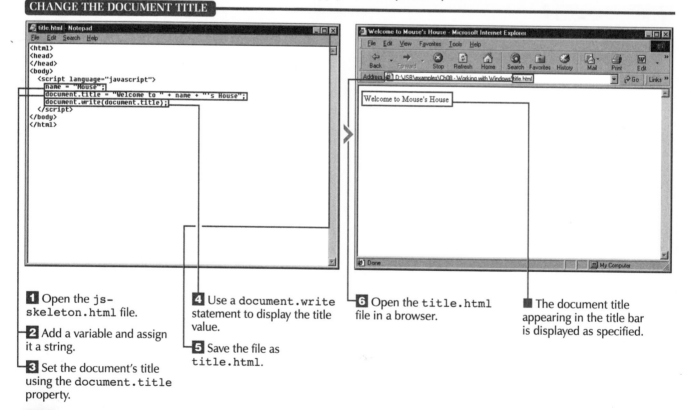

1 Open the js-skeleton.html file.

2 Add a variable and assign it a string.

3 Set the document's title using the document.title property.

4 Use a document.write statement to display the title value.

5 Save the file as title.html.

6 Open the title.html file in a browser.

■ The document title appearing in the title bar is displayed as specified.

DISPLAY THE MODIFICATION DATE

I t can be very useful for users and publishers to use JavaScript to display the date that the current page was last updated. If this information is included on the Web page, then you can immediately tell how current the page is.

The `document.lastModified` property displays the date when the document was last modified.

The format of the modification date includes the month, date, and year along with the time. In Chapter 10, the `Date` object is covered in more detail.

This example uses the `js-skeleton.html` file found on the book's CD-ROM, but you can apply these steps to any file.

Extra

The `document` object includes two additional properties that are very useful. The `document.URL` property holds a string of the current URL. This can be useful for displaying the current URL for printing. Another useful property is `document.referrer`, which displays the URL of the document that contains the link that led to the current page. This is different than the history, which holds the previously visited page.

DISPLAY THE MODIFICATION DATE

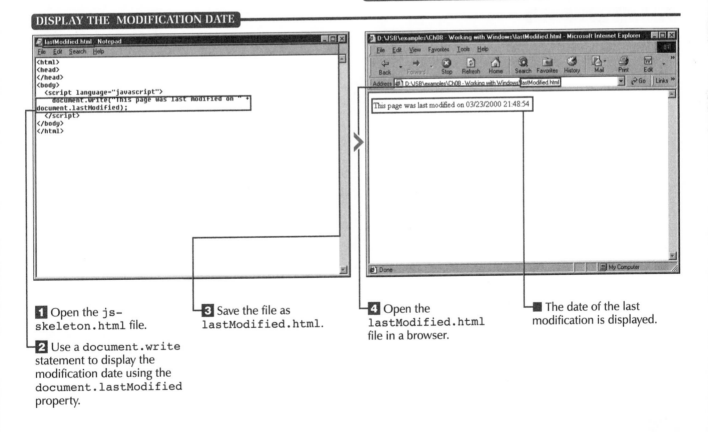

1 Open the `js-skeleton.html` file.

2 Use a `document.write` statement to display the modification date using the `document.lastModified` property.

3 Save the file as `lastModified.html`.

4 Open the `lastModified.html` file in a browser.

■ The date of the last modification is displayed.

VIEW THE URL OF THE CURRENT DOCUMENT

A useful piece of information that you can place at the bottom of every Web page is the current URL. One of the benefits of including the URL with the page is that the address of the Web page is displayed if the Web page is printed.

The property that holds the Web page address is part of the document object. This property is URL. Adding this property to the bottom of a Web page can be accomplished with the statement document.URL. This property is a

read-only property; you cannot use URL to change the URL for the current Web page.

This example uses the js-skeleton.html file found on the book's CD-ROM, but you can apply these steps to any file.

Extra

> When the URL is displayed in the browser using the document.URL statement, it is URL encoded. This is done so that any spaces or special symbols won't cause a problem. URL encoding can be undone with the unescape() statement covered in Chapter 14.

VIEW THE CURRENT URL

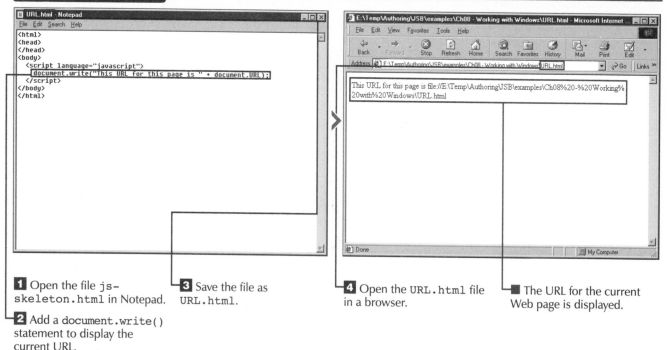

1 Open the file js-skeleton.html in Notepad.

2 Add a document.write() statement to display the current URL.

3 Save the file as URL.html.

4 Open the URL.html file in a browser.

■ The URL for the current Web page is displayed.

VIEW THE REFERRING PAGE

When two Web pages are linked together and one page loads the other page, the first page is called the *referring page* because it referred the second page.

The document object includes a property that can be used to view the referring Web page — referrer. This property displays the referring URL, which will be URL encoded.

Using document.referrer, you can determine the link that was used to send the user to your Web page.

This example uses the js-skeleton.html file found on the book's CD-ROM, but you can apply these steps to any file.

Extra

The document.referrer property can have problems in the Internet Explorer browser on different operating systems. Depending on your configuration, the property may show you nothing or the URL of the current Web page.

VIEW THE REFERRING URL

```
referrer.html - Notepad
File Edit Search Help
<html>
<head>
</head>
<body>
  <script language="javascript">
    document.write("This URL for this page is " + document.referrer);
  </script>
</body>
</html>
```

E:\Temp\Authoring\JSB\examples\Ch08 - Working with Windows\referrer.html - Microsoft Inter...

Address E:\Temp\Authoring\JSB\examples\Ch08 - Working with Windows\referrer.html

This URL for this page is file://E:\Temp\Authoring\JSB\examples\Ch08%20-%20Working%20with%20Windows\reflink.html

1 Open the file js-skeleton.html in Notepad.

2 Add a document.write() statement to display the referring URL.

3 Save the file as referrer.html.

4 Open another HTML file.

5 Add a link to the referrer.html page.

6 Save the Web page as reflink.html.

7 Open the reflink.html file in a browser.

8 Click on the link.

■ The referrer.html page loads.

■ The referring Web page (reflink.html) is displayed.

OPEN A NEW BROWSER WINDOW

Have you ever noticed while browsing the Web that some links spawn a new browser window? This technique can be accomplished in JavaScript by using the `window.open()` method.

The `window.open()` method can accept three parameters. The first parameter is the URL to open in the new window. The second parameter is the name of the new window. This name can then be used to reference the new window and is different from the document's title.

The third parameter defines the features of the window, for which you can set the following attributes: `width`, `height`, `toolbar`,

`status`, `menubar`, `scrollbars`, and `resizable`. All but the first two of these attributes can be set to either `yes` or `no`.

For example, the JavaScript statement `window.open("mypage.html", "mywindow", "width=200, height=400, toolbar=no, status=no, resizeable=yes");` opens a new 200-x-400-pixel resizable window with no toolbar or status bar and loads the `mypage.html` file in it.

This example uses the `js-skeleton.html` file found on the book's CD-ROM, but you can apply these steps to any file.

OPEN A NEW BROWSER WINDOW

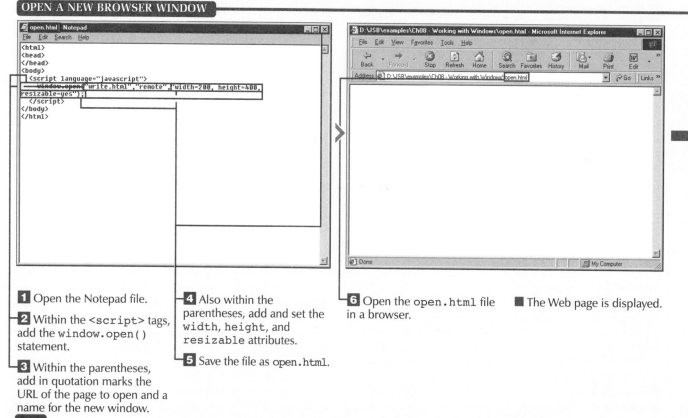

1 Open the Notepad file.

2 Within the `<script>` tags, add the `window.open()` statement.

3 Within the parentheses, add in quotation marks the URL of the page to open and a name for the new window.

4 Also within the parentheses, add and set the `width`, `height`, and `resizable` attributes.

5 Save the file as `open.html`.

6 Open the `open.html` file in a browser.

■ The Web page is displayed.

Extra

From the original Web page, you can write text to the new window. When you create a new window, one of the parameters is to give the new window a name. This name can be used to send output to the new window. For example, the `document.write()` function writes output to the current Web page, and `mywindow.write()` writes text to a new window named `mywindow`.

The JavaScript property that holds the window's name is `window.name`. You can also use the `window.opener` property to retrieve the name of the window that spawned a new window. The current window can also be accessed using the `window.self` property.

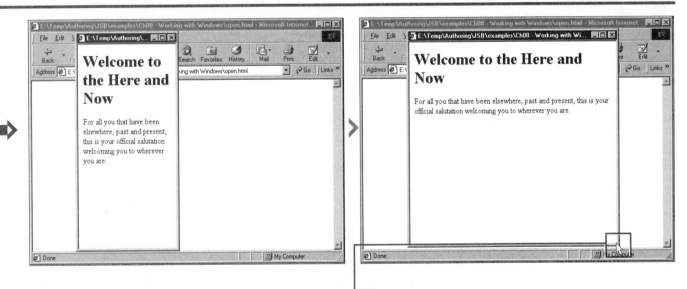

■ The new window is also opened with the specified dimensions and displays the referenced Web page.

■ If you set `resizable` to yes, you can click and drag one of the corners or sides of the new window to resize it.

CLOSE A REMOTE WINDOW

I f many browser windows are opened, then the screen can become very cluttered. You can always close a window by clicking the Close button (X) in the upper-right corner of the window, but JavaScript also includes a method for closing remote windows.

To close a remote window, you can use the window.close() function. This closes the current remote window.

If the window.close() function is used to close the original browser window, an alert dialog box will appear, asking if you wish to close the browser window. Windows that have been opened using the window.open() function automatically close without a confirmation dialog box.

This example uses the write.html and open. html files found on the book's CD-ROM, but you can apply these steps to any file.

CLOSE A REMOTE WINDOW

```
close.html - Notepad
File  Edit  Search  Help
<html>
<head>
</head>
<body>
  <script language="javascript">
    document.write('<h1>Welcome to the Here and Now</h1>');
    document.write('<p>For all you that have been elsewhere, ');
    document.write('past and present, this is your official ');
    document.write('salutation welcoming you to wherever you are.</p>');
  </script>
  <form>
    <input type="button" value="Close" onclick="window.close();"/>
  </form>
</body>
</html>
```

```
open2.html - Notepad
File  Edit  Search  Help
<html>
<head>
</head>
<body>
  <script language="javascript">
    window.open("close.html","remote","width=200, height=400,
resizable=yes");
  </script>
</body>
</html>
```

1 Open the file write.html in Notepad.

2 Add a set of <form> tags under the <script> tags.

3 Create a button within the form using an <input/> tag.

4 Add the onclick event to the <input/> tag and set it to window.close().

5 Save the file as close.html.

6 Open the open.html file in Notepad.

7 Change the URL for the new window to close.html.

8 Save the file as open2.html.

Extra

With several windows open, you can switch the focus between the different windows using the `window.focus()` method. You can also force a window to lose focus with the `window.blur()` method. You can tell which window has focus by looking at the title bar. The title bar of the window that has focus appears a different color than the other windows. You can change the window that has focus by clicking in the window with the mouse. You can also switch the focus between the different windows using the Alt+Tab keys.

In the example in this section, you add a Close button to the remote window. If you add a Close button to the original window, the difference is that closing the original window will end your session and a dialog box asking you to confirm the command will appear.

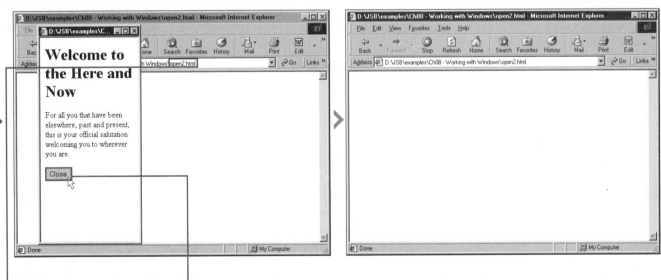

9 Open the `open2.html` file in a browser.

■ The Web page and a new window are opened and displayed.

10 Click the Close button in the remote window.

■ The remote window closes, but the window that opened it originally remains.

PRINT A WINDOW

Web browsers include a button on the main toolbar that enables you to print the current Web page. This same feature can also be made accessible using JavaScript.

The method that enables the user to print the current Web page is `window.print()`. This method opens the Print dialog box, which lets you select the printer, number of copies, and other print options.

If a printer isn't connected to the current computer, the `window.print()` method is ignored.

When a new window is opened using the `window.open()` method, one of the method parameters can set the toolbar to be hidden on the new window. If the toolbar isn't visible, then the Print button will also not be available. For this case, you can add a print feature to a Web page using the `window.print()` method.

This example uses the `close.html` file found on the book's CD-ROM (or which you may have created in the section "Close a Remote Window"), but you can apply these steps to any file.

PRINT A WINDOW

1 Open the `close.html` file.

2 Copy the `<input/>` tag to create another button for the Web page.

3 Change the button value to `Print` and the event statement to `window.print()`.

4 Save the file as `print.html`.

5 Open the `print.html` file in a browser.

■ A button that enables printing appears on the Web page.

6 Click the Print button on the Web page.

Extra

The `window.print()` button produces the same results as the browser's Print button included on the toolbar. In addition to this method, JavaScript includes several other methods that match toolbar features. These methods include the `window.back()` and `window.forward()` methods, which do the same thing as the toolbar's Back and Forward buttons. JavaScript also includes a `window.home()` method that loads the browser's home page just like the Home button on the toolbar. The function of the Stop button can also be included within a Web page by using the `window.stop()` method.

If you create a button using `window.print()` and click the button, if a printer isn't connected to your computer, then a dialog box will appear stating that you need to add a printer before you can print.

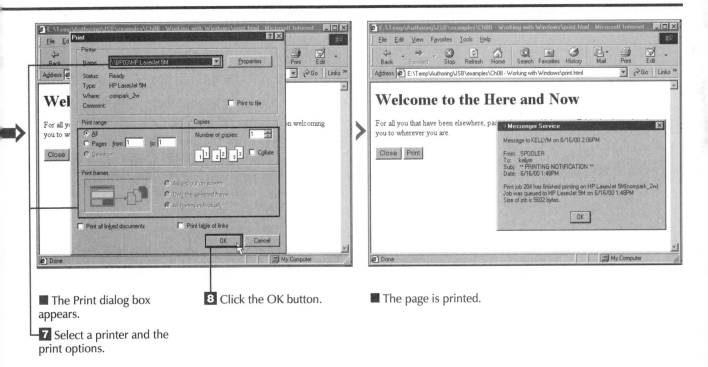

■ The Print dialog box appears.

7 Select a printer and the print options.

8 Click the OK button.

■ The page is printed.

MOVE A WINDOW

The window object includes a couple methods that can be used to move and reposition the current window.

The window.moveTo() method accepts two parameters for specifying the distance in pixels from the left edge and top of the screen where the upper-left corner of the browser should be moved to. For example, the statement window.moveTo(200, 400) positions the upper-left corner of the browser 200 pixels from the left edge of the screen and 400 pixels from the top of the screen.

The window.moveBy() method also accepts two parameters that are used to specify the

horizontal and vertical number of pixels the browser should move. For example, window.moveBy(10, 50) moves the current window to the right 10 pixels and down 50 pixels every time it is executed.

The parameters can be positive or negative values. Negative values move the window to the left and up rather than to the right and down.

This example uses the js-skeleton.html file found on the book's CD-ROM, but you can apply these steps to any file.

MOVE A WINDOW WITH WINDOW.MOVETO()

1 Open the file js-skeleton.html in Notepad.

2 Add a form with two text fields and a button.

3 Add the onclick event to the button and set it equal to window.moveTo().

4 Set the parameters of the window.moveTo() method to the value of the text fields.

5 Save the file as moveTo.html.

6 Open the moveTo.html file in a browser.

7 Click the form button.

■ The entire window moves to the specified coordinates.

134

Extra

One of the benefits of using JavaScript to move a window is control. With several windows open, the `window.moveTo` and `window.moveBy` methods enable you to position the newly opened window exactly where you want it. For example, if you open a remote window with links, you can move it to the side of the main window.

Another useful technique that you can use is to dynamically update the *x* and *y* values of the `window.moveBy()` method to animate the movement of the window — for example:

```
function moveDiag() {
   for (i=1;I<100;I++)
      window.moveBy(i,i)
}
```

This function causes the window to move to the right and down 1 pixel for each time through the loop until the 100-pixel limit is reached.

MOVE A WINDOW WITH WINDOW.MOVEBY()

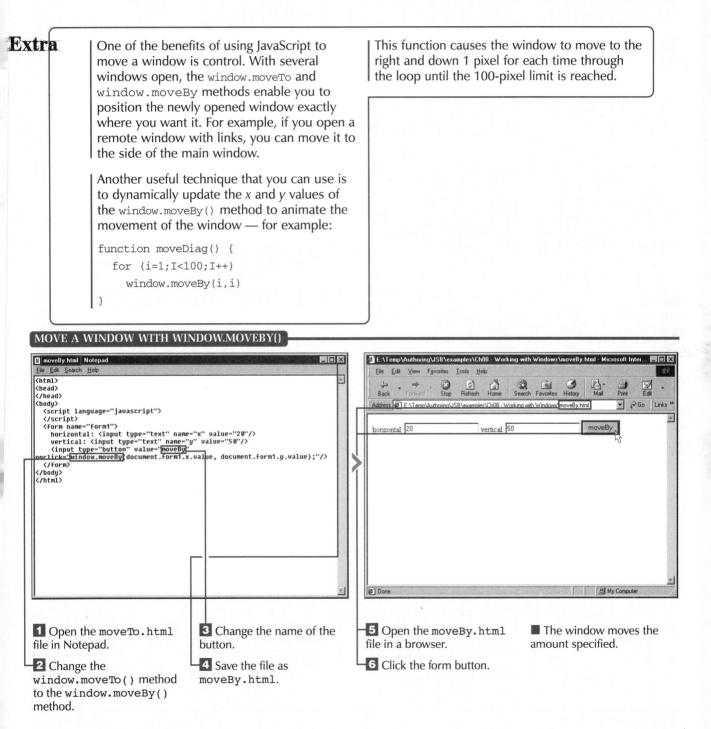

1 Open the `moveTo.html` file in Notepad.

2 Change the `window.moveTo()` method to the `window.moveBy()` method.

3 Change the name of the button.

4 Save the file as `moveBy.html`.

5 Open the `moveBy.html` file in a browser.

6 Click the form button.

■ The window moves the amount specified.

RESIZE A WINDOW

The window object also includes a couple methods that are similar to the move methods that can be used to resize the current window.

The window.resizeTo() method accepts two parameters for specifying the width and height in pixels of the browser window. For example, the statement window.resizeTo (200, 400) resizes the browser window to a width of 200 pixels and a height of 400 pixels.

The window.resizeBy() method increases the width and height of the current window. For example, window.resizeBy(10, 50)

increases the width of the window by 10 pixels and increases the height of the window by 50 pixels.

The parameters of the window.resizeBy() method can be negative values. Negative values decrease the window size.

This example uses the moveTo.html file found on the book's CD-ROM (or which you may have created in the section "Move a Window"), but you can apply these steps to any file.

RESIZE WITH RESIZETO()

1 Open the file moveTo.html in Notepad.

2 Change the window.moveTo() method to window.resizeTo().

3 Change the value of the text in the text boxes and the name of the button.

4 Save the file as resizeTo.html.

5 Open the resizeTo.html file in a browser.

6 Click the form button.

■ The window is resized to the specified coordinates.

Extra

JavaScript includes two more methods that let you control the window and are very similar to the `window.resizeTo()` and `window.resizeBy()` methods. These methods are `window.scrollTo()` and `window.scrollBy()`. These methods let you control how the page in the browser scrolls. For example, the statement `window.scrollTo (10, 200)` scrolls the window to the right 10 pixels and down 200 pixels. These methods only work if the Web page is large enough to need scrolling.

If the browser is maximized by using the Maximize button in the upper-right corner of the browser window, then the `resizeBy()` method will not have any effect.

RESIZE WITH RESIZEBY()

```
resizeBy.html - Notepad
File  Edit  Search  Help

<html>
<head>
</head>
<body>
  <script language="javascript">
  </script>
  <form name="form1">
    horizontal: <input type="text" name="x" value="200"/>
    vertical: <input type="text" name="y" value="500"/>
    <input type="button" value="resizeBy"
onclick="window.resizeBy(document.form1.x.value, document.form1.y.value);"/>
  </form>
</body>
</html>
```

E:\Temp\Authoring\JSB\examples\Ch08 - Working with Windows\resizeBy.html - Microsoft Inter...
File Edit View Favorites Tools Help

Back   Forward   Stop   Refresh   Home   Search   Favorites   History   Mail   Print   Edit

Address E:\Temp\Authoring\JSB\examples\Ch08 - Working with Windows\resizeBy.html   Go   Links

horizontal: 200   vertical: 500   resizeBy

Done   My Computer

1 Open the `resizeTo.html` file.

2 Change the `window.resizeTo()` method to the `window.resizeBy()` method.

3 Change the name of the button.

4 Save the file as `resizeBy.html`.

5 Open the `resizeBy.html` file in a browser.

6 Click the form button.

■ The window is increased by the amount specified.

INFORM THE USER WITH AN ALERT DIALOG BOX

The window object contains several methods that can be used to interact directly with the user. These methods make it possible to present dialog boxes to the user.

Many programs use dialog boxes to present information to the user. Dialog boxes can also be used to collect information from the user.

JavaScript includes three different types of dialog boxes: alert, prompt, and confirm. All these dialog boxes are window object methods.

The simplest dialog box is an alert dialog box. This dialog box presents a text message to the user and includes a single OK button. The message is defined in quotation marks as a parameter of the alert() method.

For example, the statement window.alert ("Hello") creates a dialog box with the word *Hello* in it.

This example uses the js-skeleton.html file found on the book's CD-ROM, but you can apply these steps to any file.

INFORM THE USER WITH AN ALERT DIALOG BOX

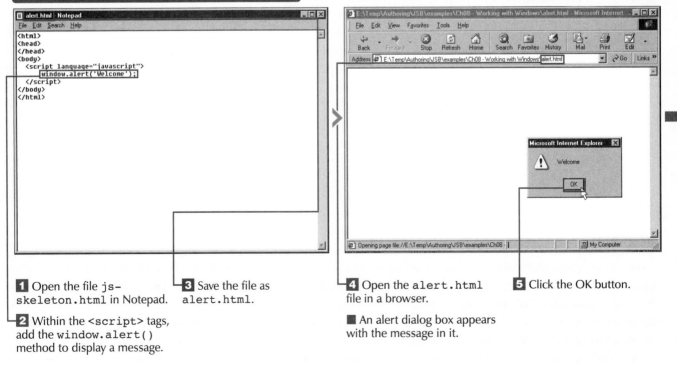

1 Open the file js-skeleton.html in Notepad.

2 Within the <script> tags, add the window.alert() method to display a message.

3 Save the file as alert.html.

4 Open the alert.html file in a browser.

■ An alert dialog box appears with the message in it.

5 Click the OK button.

Extra

Alert dialog boxes can be used for debugging purposes. For example, consider the following function for checking variables:

```
function checkVariable(varName, var1) {
  window.alert("The value of " +
varName + " is " + var1);
}
```

You can call this function using a function that looks like this:

```
checkVariable("blink", blink);
```

Whenever this function is called, an alert dialog box appears with the variable name and its value displayed. This can be very beneficial as you build your scripts. Once the script is complete, you can simply remove the function and all its related calls.

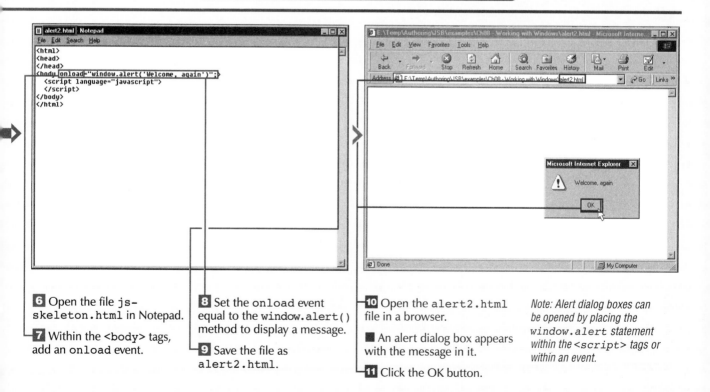

6 Open the file js-skeleton.html in Notepad.

7 Within the <body> tags, add an onload event.

8 Set the onload event equal to the window.alert() method to display a message.

9 Save the file as alert2.html.

10 Open the alert2.html file in a browser.

■ An alert dialog box appears with the message in it.

11 Click the OK button.

Note: Alert dialog boxes can be opened by placing the window.alert statement within the <script> tags or within an event.

ACCEPT INPUT WITH A PROMPT DIALOG BOX

The alert dialog box works well if you want to display a message to the user, but it doesn't let the user input information into the script. A prompt dialog box, however, enables users to enter text into a text field.

The window object includes a method for creating a prompt dialog box. This dialog box includes an OK button, a Cancel button, and a text field where the user can enter information.

Prompt dialog boxes are created using the prompt() method. This method can accept

two parameters. The first parameter defines the message text that is displayed in the dialog box. The second parameter is used to define the default text that appears within the text field. If the OK button is clicked without changing the text in the text field, then this default text is passed to the script.

When the OK button is clicked, the text in the text field of the prompt dialog box is returned to the script. You can capture this text if you assign the prompt() method to a variable.

ACCEPT INPUT WITH A PROMPT DIALOG BOX

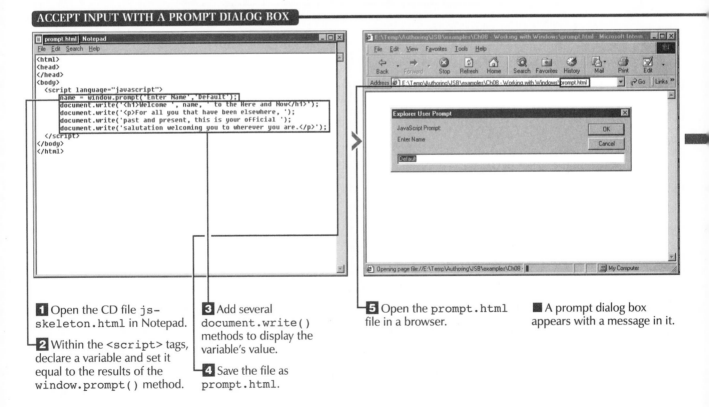

1 Open the CD file js-skeleton.html in Notepad.

2 Within the `<script>` tags, declare a variable and set it equal to the results of the window.prompt() method.

3 Add several document.write() methods to display the variable's value.

4 Save the file as prompt.html.

5 Open the prompt.html file in a browser.

■ A prompt dialog box appears with a message in it.

Extra

If you don't want to include a default text field message that appears when the dialog box is displayed, then you can simply set the second parameter to the `prompt()` method to an empty string (`""`). If you don't include the second parameter, the text `<undefined>` is displayed as the default text in the text field of the prompt dialog box.

The prompt dialog box includes an OK button and a Cancel button. If the OK button is clicked, the value within the text field of the prompt dialog is returned to the script. However, if the Cancel button is clicked, a null value is returned to the script. You check for a null value using the `if (window.prompt ("Input a value","10") != null)` statement.

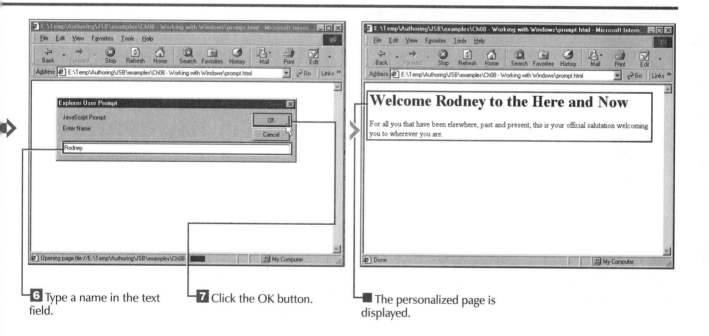

■6 Type a name in the text field.

■7 Click the OK button.

■ The personalized page is displayed.

ENABLE USER DECISIONS WITH A CONFIRM DIALOG BOX

The prompt dialog box lets you input a line of text to the script, but another type of dialog box — confirm — enables you to ask the user questions.

The confirm dialog box is also part of the `window` object. This dialog box includes both OK and Cancel buttons and can be used to enable the user to respond to questions.

Confirm dialog boxes are created using the `confirm()` method. The `confirm()` method can accept only a single parameter that is used to display the message within the dialog box.

The `confirm()` method returns a value of `true` if the OK button is clicked or `false` if the Cancel button is clicked. By setting a variable equal to the `window.confirm()` method, you can capture the user's response to the confirm dialog box.

This example uses the `js-skeleton.html` file found on the book's CD-ROM, but you can apply these steps to any file.

ENABLE USER DECISIONS WITH A CONFIRM DIALOG BOX

1 Open the file `js-skeleton.html` in Notepad.

2 Declare a variable and set it equal to the results of the `window.confirm()` method.

3 Add an `if-else` statement that checks the value of the confirm dialog box and displays appropriate text.

4 Save the file as `confirm.html`.

5 Open the `confirm.html` file in a browser.

■ A confirm dialog box appears with a question in it.

6 Click the OK button.

Apply It

One place that the confirm dialog box can be used is to double-check with the user before an action is taken. For instance, Web page forms typically have a Reset button that resets all the form elements to their default values. A function can be created that enables the user to confirm the Reset action:

```
function confirmReset() {
   check = window.confirm("Are you sure
you want to reset this form?");
   if (check)
      document.form1.reset1.click();
}
<form name="form1">
   <input type="reset" name="reset1"
onclick="confirmReset()">
</form>
```

When this reset button is clicked, the `confirmReset()` function is called and a confirm dialog box is displayed. If the user clicks OK, the page form is reset. If the Cancel button is clicked, the form is not reset.

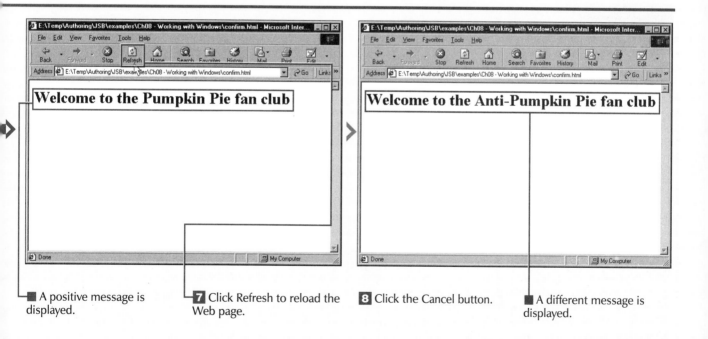

■ A positive message is displayed.

7 Click Refresh to reload the Web page.

8 Click the Cancel button.

■ A different message is displayed.

USING THE STRING OBJECT

The `string` object includes properties and methods that let you work with text.

The `string` object has a single property — `length` — which returns the number of characters in the string. This information is valuable as you work with strings because it lets you know how many characters are in the string. The `string` object also has numerous methods that can be applied to text. A number of these methods can be used to format the text with HTML tags. For example, the `bold()` method returns a string of text surrounded by opening and closing `<bold>` tags. Other string-formatting methods include `big()`, `fontColor(color)`, `fontSize(size)`, `italics()`, `link(href)`, `small()`, `strike()`, `sub()`, `sup()`, `toLowerCase()`, and `toUpperCase()`. See the section "Format String Variables" later in this chapter for an example of using these methods.

Other methods enable you to combine, locate, and extract portions of text. These methods include `charAt(index)`, `concat(text)`, `replace(text1, text2)`, and `substring(index1, index2)`.

This example uses the `js-skeleton.html` file found on the book's CD-ROM, but you can apply these steps to any file.

FORMAT TEXT

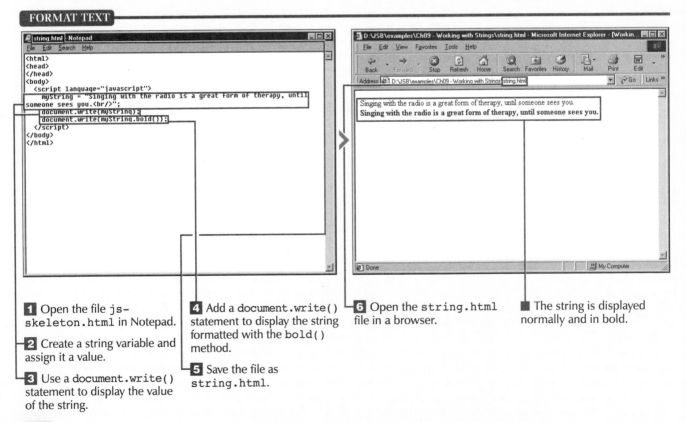

1 Open the file `js-skeleton.html` in Notepad.

2 Create a string variable and assign it a value.

3 Use a `document.write()` statement to display the value of the string.

4 Add a `document.write()` statement to display the string formatted with the `bold()` method.

5 Save the file as `string.html`.

6 Open the `string.html` file in a browser.

■ The string is displayed normally and in bold.

Extra

`string` objects by default are created whenever a string variable is declared. Strings are assigned to any variable that has a pair of quotes in the definition. You can also create `string` objects using the `new` keyword, but it is not necessary. To do this, you need to list a name for the string and set it equal to `new String()`. For example, the JavaScript statement `string1 = new String();` creates a new string object, and `string1.bold();` calls the `bold()` method for that string.

Single-quote marks can be used in place of double-quote marks. In some places, you may want to use a set of each. For example, if you specify a `document.write` statement within an event, the quotes for the `document.write` statement need to be different from the event quotes.

CHANGE TEXT CASE

```html
<html>
<head>
</head>
<body>
  <script language="javascript">
    myString = "Singing with the radio is a great form of therapy, until
someone sees you.<br/>";
    document.write(myString);
    document.write(myString.bold());
    document.write(myString.toUpperCase());
  </script>
</body>
</html>
```

1 Open the `string.html` file in Notepad.

2 Add a document.write() statement to display the string converted to uppercase.

3 Save the file as `string2.html`.

4 Open the `string2.html` file in a browser.

■ The string is displayed in uppercase.

WORK WITH SUBSTRINGS

A *substring* is a portion of a string. To extract a section of a string, you can use the substring() method.

The substring() method accepts two parameters, which correspond to the first and last characters to extract from the base string.

For example, if a string is defined as str1 = "useful handbook", the statement str1.substring(0,10) equals the string "useful hand".

JavaScript includes another useful substring method, substr(), which also accepts two parameters. The first parameter marks the beginning of the substring, and the second parameter marks the length to extract.

For example, if a string is defined as str2 = "boring dialogue", the statement str2.substr(7,4) would result in "dial". Remember that spaces count as characters and the string index starts with 0.

This example uses the js-skeleton.html file found on the book's CD-ROM, but you can apply these steps to any file.

WORK WITH SUBSTRINGS

```
substring.html - Notepad
File  Edit  Search  Help
<html>
<head>
</head>
<body>
  <script language="javascript">
    str1 = "April showers bring May flowers.<br/>";
    document.write(str1);
    document.write(str1.substring(0,13) + "<br/>");
  </script>
</body>
</html>
```

```
D:\JSB\examples\Ch09 - Working with Strings\substring.html - Microsoft Internet Explorer - [Wo...
File  Edit  View  Favorites  Tools  Help
Back   Forward  Stop  Refresh  Home   Search  Favorites  History   Mail   Print   Edit
Address  D:\JSB\examples\Ch09 - Working with Strings\substring.html            Go   Links

April showers bring May flowers.
April showers

Done                                                             My Computer
```

1 Open the file js-skeleton.html in Notepad.

2 Create a string variable and assign it a value.

3 Use a document.write() statement to display the value of the string.

4 Add a document.write() statement to display the substring created with the substring() method.

5 Save the file as substring.html.

6 Open the substring.html file in a browser.

■ The string and its substring are displayed.

Note: The substring started at the first position, as specified by the first parameter, 0, and ended at string index 13 (a space), as specified by the second parameter.

Extra

JavaScript includes another method that works just like the `substring()` method with an additional feature. The `slice()` method works on strings the same way that it works on arrays. It accepts two parameters. The first parameter is the starting index value where the string should be sliced. The second value is the ending index where the slice should end. The difference between this method and the `substring()` method is that the second parameter can be a negative value. Negative values are counted from the end of the string backwards. For example, a string is defined as `str1 = "out to lunch"` before the statement `str1.slice(3, -2)` returns the substring `"to lun"`.

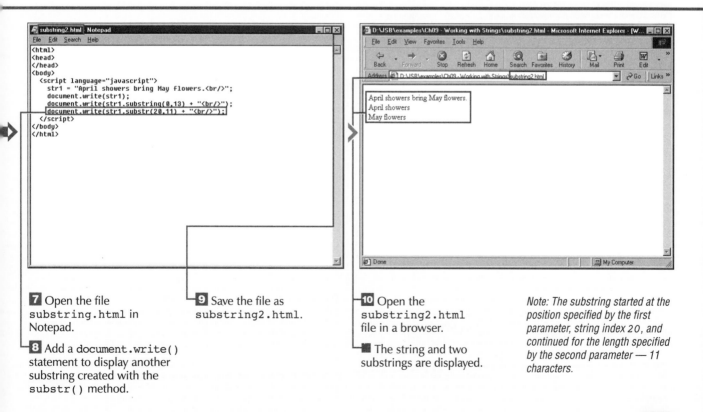

7 Open the file `substring.html` in Notepad.

8 Add a `document.write()` statement to display another substring created with the `substr()` method.

9 Save the file as `substring2.html`.

10 Open the `substring2.html` file in a browser.

■ The string and two substrings are displayed.

Note: The substring started at the position specified by the first parameter, string index 20, and continued for the length specified by the second parameter — 11 characters.

CONCATENATE STRINGS

The substring() and substr() methods are used to break strings apart, but JavaScript includes another method that is used to combine *(concatenate)* strings.

The concat() method tacks a second string onto the end of the first. The second string that is attached is identified as a parameter to the concat() method.

For example, if a string is defined as str1 = "Thanks for the ", and another string is defined as str2 = "work well done.", these two strings can be combined with the statement str1.concat(str2).

Another easy way to combine strings is with the addition assignment (+=) operator. This operator is used a lot in earlier examples and simply needs to be placed between two strings to add the second string to the first one.

For example, str1 and str2 can also be combined using the statement str1 += str2.

This example uses the js-skeleton.html file found on the book's CD-ROM, but you can apply these steps to any file.

CONCATENATE STRINGS

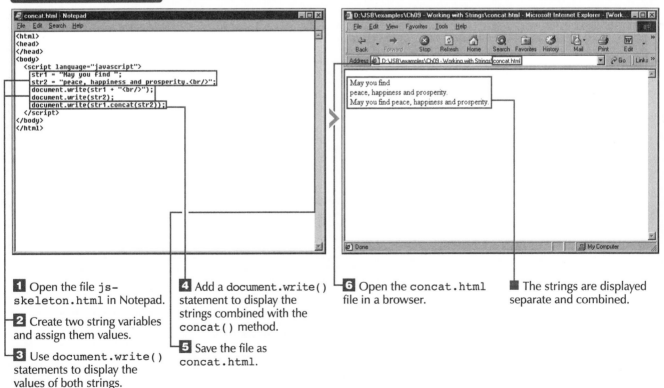

1 Open the file js-skeleton.html in Notepad.

2 Create two string variables and assign them values.

3 Use document.write() statements to display the values of both strings.

4 Add a document.write() statement to display the strings combined with the concat() method.

5 Save the file as concat.html.

6 Open the concat.html file in a browser.

■ The strings are displayed separate and combined.

Extra

Strings are enclosed within quote marks, so how do you display a quote mark? Any character that cannot be printed by including it within the string quotes is called an *escaped character*. When working with strings, you can include special escape characters such as the quote mark if it is preceded by a backslash (\). For example, to include quotes around a word in a string, use the backslash character like this:

```
str1 = "He responded, \"Hooray\"
when he was finished."
```

This statement displays the quote marks around the quoted word. Other escape characters include the single quote (\'), the backslash (\\), the backspace (\b), the tab (\t), the new line (\n), the carriage return (\r), and a form feed (\f).

For example, `str2 =   "The file is located in the C:\\temp\\test directory.";` correctly displays the backspace characters.

USING THE ADDITION ASSIGNMENT OPERATOR

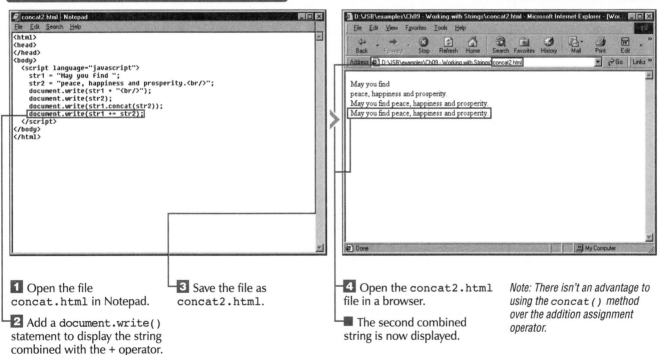

1 Open the file `concat.html` in Notepad.

2 Add a `document.write()` statement to display the string combined with the + operator.

3 Save the file as `concat2.html`.

4 Open the `concat2.html` file in a browser.

■ The second combined string is now displayed.

Note: There isn't an advantage to using the `concat()` method over the addition assignment operator.

FORMAT STRING VARIABLES

JavaScript could be used to create functions that would format strings using HTML tags, but many of the basic formatting options are already available as methods of the `string` object.

These string-formatting methods simply add the correct formatting tags on the beginning and end of the string. For example, for the string `str1 = "Little John"`, the statement `str1.big()` equals `<big>Little John</big>`.

Other string-formatting methods include `big()`, `bold()`, `italics()`, `small()`, `strike()`, `sub()`, and `sup()`. The `sub()`

and `sup()` methods are used to format string characters as subscripts or superscripts.

You can also change the font size using the `fontsize()` method, which accepts a size parameter. The size parameter can be an integer between 1 and 7, with 7 being the largest. The font color can be set with the `fontcolor()` method, which accepts a color parameter including a color name or a hexadecimal color value.

This example uses the `js-skeleton.html` file found on the book's CD-ROM, but you can apply these steps to any file.

FORMAT STRING VARIABLES

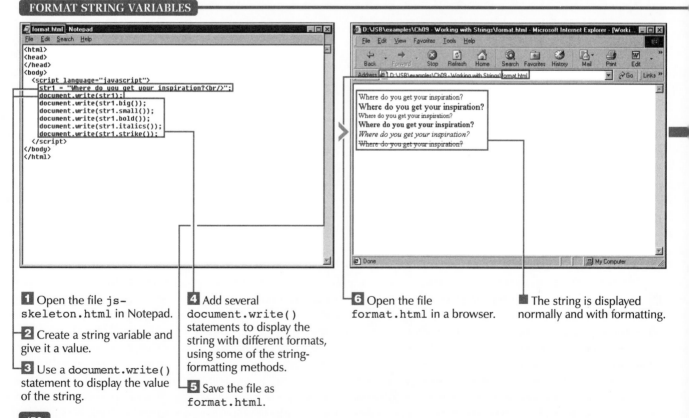

1 Open the file `js-skeleton.html` in Notepad.

2 Create a string variable and give it a value.

3 Use a `document.write()` statement to display the value of the string.

4 Add several `document.write()` statements to display the string with different formats, using some of the string-formatting methods.

5 Save the file as `format.html`.

6 Open the file `format.html` in a browser.

■ The string is displayed normally and with formatting.

Extra

If an entire string is formatted using the `sub()` or `sup()` methods, it is difficult to notice how the string looks any different from a normal string unless it can be compared to another string on the page. A more reasonable way to use the `sub()` method is to build a string:

```
water = "H" + "2".sub() + "O";
```

This statement creates a string variable named `water` that includes an H and the string for 2 that is returned from the `sub()` method and an O. The resulting string displays the number as a subscript to the letter *H*. An example of the `sup()` method would be

```
squared = "x" + "2".sup();
```

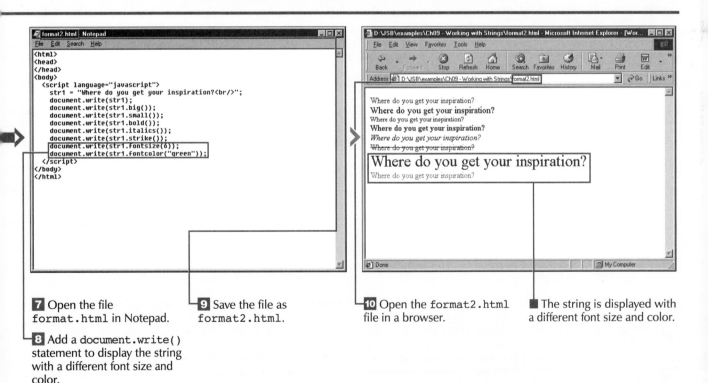

7 Open the file `format.html` in Notepad.

8 Add a `document.write()` statement to display the string with a different font size and color.

9 Save the file as `format2.html`.

10 Open the `format2.html` file in a browser.

■ The string is displayed with a different font size and color.

BUILD ANCHORS AND LINKS

A ny defined `string` object can be changed into an anchor or a link using the `anchor()` and `link()` methods of the `string` object.

The `anchor()` method accepts a name parameter that is used to specify the name of the anchor. The `link()` method accepts an `href` parameter that defines where the link points.

For example, if you define a string using the statement `str1 = "This is the start"`, you can change this string into an anchor with the name `"start"` by using the

following statement:
`str1.anchor("start")`.

An example of the `link()` method would be as follows. Given the string `str2 = "fun for kids"`, the following statement converts this string into a link:
`str2.link("www.animabets.com")`.

This example uses the `js-skeleton.html` file found on the book's CD-ROM, but you can apply these steps to any file.

BUILD ANCHORS AND LINKS

1 Open the file `js-skeleton.html` in Notepad.

2 Create string variables and assign each a value.

3 Use `for` and `document.write()` statements to display the strings' values.

4 Create a couple anchors and links by using the `anchor()` and `link()` methods. Set the links to point to the anchors, including the number symbol (#) in front of them.

5 Save the file as `link.html`.

6 Open the `link.html` file in a browser.

■ The anchors and links are displayed.

Extra

The `anchor()` method can accept any string or variable value to be used as the anchor name. The parameters to the `link()` method must be a valid URL or location. Using the `link()` method with an invalid URL does not cause the script to error, but the link will not be available when clicked.

If you use an anchor name within the `link()` method, a link will be established to the anchor. The anchor needs to include a number symbol (#) in front of the anchor name. The `href` parameter that is passed to the `link()` method can be either a relative URL or an absolute URL. Absolute URLs must include a protocol such as `http`.

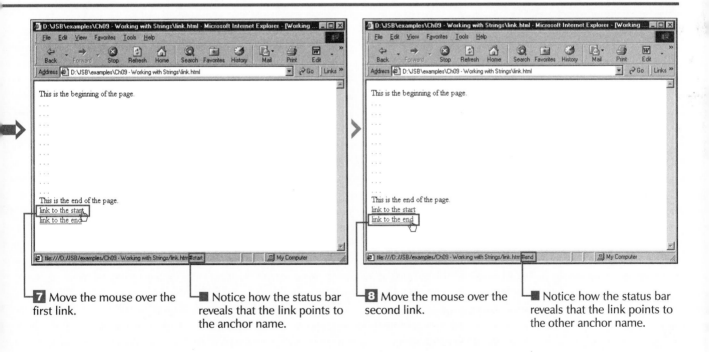

7 Move the mouse over the first link.

■ Notice how the status bar reveals that the link points to the anchor name.

8 Move the mouse over the second link.

■ Notice how the status bar reveals that the link points to the other anchor name.

DETERMINE STRING LENGTH

The `string` object includes a single property — `length`. This property is useful because it can be used as part of a `for` loop to look at each letter in a string.

For example, for the string defined as `str1 = "hello"`, the `str1.length` is equal to 5.

The `length` property counts all characters within the quotation marks including spaces and any HTML code.

This example uses the `js-skeleton.html` file found on the book's CD-ROM, but you can apply these steps to any file.

Extra

Escaped characters such as `\"` or `\t` count as only a single character when the `length` property is used.

DETERMINE STRING LENGTH

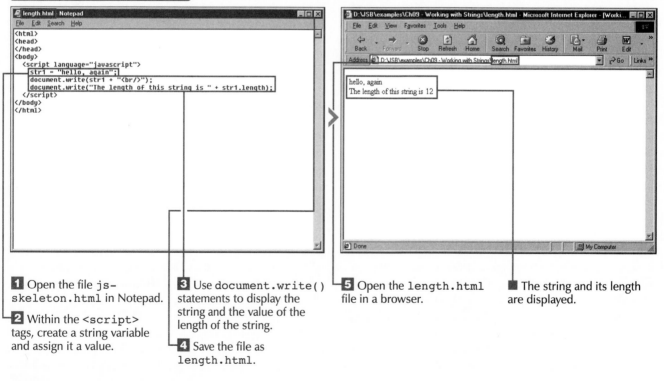

1 Open the file `js-skeleton.html` in Notepad.

2 Within the `<script>` tags, create a string variable and assign it a value.

3 Use `document.write()` statements to display the string and the value of the length of the string.

4 Save the file as `length.html`.

5 Open the `length.html` file in a browser.

■ The string and its length are displayed.

CHANGE CASE

If a string is inputted to your script in all lowercase (or all uppercase) letters, you can convert the string to all uppercase (or all lowercase) letters.

The toLowerCase() method can be used to convert a string to all lowercase letters. Remember that even initial capitals (first letter of each word is capitalized) are changed to lowercase. The toUpperCase() method can be used to convert a string to all capital letters.

This example uses the js-skeleton.html file found on the book's CD-ROM, but you can apply these steps to any file.

Extra

It is common when validating form input such as the value of a text field, to use the toUpperCase() or toLowerCase() methods before checking any data. This ensures that the data isn't case-sensitive. Case-sensitivity is important for some strings such as passwords. If the server expects the password in all capitals or all lowercase, then you can force the string to be either.

CHANGE CASE

1 Open the file js-skeleton.html in Notepad.

2 Within the <script> tags, create a string variable and assign it a value.

3 Add document.write() statements to display the string as it appears initially and then converted to uppercase and lowercase.

4 Save the file as case.html.

5 Open the case.html file in a browser.

■ The string is displayed in all lower- and uppercase.

SEARCH WITHIN A STRING

Using JavaScript, you can search within a string for a section of text. This capability is essential for being able to parse through a string.

The `string` object method to accomplish a string search is `search()`. The parameter for this method is the string for which you're searching. The method returns the index for the position of the search string.

For example, if you have a string defined as `str1 = "Your name is mud."`, you can locate the word *mud* with the following statement `str1.search("mud")`. The

results of this last method are 13. Remember that the string index numbers always start with 0.

If the search string cannot be found within the string, the method returns a value of -1.

This example uses the `js-skeleton.html` file found on the book's CD-ROM, but you can apply these steps to any file.

SEARCH WITHIN A STRING

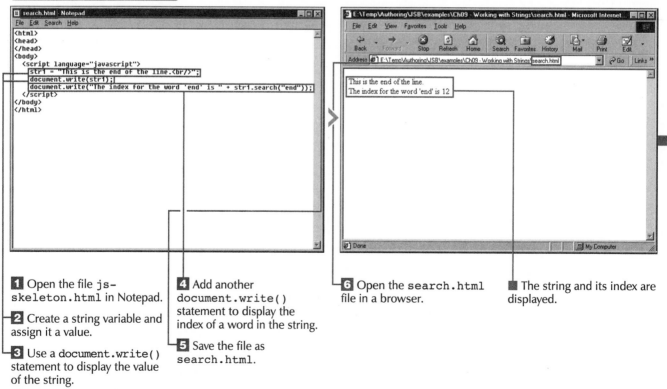

1 Open the file `js-skeleton.html` in Notepad.

2 Create a string variable and assign it a value.

3 Use a `document.write()` statement to display the value of the string.

4 Add another `document.write()` statement to display the index of a word in the string.

5 Save the file as `search.html`.

6 Open the `search.html` file in a browser.

■ The string and its index are displayed.

Apply It

When search features are added to a Web page, you will want to validate the existence of the string in the text before continuing with the search. This validation can be done by checking to see if the text exists using the `search()` method — for example:

```
function
checkSearch(searchString, text) {

  if (text.search(searchString)
== -1)

    document.write("The search
string doesn't exist within this
section of text.")
```

```
  else {

    searchIndex =
text.search(searchString);

    return searchIndex;

  }

}
```

This function checks first to see if the search string exists in the section of text. If it doesn't exist, a message is displayed; if it does, however, the search is executed, and the index is returned.

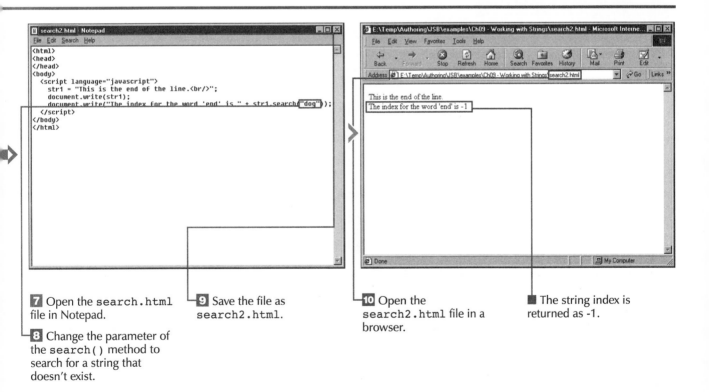

7 Open the `search.html` file in Notepad.

8 Change the parameter of the `search()` method to search for a string that doesn't exist.

9 Save the file as `search2.html`.

10 Open the `search2.html` file in a browser.

■ The string index is returned as -1.

LOCATE CHARACTERS IN A STRING

J avaScript includes some methods additional to `search()` for precisely locating characters and strings.

The `indexOf()` method, like the `search()` method, can be used to locate the first occurrence of a string, but you can also specify where the method begins looking. Remember that the first index value in a string starts with 0.

For example, if a string is defined as `str1 = "I like spaghetti and meatballs and garlic bread"`, you can find the first `"and"` string using the

`str1.indexOf("and")` statement. You can then find the second `"and"` in the string by using the statement `str1.indexOf("and", 20)`. This statement will start looking for the `"and"` string starting at the 20th character in the string.

You can also search from the end of the string using the `lastIndexOf()` method. If you provide a second parameter to this method, it searches backward toward the beginning of the string from the index specified in the second parameter.

USING THE INDEXOF() METHOD

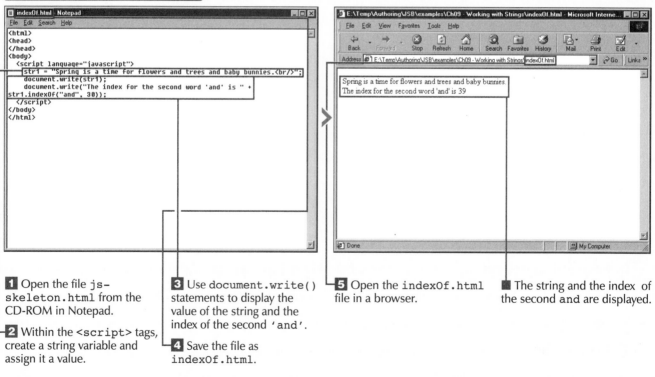

1 Open the file `js-skeleton.html` from the CD-ROM in Notepad.

2 Within the `<script>` tags, create a string variable and assign it a value.

3 Use `document.write()` statements to display the value of the string and the index of the second `'and'`.

4 Save the file as `indexOf.html`.

5 Open the `indexOf.html` file in a browser.

■ The string and the index of the second `and` are displayed.

Apply It

Using the `indexOf()` method, you can write a function to find all the occurrences of a search string within a string. To do this, you can use an `if` or `while` statement. Such a function looks like this:

```
function findAll(searchString,
text) {

  num = 0;

  index = 0;

  pos = new Array();

  while
(text.indexOf(searchString)
!= -1) {
```

```
    pos[num] =
text.indexOf(searchString, pos[

    index = pos[num];

    num++;

    }

}
```

This function stores the position of each search string in an array. Each time through the `while` loop, the `indexOf()` method starts searching from the index of the last search string. This search continues until the search string is no longer found.

USING THE LASTINDEXOF() METHOD

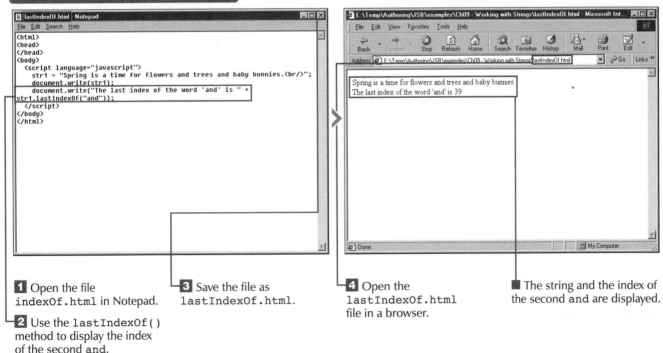

1 Open the file `indexOf.html` in Notepad.

2 Use the `lastIndexOf()` method to display the index of the second and.

3 Save the file as `lastIndexOf.html`.

4 Open the `lastIndexOf.html` file in a browser.

■ The string and the index of the second and are displayed.

REPLACE TEXT IN A STRING

Sometimes finding the index of a search string just isn't enough. You may want to replace the string with another string. You can do this manually, but JavaScript also includes a method that does this.

The `replace()` method can be used to replace an existing string with another one. The `replace()` method accepts the string to search for as its first parameter. The second parameter is the string to replace the first one with.

For example, if a string is defined as `str1 = "I like spaghetti and meatballs`

and garlic bread", you can replace all the `'and'` string with the word *or* by using the statement `str1.replace("and","or")`.

This method replaces only a single instance of the search string, not all instances, in the entire string. To replace all instances, you need to use the method several times.

This example uses the `js-skeleton.html` file found on the book's CD-ROM, but you can apply these steps to any file.

REPLACE TEXT IN A STRING

```html
<html>
<head>
</head>
<body>
  <script language="javascript">
    str1 = "Spring is a time for flowers and trees and baby bunnies.<br/>";
    document.write(str1);
    document.write(str1.replace(" and", ", "));
  </script>
</body>
</html>
```

Spring is a time for flowers and trees and baby bunnies.
Spring is a time for flowers, trees and baby bunnies.

1 Open the file `js-skeleton.html` in Notepad.

2 Create a string variable and assign it a value.

3 Use a `document.write()` statement to display the value of the string.

4 Use the `replace()` method within another `document.write()` statement to replace the word *and* with a comma.

5 Save the file as `replace.html`.

6 Open the `replace.html` file in a browser.

■ The string is displayed normally and with the replacement.

Note: Only the first and *was replaced because the* `replace()` *method was used only once.*

All the search strings within a string can be replaced at once using a `while` loop such as the following:

```
str1 = "standard string";

searchStr = "str";

repStr = "tr";

while (str1.search(searchStr) != -1) {

   str1.replace(searchStr, repStr);

}
```

This code checks for the existence of the search string, and if found, it uses the replace() method to replace it. If the search string isn't found within the string, the loop condition fails and the program continues.

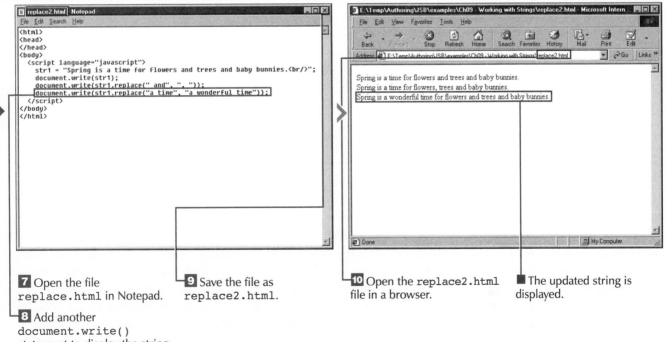

7 Open the file `replace.html` in Notepad.

8 Add another `document.write()` statement to display the string with another replacement.

9 Save the file as `replace2.html`.

10 Open the `replace2.html` file in a browser.

■ The updated string is displayed.

SPLIT A STRING

Using JavaScript, you can split a string into an array of strings. You may find this capability useful for extracting all the separate words within a string.

The `split()` method does this. This method takes a single parameter that is the separator to locate and use to split the string. The method returns an array of strings and can be captured if the method statement is assigned to a variable. None of the array elements include the separator.

For example, if a string is defined as `vocab = "paradigm convolution exception"`,

the `split()` method with the space as a separator can split these words into an array of strings. The method statement looks like `myArray = vocab.split(" ")` and the array includes three elements.

The strings are placed within the array named `myArray` in the order that they appear in the string. For example, `myArray[0]` would equal `"paradigm"`.

This example uses the `js-skeleton.html` file found on the book's CD-ROM, but you can apply these steps to any file.

SPLIT A STRING

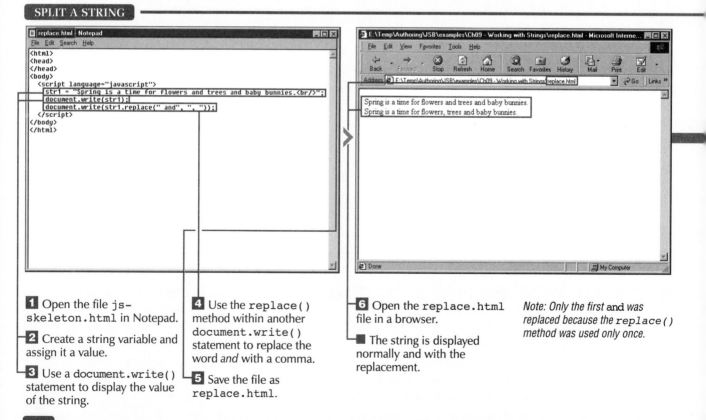

1 Open the file `js-skeleton.html` in Notepad.

2 Create a string variable and assign it a value.

3 Use a `document.write()` statement to display the value of the string.

4 Use the `replace()` method within another `document.write()` statement to replace the word *and* with a comma.

5 Save the file as `replace.html`.

6 Open the `replace.html` file in a browser.

■ The string is displayed normally and with the replacement.

Note: Only the first and *was replaced because the* `replace()` *method was used only once.*

Apply It

You can use a textarea to obtain a list of items. If you have the user place a symbol such as an asterisk (*) in front of each list item in the textarea box, you can use the split() method to separate the list items into an array. A function to do this would look like this:

```
function textList(text) {

    listArray = text.split("*");

}
```

This simple function separates list items using the split() method and places each item as an element in an array. You can view the list using this code:

```
for (j=0;j<listArray.length;j++) {

    document.write("List item " + j
+ ": " + listArray[j]);

}
```

split2.html - Notepad

```
<html>
<head>
</head>
<body>
  <script language="javascript">
    str1 = "Oscar the Grouch, Big Bird, Cookie Monster<br/>";
    document.write(str1);
    str1Array = str1.split(" ");
    document.write(str1Array[0] + "<br/>");
    document.write(str1Array[1] + "<br/>");
    document.write(str1Array[2] + "<br/>");
  </script>
</body>
</html>
```

Browser output:
```
Oscar the Grouch, Big Bird, Cookie Monster
Oscar
the
Grouch,
```

8 Open the file split.html in Notepad.

9 Change the separator to a space.

10 Save the file as split2.html.

11 Open the split2.html file in a browser.

■ The array elements are now different.

Note: The string in this example has been split into more elements because there are more spaces in this string than commas. You can see only the first three because there are only three document.write statements.

USING THE DATE OBJECT

The date object isn't associated with a Web page element, but it is included as part of the default JavaScript syntax.

Before you can use the date object, you must create it. To create a date object, you need to give it a variable name and set it equal to the new keyword followed by Date(). For example, myDate = new Date() creates a new date object called myDate.

By defining a parameter to the Date() object, you can set the date format. The date format accepts three definitions. The first must be placed in quotes and include "month day, year hours:minutes:seconds."

The second definition includes just numbers for the year, month, and day. The third definition is like the second except it also includes values for the hours, minutes, and seconds — for example, Date("Jul 29, 1982 06:30:00"), Date(1993, 4, 17) for May 17, 1993, and Date(1997, 3, 4, 10, 37, 00) for April 4, 1997 at 10:37 a.m. Months are specified starting with 0, so 0 is January, 1 is February, and so on.

This example uses the js-skeleton.html file found on the book's CD-ROM, but you can apply these steps to any file.

USING THE DATE OBJECT AND DATE FORMATS

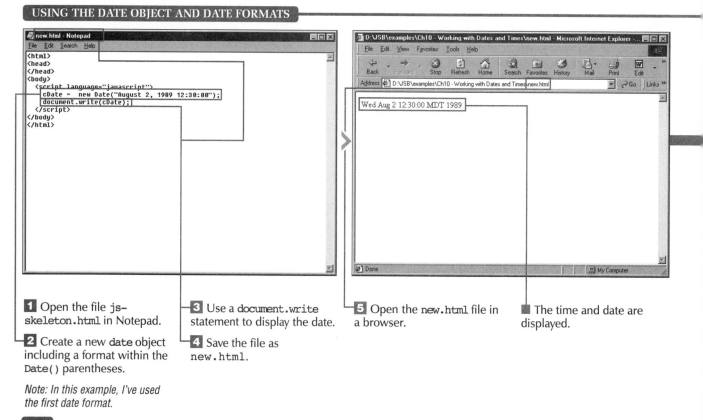

1 Open the file js-skeleton.html in Notepad.

2 Create a new date object including a format within the Date() parentheses.

Note: In this example, I've used the first date format.

3 Use a document.write statement to display the date.

4 Save the file as new.html.

5 Open the new.html file in a browser.

■ The time and date are displayed.

Extra

The date object, when unformatted, holds only a single piece of data — an integer. This integer is the number of milliseconds that have transpired since January 1, 1970. This number for the current time is a rather large number.

To compare date objects, both objects need to be converted to the standard date object format, which is the number of milliseconds since January, 1970. Any new date object that is created automatically appears in this format, and you can convert a date to this format using the Date.UTC() method. This method accepts the same formats as a new date object. For example, Date.UTC(86, 2, 16, 8, 45, 00) sets a date object equal to March 16, 1986 at 8:45:00.

```
new2.html - Notepad
File  Edit  Search  Help
<html>
<head>
</head>
<body>
  <script language="javascript">
    cDate =  new Date(2000, 1, 1, 12, 00, 00);
    document.write(cDate);
  </script>
</body>
</html>
```

Tue Feb 1 12:00:00 MST 2000

6 Open the new.html file in Notepad.

7 Change the format in the Date() object.

Note: In this example, I've used the third date format.

8 Save the file as new2.html.

9 Open the new2.html file in a browser.

■ The new time and date are displayed.

Note: The index for months starts with 0, so 0 is January, 1 is February, and so on, which is why February is returned in this example.

DISPLAY THE LOCAL TIME AND DATE

After creating a new date object, you can use one of many methods to get information about the current date and time.

One very useful date object method is the toGMTString() method, which will return the current Greenwich mean time (GMT). *Greenwich mean time* is the time zone where all other time zones are measured from. Another useful method is toLocaleString(). This method returns the current date and time for the local time zone.

The format for these dates and times lists the day, the date, the month, and then the year. After the year comes the hours, minutes, and seconds, and finally the time zone.

For example, Wed, 12 Apr 2000 03:37:38 UTC is the date and time format for Wednesday, April 12 of the year 2000 at 3:37 and 38 seconds. UTC is short for Universal Coordinated Time, which is another name for GMT.

This example uses the js-skeleton.html file found on the book's CD-ROM, but you can apply these steps to any file.

DISPLAY GREENWICH MEAN TIME

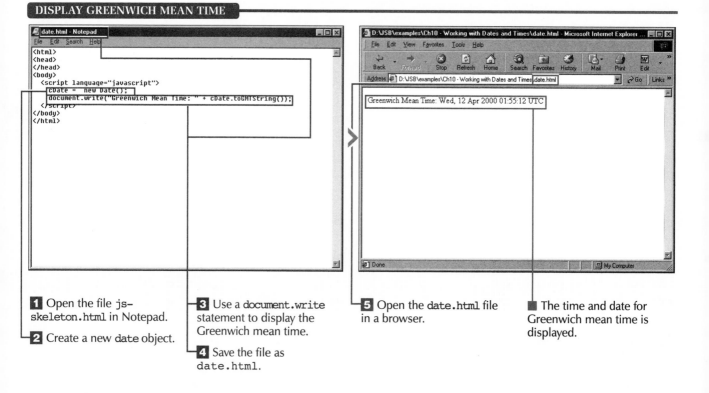

1 Open the file js-skeleton.html in Notepad.

2 Create a new date object.

3 Use a document.write statement to display the Greenwich mean time.

4 Save the file as date.html.

5 Open the date.html file in a browser.

■ The time and date for Greenwich mean time is displayed.

Extra

The format of the date object remains the same displaying the day, date, time, and time zone if you use the `toGMTString()` method. This method displays the day and month using three characters, such as Fri for Friday and Apr for April. For example, this format looks like this: `Fri, 14 Apr 2000 19:01:54 UTC`. The date format for the `toLocaleString()` method is a little different. This method displays only numbers with the date first and then the time. Slash

symbols (/) are placed between the date numbers. For example, the format for this method is `04/14/2000 13:05:13`. You can also use the `toString()` method to display the date object. This format looks different still with the year at the end of the string. For example, this format looks like `Fri Apr 14 13:06:23 MDT 2000`. If you want to use a custom format, you can use the get methods to format the date, as shown in the next section, "Get Time and Date Values."

DISPLAY LOCAL TIME AND DATE

```
<html>
<head>
</head>
<body>
  <script language="javascript">
    cDate = new Date();
    document.write("Local Time: " + cDate.toLocaleString());
  </script>
</body>
</html>
```

Local Time: 04/11/2000 19:59:26

1 Open the date.html file in Notepad.

2 Change the toGMTString() method to toLocaleString() and update the displayed text.

3 Save the file as date2.html.

4 Open the date2.html file in a browser.

■ The local time and date are displayed.

GET TIME AND DATE VALUES

JavaScript includes several methods that enable you to retrieve specific date and time information from a date object. These methods all begin with the word *get* and return integer values.

The getDate() method returns the date, so on January 24, this method would return 24. The getDay() method returns an integer representing the day of the week; that is, 1 is for Monday, 2 is for Tuesday, and so on, through 7 for Sunday.

The getHours() method returns the hour of day in 24-hour military time format. For

example, 3:00 p.m. returns 15. The getMinutes() and getSeconds() methods return the number of minutes and seconds.

The getMonth() method returns an integer representing the month of the year starting with 0 for January, so July returns a 6 and December returns 11. The getYear() method returns a two-digit value for the year, so 1996 would return 96.

This example uses the js-skeleton.html file found on the book's CD-ROM, but you can apply these steps to any file.

GET DATE VALUES

```
getDate.html - Notepad
File  Edit  Search  Help
<html>
<head>
</head>
<body>
  <script language="javascript">
    cDate =  new Date();
    document.write("The current day value is " + cDate.getDay() + "<br/>");
    document.write("The current month value is " + cDate.getMonth() +
"<br/>");
    document.write("The current date value is " + cDate.getDate() +
"<br/>");
    document.write("The current year value is " + cDate.getYear() +
"<br/>");
  </script>
</body>
</html>
```

```
D:\JSB\examples\Ch10 - Working with Dates and Times\getDate.html - Microsoft Internet Explo...
File  Edit  View  Favorites  Tools  Help
Back  Forward  Stop  Refresh  Home  Search  Favorites  History  Mail  Print  Edit
Address  D:\JSB\examples\Ch10 - Working with Dates and Times\getDate.html        Go  Links

The current day value is 3
The current month value is 3
The current date value is 12
The current year value is 2000

Done                                                    My Computer
```

■1 Open the file js-skeleton.html in Notepad.

■2 Create a new date object.

■3 Use document.write statements to display the get methods for the current date.

■4 Save the file as getDate.html.

■5 Open the getDate.html file in a browser.

■ The values for the current date are displayed.

Apply It

Using the `get` methods, you can create a simple clock. The key to this clock is the `setTimeout()` method that is set to call the `clock` function every 1000 milliseconds. The `clock` function can display the time to a text field named `text1` located within a form named `form1`:

```
function clock() {
  cTime = new Date();
  cHours = cTime.getHours();
  cMinutes = cTime.getMinutes();
  cSeconds = cTime.getSeconds();
  document.form1.text1.value =
cHours + ":" + cMinutes + ":" +
cSeconds;
  setTimeout("clock()", 1000);
}
```

This function creates a new `date` object, gets the hours, minutes, and seconds, and displays these values in a text field. It then calls the same function again after 1,000 milliseconds, and the clock is updated again.

GET TIME VALUES

```html
<html>
<head>
</head>
<body>
  <script language="javascript">
  cDate = new Date();
  document.write("The current day value is " + cDate.getDay() + "<br/>");
  document.write("The current month value is " + cDate.getMonth() +
"<br/>");
  document.write("The current date value is " + cDate.getDate() +
"<br/>");
  document.write("The current year value is " + cDate.getYear() +
"<br/>");
  document.write("The current hour value is " + cDate.getHours() +
"<br/>");
  document.write("The current minutes value is " + cDate.getMinutes() +
"<br/>");
  document.write("The current seconds value is " + cDate.getSeconds() +
"<br/>");
  </script>
</body>
</html>
```

The current day value is 3
The current month value is 3
The current date value is 12
The current year value is 2000
The current hour value is 7
The current minutes value is 39
The current seconds value is 52

1 Open the getDate.html file in Notepad.

2 Add several additional `document.write` statements to display the values of the `get` methods for the current time.

3 Save the file as getDate2.html.

4 Open the getDate2.html file in a browser.

■ The values for the current time are displayed.

SET TIME AND DATE VALUES

When working with the date object, you can also set dates and times using one of several methods that begin with the word *set*. These methods place an integer value into a date object.

The setDate() method sets the date for the object and can be a value between 1 and 31. The setMonth() sets the value for the month. It accept values 0 through 11 with 0 for January (so July returns 6 and December returns 11). setYear() can accept a two-digit or four-digit year value, so 96 would set the year to 1996.

The setHours() method sets the hour of day in 24-hour military time format. For example, setHours(15) would set the hour to 3:00 p.m. The setMinutes() and setSeconds() methods set the number of minutes and seconds for the time.

This example uses the js-skeleton.html file found on the book's CD-ROM, but you can apply these steps to any file.

SET DATE VALUES

```
<html>
<head>
</head>
<body>
  <script language="javascript">
    cDate = new Date("December 25, 1984");
    document.write("The date is initially set to " + cDate + "<br/>");
    cDate.setMonth(10);
    document.write("The month value has been changed: " + cDate + "<br/>");
    cDate.setDate(17);
    document.write("The date value has been changed: " + cDate + "<br/>");
    cDate.setYear(97);
    document.write("The year value has been changed: " + cDate + "<br/>");
  </script>
</body>
</html>
```

The date is initially set to Tue Dec 25 00:00:00 MST 1984
The month value has been changed: Sun Nov 25 00:00:00 MST 1984
The date value has been changed: Sat Nov 17 00:00:00 MST 1984
The year value has been changed: Mon Nov 17 00:00:00 MST 1997

1 Open the file js-skeleton.html in Notepad.

2 Create a new date object and set the initial date within the parentheses.

3 Use a document.write statement to display the initial date.

4 Change the month, date, and year values using the set methods and display the results.

5 Save the file as setDate.html.

6 Open the setDate.html file in a browser.

■ The date before and after the changes is shown.

Apply It

If you enable a user to enter a date such as their birthday using a Web page form, you can create and save the entire date object. The date object can then be manipulated and used as needed. For example, you could compute how many days until their next birthday or display a unique page on their birthday. A function to create such a date would look like this:

```
function birthday() {

  myBirthday = new Date();

myBirthday.setMonth(document.form1.
text1.value);.
myBirthday.setDate(document.form1.
text2.value);.
myBirthday.setYear(document.form1.
text3.value);

  document.write("Your birthday is
" + myBirthday);

}
```

This function creates a new date object and sets the date's month, date, and year based on the values of three text fields found on a Web page form named form1.

SET TIME VALUES

```
setDate2.html - Notepad
File  Edit  Search  Help
<html>
<head>
</head>
<body>
  <script language="javascript">
    cDate =  new Date("December 25, 1984");
    document.write("The date is initially set to " + cDate + "<br/>");
    cDate.setMonth(10);
    document.write("The month value has been changed: " + cDate + "<br/>");
    cDate.setDate(17);
    document.write("The date value has been changed: " + cDate + "<br/>");
    cDate.setYear(97);
    document.write("The year value has been changed: " + cDate + "<br/>");
    cDate.setHours(13);
    cDate.setMinutes(47);
    cDate.setSeconds(23);
    document.write("The time values have been changed: " + cDate + "<br/>");
  </script>
</body>
</html>
```

Browser window (D:\JSB\examples\Ch10 - Working with Dates and Times\setDate2.html - Microsoft Internet Expl...):

The date is initially set to Tue Dec 25 00:00:00 MST 1984
The month value has been changed: Sun Nov 25 00:00:00 MST 1984
The date value has been changed: Sat Nov 17 00:00:00 MST 1984
The year value has been changed: Mon Nov 17 00:00:00 MST 1997
The time values have been changed: Mon Nov 17 13:47:23 MST 1997

1 Open the setDate.html file in Notepad.

2 Change the hours, minutes, and seconds using the set methods and display the results.

3 Save the file as setDate2.html.

4 Open the setDate2.html file in a browser.

■ The initial time and changed time are displayed.

WORK WITH TIME

A long with the `get` and `set` methods used to control months, dates, years, hours, minutes, and seconds are two more methods for controlling the time.

The `getTime()` method returns an integer value that is equal to the number of milliseconds that have passed since January 1, 1970. This is the standard format for dates and times. You can also use the `setTime()` method to set the time of a `date` object. This method accepts the number of milliseconds that have passed since January 1, 1970.

You can also change a date into this standard format using the `Date.parse()` method. This method accepts a month, date, and year such as February 14, 1980 or a more descriptive format like `Mon Nov 17 1997 13:47:23 MST` and returns the number of milliseconds since January 1, 1970.

To convert the number of milliseconds since January 1, 1970 to a recognizable format, you can use the `toGMTString()` method.

This example uses the `js-skeleton.html` file found on the book's CD-ROM, but you can apply these steps to any file.

WORK WITH TIME

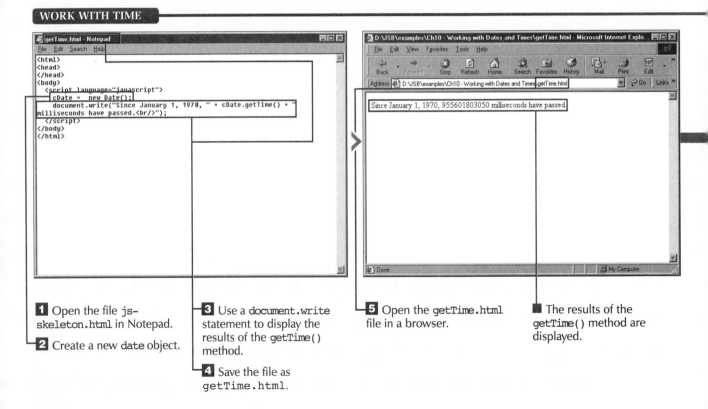

1 Open the file `js-skeleton.html` in Notepad.

2 Create a new `date` object.

3 Use a `document.write` statement to display the results of the `getTime()` method.

4 Save the file as `getTime.html`.

5 Open the `getTime.html` file in a browser.

■ The results of the `getTime()` method are displayed.

Apply It

You may sometimes want to perform some arithmetic on a date object. For example, to figure out how many days are between two dates, you could subtract the two dates and then calculate the number of days. Such a script looks like this:

```
function compDates(date1, date2)
  {
  diffMilliseconds = date2 -
  date1;
  diffSeconds = diffMilliseconds
  / 1000;
  diffMinutes = diffSeconds /
  60;
```

```
  diffHours = diffMinutes / 60;
  diffDays = diffHours / 24;
  return diffDays;

}
```

This function accepts two dates and returns the difference in the number of days between them.

Notepad — parse.html

```
<html>
<head>
</head>
<body>
  <script language="javascript">
    cDate = new Date();
    nDate = new Date("Sep 12, 1974");
    document.write("Since January 1, 1970, " + cDate.getTime() + "
milliseconds have passed.<br/>");
    document.write("Between January 1, 1970 and " + nDate + ", " +
Date.parse(nDate) + " milliseconds have passed.<br/>");
  </script>
</body>
</html>
```

Browser — parse.html

Since January 1, 1970, 955602529000 milliseconds have passed.
Between January 1, 1970 and Thu Sep 12 00:00:00 MDT 1974, 148197600000 milliseconds have passed.

6 Open the file getTime.html in Notepad.

7 Create another date object and set its date.

8 Use a document.write and a Date.parse() statement to display the number of milliseconds since January 1, 1970 for this date.

9 Save the file as parse.html.

10 Open the parse.html file in a browser.

■ The number of milliseconds since January 1, 1970 for this date are displayed.

WORK WITH TIME ZONES

JavaScript includes a method that can be used to compute the time difference for different time zones. All times zones are computed relative to *Greenwich mean time* (GMT). GMT is also referred to as UTC, which stands for *Universal Time Coordinated.*

The getTimezoneOffset() returns the number of minutes between GMT and the local time zone. The returned value could be positive or negative, depending on whether the current time zone is ahead of or behind Greenwich mean time.

For example, if the user's computer is located within the Pacific standard time zone, then for the date object named myDate, the statement myDate.getTimezoneOffset() returns a value of 480. This value represents an offset of 8 hours from GMT.

This example uses the js-skeleton.html file found on the book's CD-ROM, but you can apply these steps to any file.

WORK WITH TIME ZONES

```
getTimezoneOffset.html - Notepad
File  Edit  Search  Help
<html>
<head>
</head>
<body>
  <script language="javascript">
    cDate =  new Date();
    document.write("The local time and date is: " + cDate.toLocaleString() +
".<br/>");
    document.write("The time zone offset between local time and GMT is " +
cDate.getTimezoneOffset() + ".<br/>");
  </script>
</body>
</html>
```

```
D:\JSB\examples\Ch10 - Working with Dates and Times\getTimezoneOffset.html - Microsoft Int...
File  Edit  View  Favorites  Tools  Help
Back   Forward   Stop   Refresh   Home   Search   Favorites   History   Mail   Print   Edit
Address  D:\JSB\examples\Ch10 - Working with Dates and Times\getTimezoneOffset.html          Go   Links

The local time and date is: 04/12/2000 23:29:12.
The time zone offset between local time and GMT is 360.

Done                                                                    My Computer
```

1 Open the file js-skeleton.html in Notepad.

2 Create a new date object.

3 Use a document.write statement to display the current local time and date.

4 Add another document.write statement to display the time zone offset.

5 Save the file as getTimezoneOffset.html.

6 Open the file getTimezoneOffset.html in a browser.

■ The local time and date and the time zone offset are displayed.

Extra

The time zone offset value that is returned by the `getTimezoneOffset()` method is based on the user's internal computer system. For a Windows-based system, this value is retrieved from the system setting that is configured using the Control Panel Date application. If the date and time specified in this system application is incorrect, the `date` object methods will return incorrect values for the `date` object.

The `getTimezoneOffset()` method doesn't need to directly handle daylight saving time because DST is computed and controlled by the operating system. Because JavaScript queries the system for this information, it automatically converts your date and time settings to accommodate for the changes caused by daylight saving time.

```
<html>
<head>
</head>
<body>
  <script language="javascript">
    cDate = new Date();
    document.write("The local time and date is: " + cDate.toLocaleString() +
".<br/>");
    document.write("The time zone offset between local time and GMT is " +
cDate.getTimezoneOffset() + ".<br/>");
    document.write("The time for the neighboring time zone is " +
(cDate.getHours() + 1) + ":" + cDate.getMinutes() + ".<br/>");
  </script>
</body>
</html>
```

The local time and date is: 04/13/2000 07:11:25.
The time zone offset between local time and GMT is 360.
The time for the neighboring time zone is 8:11.

7 Open the `getTimezoneOffset.html` file in Notepad.

8 Add another `document.write` statement to display the time in the neighboring time zone.

Note: To display the time in a neighboring time zone, you typically only need to add or subtract an hour from the time.

9 Save the file as `getTimezoneOffset2.html`.

10 Open the `getTimezoneOffset2.html` file in a browser.

■ The local and neighboring time zone times are displayed.

USING THE MATH OBJECT

The `Math` object includes properties and methods that make it possible to work with mathematical equations and computations.

The `Math` object includes properties for representing various mathematical values, such as Euler's constant (E), base-10 logarithms (LOG10E), natural logarithms (LN10), pi (PI), and the square root of two (SQRT2).

The `Math` object methods include a variety of advanced mathematical functions. These functions include, but are not limited to,

`abs(x)`, `ceil(x)`, `floor(x)`, `sin(x)`, `cos(x)`, `tan(x)`, `log(x)`, `min(x)`, `max(x)`, `pow(x,y)`, `random()`, and `sqrt(x)`, where *x* and *y* are numbers.

The `Math` object doesn't need to be specified as a sub-object of the `document` or `window` objects, but it does need to be capitalized. For example, to specify the value of pi, you must use the `Math.PI` syntax.

This example uses the `js-skeleton.html` file found on the book's CD-ROM, but you can apply these steps to any file.

USING THE MATH OBJECT

```html
<html>
<head>
</head>
<body>
  <script language="javascript">
  </script>
  <form name="form1">
    Circle Radius:<input type="text" name="rad"/><br/>
    Circle Area:<input type="text" name="area"/><br/>
    <input type="button" name="button1" value="Compute Area"
    onclick="document.form1.area.value=document.form1.rad.value*
    document.form1.rad.value*Math.PI;"/>
  </form>
</body>
</html>
```

Circle Radius:
Circle Area:
Compute Area

1 Open the file js-skeleton.html in Notepad.

2 Add a form with two text boxes and a button.

3 Add the onclick event to the button.

4 Add a statement for the onclick event that computes the area of a circle based on the text box value.

5 Save the file as math.html.

6 Open the math.html file in a browser.

■ A form with two text boxes and a button is displayed.

Extra

Each `Math` object method returns a value based on the number that is passed as a parameter. The number passed in as a parameter could be an actual number or another object. For example, `Math.pow(2,3)` returns a value of 8, which is the value of 2 raised to the power of 3. The JavaScript statement `Math.cos(document.form1.text1.value)` returns the cosine of the value found in the text box named `text1` on the form named `form1`.

The `Math` object keyword that appears in front of the properties and methods always needs to be capitalized. JavaScript is case-sensitive and does not work if capitalized incorrectly.

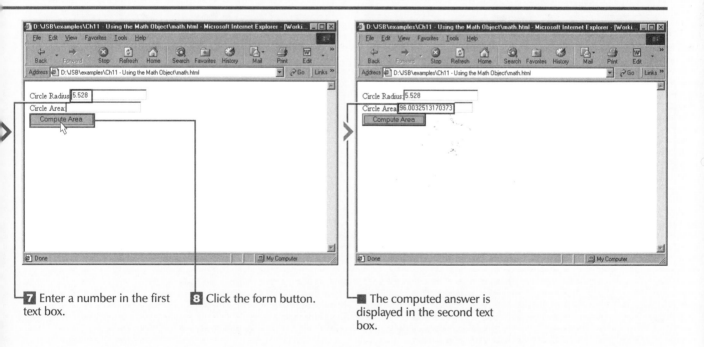

7 Enter a number in the first text box.

8 Click the form button.

■ The computed answer is displayed in the second text box.

GENERATE RANDOM NUMBERS

Random numbers can be used within JavaScript scripts for a number of different purposes, such as randomly selecting an option for the user.

The `Math.random()` method returns a random number between 0 and 1. If you multiply the number generated by this method by another number, you can get a random number that is between 0 and the other number. For example, the statement `Math.random() * 5` generates a number between 0 and 5.

The random number will not be an integer, but you can make it an integer using the `Math.floor()` method. This method truncates the numbers after the decimal point and returns an integer. For example, `Math.floor(Math.random() * 5)` returns a random integer between 0 and 4.

This example uses the `js-skeleton.html` file found on the book's CD-ROM, but you can apply these steps to any file.

GENERATE RANDOM NUMBERS

```
<html>
<head>
</head>
<body>
<script language="javascript">
QuoteArray = new Array(
   "Now is the time for all good men to come to the aid of their country.",
   "I have not yet begun to fight.",
   "Give me liberty or give me death.",
   "One if by land, two if by sea.",
   "We, the people, in order to form a more perfect union,",
   "Life, liberty and pursuit of happiness.");
RandomNo = Math.floor(QuoteArray.length * Math.random());
document.write("<b>" + QuoteArray[RandomNo] + "</b>");
</script>
</body>
</html>
```

I have not yet begun to fight.

1 Open the file `js-skeleton.html` in Notepad.

2 Within the `<script>` tags, create a new array using the `Array` keyword.

3 Add several quotes to the array enclosed in quotation marks and separated with commas.

4 Create a variable using the `Math.floor()` and `Math.random()` methods and multiply `Math.random()` by the array's length.

5 Display a quote using `document.write()`.

6 Save the file as `random.html`.

7 Open the `random.html` file in a browser.

■ A quote is displayed in the browser.

8 Click the Refresh button on the browser.

Apply It

To select options based on random numbers, you can use a series of `if` and `else if` statements. For example, consider the following function:

```
function threeOptions() {
    rand =
Math.floor(Math.random() * 3);
  if (rand == 1) {
     document.write("option 1");
  }
  else if (rand == 2) {
     document.write("option 2");
  }
  else {
     document.write("option 3");
  }
}
```

The first statement generates a random number between 1 and 3. Statements can be placed in the braced sections for each option.

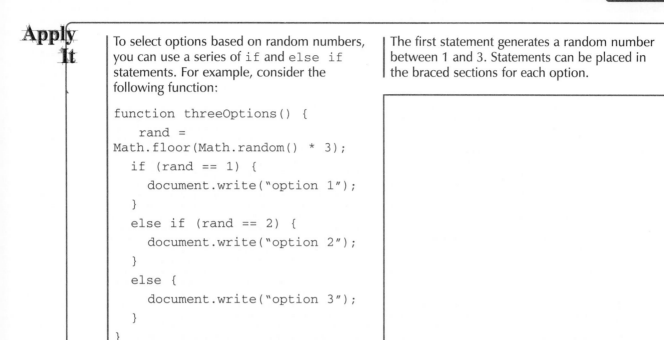

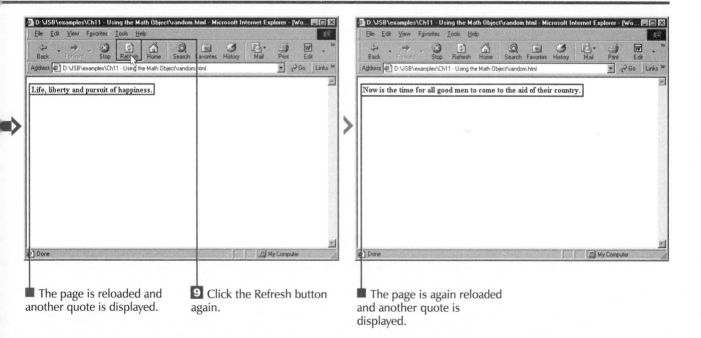

■ The page is reloaded and another quote is displayed.

9 Click the Refresh button again.

■ The page is again reloaded and another quote is displayed.

USING MATHEMATICAL CONSTANTS

The properties of the Math object are used to represent several standard mathematical constants. Various mathematical equations rely on these constants.

These constants include Euler's constant (Math.E), the natural logarithm of 10 (Math.LN10), the natural logarithm of 2 (Math.LN2), the base-10 logarithm of Euler's constant (Math.LOG10E), the base-2 logarithm of Euler's constant (Math.LOG2E), pi (Math.PI), the square root of one half (Math.SQRT1_2), and the square root of two (Math.SQRT2).

These properties can be inserted wherever the constant would normally appear in the equation. JavaScript computes the value of the constant to roughly 17 digits. Using these constants enables a high level of accuracy without having to type in all the digits.

For example, to compute the perimeter of a circle, you can use the statement perimeter = 2 * radius * Math.PI.

This example uses the js-skeleton.html file found on the book's CD-ROM, but you can apply these steps to any file.

DISPLAY THE MATH OBJECT CONSTANTS

```
constants.html - Notepad
File  Edit  Search  Help
<html>
<head>
</head>
<body>
<script language="javascript">
   document.write("<h2>Mathematical Constants</h2>");
   document.write("Euler's constant: " + Math.E + "<br/>");
   document.write("natural logarithm of 10: " + Math.LN10 + "<br/>");
   document.write("natural logarithm of 2: " + Math.LN2 + "<br/>");
   document.write("base 10 logarithm of Euler's constant: " + Math.LOG10E +
"<br/>");
   document.write("base 2 logarithm of Euler's constant: " + Math.LOG2E +
"<br/>");
   document.write("Pi: " + Math.PI + "<br/>");
   document.write("square root of one half: " + Math.SQRT1_2 + "<br/>");
   document.write("square root of two: " + Math.SQRT2 + "<br/>");
</script>
</body>
</html>
```

D:\JSB\examples\Ch11 - Using the Math Object\constants.html - Microsoft Internet Explorer - [...]
File Edit View Favorites Tools Help
Back Forward Stop Refresh Home Search Favorites History Mail Print Edit
Address D:\JSB\examples\Ch11 - Using the Math Object\constants.html

Mathematical Constants

Euler's constant: 2.718281828459045
natural logarithm of 10: 2.302585092994046
natural logarithm of 2: 0.6931471805599453
base 10 logarithm of Euler's constant: 0.4342944819032518
base 2 logarithm of Euler's constant: 1.4426950408889633
Pi: 3.141592653589793
square root of one half: 0.7071067811865476
square root of two: 1.4142135623730951

■1 Open the file js-skeleton.html in Notepad.

■2 Use **document.write** statements to display the values of all the mathematical constants and a heading.

■3 Save the file as constants.html.

■4 Open the file constants.html in a browser.

■ All the Math object constants are displayed.

Many different mathematical equations rely on these constants. Some of these constants can be computed using the other `Math` object methods. For example, the `Math.LN10` constant can be computed using the `Math.log()` method that is used to compute the natural logarithm of a number. The reason this number is defined as a constant is that it appears in many useful equations and, as a constant, it can be quickly included and computed as part of a JavaScript statement.

If the Math object doesn't include a specific constant that you need, you can create a global variable and assign it the needed variable. This variable could then be used throughout the script.

USING THE MATH.PI CONSTANT

```
<html>
<head>
</head>
<body>
  <script language="javascript">
  </script>
  <form name="form1">
    Circle Radius:<input type="text" name="rad"/><br/>
    Circle Area:<input type="text" name="area"/><br/>
    <input type="button" name="button1" value="Compute Area"
      onclick="document.form1.area.value=4/3*document.form1.rad.value*
      document.form1.rad.value*document.form1.rad.value*Math.PI;"/>

  </form>
</body>
</html>
```

Circle Radius 2.5
Circle Area 65.44984694978734
Compute Area

1 Open the file js-skeleton.html in Notepad.

2 Add a form with two text boxes and a button.

3 Add the onclick event to the button.

4 Add a statement for the onclick event that computes the area of a sphere based on the text box value.

5 Save the file as sphere.html.

6 Open the file sphere.html in a browser.

7 Enter a number in the first text box.

8 Click the form button.

■ The computed answer is displayed in the second text box.

USING TRIGONOMETRIC FUNCTIONS

D o you remember the trigonometric functions from your geometry class? JavaScript supports these as methods of the `Math` object, including the cosine, sine, and tangent functions. JavaScript also supports their opposite functions: arc-cosine, arc-sine, and arc-tangent.

The methods for these functions are `cos()`, `sin()`, `tan()`, `acos()`, `asin()`, and `atan()`. All these functions take a single parameter value and return an angular value in radians.

Radians are a mathematical measure of an angle. 360 degrees is equal to 2 Pi radians. You can compute the more common angular measurement of degrees by multiplying the number of radians by 57.3.

JavaScript also includes one additional trigonometric method that can convert standard x and y coordinate values to an angular measurement. This method is `atan2()`, and it takes two coordinate values as parameters.

This example uses the `js-skeleton.html` file found on the book's CD-ROM, but you can apply these steps to any file.

USING TRIGONOMETRIC FUNCTIONS

1 Open the file js-skeleton.html in Notepad.

2 Add a heading and a form with six text boxes. Make three text boxes to hold the values of the sides of a triangle and three to hold the trigonometric angle values.

3 Add the onchange event to each text box for the side lengths.

4 Set each onchange event equal to the trigonometric equation for computing the angle values.

5 Save the file as trig.html.

6 Open the trig.html file in a browser.

■ A form with six text boxes is displayed.

Apply It

To convert the angles measured in radians to degrees, you can use a function like this one:

```
function radiansToDegrees(rads) {

  degrees = (360 * rads / (2 *
Math.PI));

  return degrees;

}
```

The function takes a radian value and returns an equivalent value in degrees. A similar function can be created to convert degrees back to radians. Such a function looks like this:

```
function degreesToRadians(degrees)
{

  radians = (2 * Math.PI *
degrees) / 360);

  return radians;

}
```

This function takes a value in degrees as a parameter and returns the same value measured in radians.

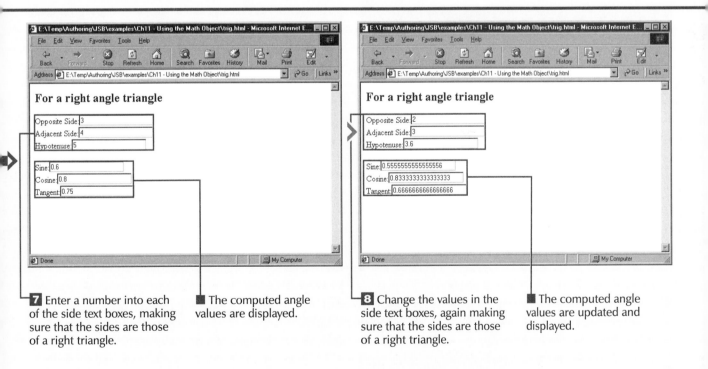

7 Enter a number into each of the side text boxes, making sure that the sides are those of a right triangle.

■ The computed angle values are displayed.

8 Change the values in the side text boxes, again making sure that the sides are those of a right triangle.

■ The computed angle values are updated and displayed.

USING LOGARITHMIC AND EXPONENTIAL METHODS

JavaScript includes two methods for working with natural logarithms and exponentials based on *Euler's constant.*

The log() method takes a number as a parameter and returns the natural logarithm (base e) of the number.

The exp() method takes a number as a parameter and returns the value of Euler's constant raised to the power of the number.

These two methods are complementary where the log(x) = y and the exp(y) = x.

This example uses the js-skeleton.html file found on the book's CD-ROM, but you can apply these steps to any file.

Extra

The Math.LN10 and Math.LN2 properties are constants for values returned by Math.log(10) and Math.log(2). The Math.log() method can be used to return the natural logarithm of any number.

USING LOGARITHMIC AND EXPONENTIAL METHODS

```
log.html - Notepad
File  Edit  Search  Help
<html>
<head>
</head>
<body>
  <script language="javascript">
  </script>
  <form name="form1">
    value:<input type="text" name="val"/><br/>
    log(value):<input type="text" name="res1"/><br/>
    exp(value):<input type="text" name="res2"/><br/>
    <input type="button" name="button1" value="Compute"
onclick="document.form1.res1.value=Math.log(document.form1.val.value);
document.form1.res2.value=Math.exp(document.form1.val.value);"/>
  </form>
</body>
</html>
```

D:\JSB\examples\Ch11 - Using the Math Object\log.html - Microsoft Internet Explorer - [Workin...

value 5.5
log(value): 1.7047480922384252
exp(value): 244.69193226422038
Compute

■1 Open the file js-skeleton.html in Notepad.

■2 Add a form with three text boxes and a button.

■3 Add the onclick event to the button.

■4 Add a statement for the onclick event that computes the log and the exp of the value.

■5 Save the file as log.html.

■6 Open the log.html file in a browser.

■7 Enter a number in the first text box.

■8 Click the form button.

■ The computed answers are displayed in the other text boxes.

USING THE SQUARE ROOT METHOD

JavaScript also includes a method for computing the square root of a number. This computation is accomplished with the `sqrt()` method.

The `sqrt()` method receives a number as a parameter and returns its square root.

An example of where the `sqrt()` method is used is in computing the Pythagorean theorem (the square of two sides of a right triangle equals the square of the hypotenuse).

This example uses the `js-skeleton.html` file found on the book's CD-ROM, but you can apply these steps to any file.

USING THE SQUARE ROOT METHOD

1 Open the file js-skeleton.html in Notepad.

2 Add a form with two text boxes and a button.

3 Add the `onclick` event to the button.

4 Add a statement for the `onclick` event that computes the square root of the value in the first text box.

5 Save the file as sqrt.html.

6 Open the sqrt.html file in a browser.

7 Enter a number in the first text box.

8 Click the form button.

■ The computed value is displayed in the second text box.

ROUND NUMBERS

If you're dealing with floating-point numbers that include a decimal point, you can eliminate the numbers after the decimal point by using the `round()` method.

This method changes any floating-point number to the closest integer. Any decimal value less than 0.5 converts the number to the lower integer value. Any decimal value equal to or greater than 0.5 rounds up to the next greatest integer.

For example, the number 4.45 rounds down to the integer 4, and a value of 4.50 rounds up to the integer 5.

Extra

JavaScript also includes a couple of methods that enable you to round numbers up to the next nearest integer or down to the nearest integer. These methods are `ceil()` and `floor()`. For example, the following statements are both rounded to a value of 5:

```
ceil(4.65);

floor(5.76);
```

ROUND NUMBERS

1 Open the file js-skeleton.html from the CD-ROM in Notepad.

2 Add a form with two text boxes and a button.

3 Add the onclick event to the button.

4 Add a statement for the onclick event that rounds the value.

5 Save the file as round.html.

6 Open the round.html file in a browser.

7 Enter a number in the first text box.

8 Click the form button.

■ The rounded value is displayed in the second text box.

RAISE NUMBERS TO A POWER

JavaScript includes another Math object method that can be used to raise one number to the power of another.

This method is the pow() method. It accepts two parameters. The first parameter is the number, and the second parameter is the power that the number is raised to.

For example, the statement Math.pow(5, 2) raises the number 5 to the power of 2, resulting in a value of 25.

This example uses the js-skeleton.html file found on the book's CD-ROM, but you can apply these steps to any file.

Extra

Raising a number to the power of ½ is the same as computing the square root of the number. You can include any value as the second parameter including variables, but the parameter must be a number.

RAISE NUMBERS TO A POWER

```
<html>
<head>
</head>
<body>
  <script language="javascript">
  </script>
  <form name="form1">
    value:<input type="text" name="val"/><br/>
    power:<input type="text" name="power"/><br/>
    result:<input type="text" name="result"/><br/>
    <input type="button" name="button1" value="Compute"
onclick="document.form1.result.value=Math.pow(document.form1.val.value,docum
ent.form1.power.value);"/>
  </form>
</body>
</html>
```

value: 12.5
power: 3
result: 1953.125
Compute

1 Open the file js-skeleton.html in Notepad.

2 Add a form with three text boxes and a button.

3 Add the onclick event to the button.

4 Add a statement for the onclick event that computes the value of the first text box raised to the power of the second text box.

5 Save the file as pow.html.

6 Open the pow.html file in a browser.

7 Enter numbers in the first two text boxes.

8 Click the form button.

■ The resulting value is displayed in the third text box.

FIND MINIMUM AND MAXIMUM VALUES

I f you ever want to determine if one number or another is greater, you could use a series of `if` statements, but a simpler method is to use the `min()` and `max()` methods.

These `Math` object methods accept two parameters and return the number that is smaller or greater.

For example, the `min(3, 4)` statement returns the value of 3, because 3 is the smaller number of the two. The statement `max(3, 4)` returns the value of 4, because 4 is larger than 3.

Apply It

To use an `if-else` statement to determine maximum values, the code looks like this:

```
function maximum(val1, val2) {
   if (val1 > val2)
      return val1;
   else
      return val2;
}
```

FIND MINIMUM AND MAXIMUM VALUES

1 Open the file js-skeleton.html from the CD-ROM in Notepad.

2 Add a form with four text boxes and a button.

3 Add the `onclick` event to the button.

4 Add a statement for the `onclick` event that determines the maximum and minimum values in the first two text boxes.

5 Save the file as min-max.html.

6 Open the min-max.html file in a browser.

7 Enter numbers in the first two text boxes.

8 Click the form button.

■ The minimum and maximum values are displayed.

USING ABSOLUTE VALUES

JavaScript includes another Math object method that can be used to return the *absolute value* of a number. Absolute value ensures that a number is positive. If a negative number is sent, then the negative sign is removed, and the positive value is returned.

This method is the abs() method. It accepts a single parameter and returns the absolute value of the number.

For example, the statement Math.abs(-25) returns a positive value of 25.

This example uses the js-skeleton.html file found on the book's CD-ROM, but you can apply these steps to any file.

Extra

> The abs() method works on any number including integers and floating-point numbers, but it returns NaN if it is sent a string.

USING ABSOLUTE VALUES

```html
<html>
<head>
</head>
<body>
  <script language="javascript">
  </script>
  <form name="form1">
    value1:<input type="text" name="val1"/><br/>
    absolute value:<input type="text" name="abs"/><br/>
    <input type="button" name="button1" value="Compute"
onclick="document.form1.abs.value=Math.abs(document.form1.val1.value);"/>
  </form>
</body>
</html>
```

1 Open the file js-skeleton.html in Notepad.

2 Add a form with two text boxes and a button.

3 Add the onclick event to the button.

4 Add a statement for the onclick event that computes the absolute value of the value in the first text box.

5 Save the file as abs.html.

6 Open the abs.html file in a browser.

7 Enter a number in the first text box.

8 Click the form button.

■ The absolute value of the number is displayed.

USING TEXT BOXES

Using HTML, you can interact with the user using *forms*. Forms enable the user to input simple data types using elements such as text boxes, radio and check box buttons, and selection lists.

Using JavaScript, you can dynamically alter the contents of a form element such as a text box.

Text boxes are defined in HTML using the `<input>` tag and setting the `type` attribute to `text`. Text boxes also include `name` and `value` attributes.

To reference a text box in JavaScript, you need to refer to the form name and the text box name. For example, you can get the value of a text box named `text1` within a form named `form1` by using the syntax `document.form1.text1.value`.

Properties for the text box object include `defaultValue`, `enabled`, `form`, `name`, `size`, `type`, and `value`. The methods include `focus()`, `blur()`, and `select()`.

This example uses the `js-skeleton.html` file found on the book's CD-ROM, but you can apply these steps to any file.

DISPLAY TEXT BOX OBJECT PROPERTIES

```html
<html>
<head>
</head>
<body>
    <form name="form1">
        <input type="text" name="text1" value="information, please">
    </form>
    <script language="javascript">
        document.write("The field type is: " + document.form1.text1.type +
"<br/>");
        document.write("The name of this field is: " + document.form1.text1.name
+ "<br/>");
        document.write("The value of this field is: " +
document.form1.text1.value + "<br/>");
        document.write("The size of this field is: " + document.form1.text1.size
+ "<br/>");
    </script>
</body>
</html>
```

1 Open the file js-skeleton.html in Notepad.

2 Before the `<script>` tags, add a form with a single text box.

3 Add several `document.write` statements to display some of the text box object properties.

4 Save the file as `text.html`.

5 Open the `text.html` file in a browser.

■ A text box is displayed with its property values.

Extra

The defaultValue property of the text object is different from the value property. The defaultValue property is the value that is included as part of the <input/> tag. The value property is the text that exists inside the text box. Initially, this text is the same as the defaultValue, but the user can change it. If the user changes a value, you can retrieve its initial value from the defaultValue property.

It is okay to have a text box without any default text. If the value attribute isn't included, then the text box will appear blank without any displayed text.

Using the select() method, you can automatically select the contents of a text box.

USING TEXT BOX OBJECT METHODS

text2.html - Notepad

File Edit Search Help

```
<html>
<head>
</head>
<body>
  <script language="javascript">
  </script>
  <form name="form1">
    <input type="text" name="text1" value="click here!"
onfocus="document.form1.text1.select()">
  </form>
</body>
</html>
```

E:\Temp\Authoring\JSB\examples\Ch12 - Working with Forms\text2.html - Microsoft Internet Ex...

File Edit View Favorites Tools Help

Back | Forward | Stop | Refresh | Home | Search | Favorites | History | Mail | Print | Edit

Address E:\Temp\Authoring\JSB\examples\Ch12 - Working with Forms\text2.html

click here!

Done | My Computer

■1 Open the file js-skeleton.html in Notepad.

■2 Add a form with a text box to the Web page.

■3 Add the onfocus event to the text box and assign it the select() method.

■4 Save the file as text2.html.

■5 Open the text2.html file in a browser.

■6 Click in the text box.

■ The text within the text box is selected.

WORK WITH PASSWORD BOXES

Password boxes are similar to text boxes, except all characters typed in a password box are displayed as asterisks (*). This password masking is useful for inputting sensitive information such as a password without revealing the information to a bystander looking over your shoulder.

The password box object includes properties for `defaultValue`, `enabled`, `form`, `name`, `size`, `type`, and `value`. It also includes methods for `focus()`, `blur()`, and `select()`.

This example uses the `js-skeleton.html` file found on the book's CD-ROM, but you can apply these steps to any file.

Extra

You need to be careful to keep the contents of a password box secure. If you view the contents of a password box with the `document.form1.password1.value` statement, the password is visible. To maintain password security, you should pass any passwords directly to the server.

WORK WITH PASSWORD BOXES

1 Open the file js-skeleton.html in Notepad.

2 Before the `<script>` tags, add a form with a single password box.

3 Add several `document.write` statements to display some of the `password` object properties.

4 Save the file as `password.html`.

5 Open the `password.html` file in a browser.

■ A password box is displayed with its property values.

192

WORK WITH HIDDEN FIELDS

Hidden fields are a special type of form element. You create them using the `<input/>` tag with the `type` attribute set to `hidden`. Hidden fields do not display anything within a browser, but can be used to pass data to the form-processing script.

The `hidden` object includes only three properties — `name`, `type`, and `value` — and no methods.

This example uses the `js-skeleton.html` file found on the book's CD-ROM, but you can apply these steps to any file.

Extra

Hidden fields are not visible within a browser, but they can be viewed as part of code within a Web page file. If you use the browser's View Source option, you can see any hidden fields and their values.

WORK WITH HIDDEN FIELDS

```
hidden.html - Notepad
File  Edit  Search  Help
<html>
<head>
</head>
<body>
  <form name="Form1">
    <input type="hidden" name="hid1" value="pieces of eight">
  </form>
  <script language="javascript">
    document.write("The field type is: " + document.form1.hid1.type +
"<br/>");
    document.write("The name of this field is: " + document.form1.hid1.name
+ "<br/>");
    document.write("The value of this field is: " +
document.form1.hid1.value + "<br/>");
  </script>
</body>
</html>
```

```
E:\Temp\Authoring\JSB\examples\Ch12 - Working with Forms\hidden.html - Microsoft Internet ...
File  Edit  View  Favorites  Tools  Help
Back   Forward   Stop   Refresh   Home   Search  Favorites  History   Mail   Print   Edit
Address  E:\Temp\Authoring\JSB\examples\Ch12 - Working with Forms\hidden.html      Go   Links

The field type is: hidden
The name of this field is: hid1
The value of this field is: pieces of eight

Done                                                      My Computer
```

1 Open the file js-skeleton.html in Notepad.

2 Before the `<script>` tags, add a form with a `hidden` field.

3 Add several `document.write` statements to display some of the hidden object properties.

4 Save the file as `hidden.html`.

5 Open the `hidden.html` file in a browser.

■ The hidden object properties are displayed.

WORK WITH TEXTAREA BOXES

Textarea boxes are like multiple-line text boxes. They are created using beginning and ending `<textarea>` tags and can be used to display full paragraphs of text.

You can specify the size of a textarea box by using the `rows` and `cols` attributes. The `cols` attribute is similar to the text box's `size` attribute. It defines the width of the element in number of characters. You can also specify the number of rows of text that are available using the `rows` attribute. Both of these attributes are accessible as properties to the `textarea` object.

The `textarea` object is very similar to the `text` object and includes properties for identifying `defaultValue`, `enabled`, `form`, `name`, `rows`, `cols`, `type`, and `value`.

The `textarea` object also includes, like the `text` object, methods for `focus()`, `blur()`, and `select()`.

This example uses the `js-skeleton.html` file found on the book's CD-ROM, but you can apply these steps to any file.

DISPLAY TEXTAREA BOX PROPERTIES

```
textarea.html - Notepad
File  Edit  Search  Help
<html>
<head>
</head>
<body>
<form name="form1">
    <textarea name="ta1">How many grains of sand are there in the Sahara
desert?</textarea>
</form>
<script language="javascript">
    document.write("The field type is: " + document.form1.ta1.type +
"<br/>");
    document.write("The name of this field is: " + document.form1.ta1.name +
"<br/>");
    document.write("The value of this field is: " + document.form1.ta1.value
+ "<br/>");
    document.write("The value of this field is: " + document.form1.ta1.cols
+ "<br/>");
    document.write("The value of this field is: " + document.form1.ta1.rows
+ "<br/>");
</script>
</body>
</html>
```

```
E:\Temp\Authoring\JSB\examples\Ch12 - Working with Forms\textarea.html - Microsoft Internet...
File  Edit  View  Favorites  Tools  Help
Back   Forward   Stop   Refresh   Home   Search   Favorites   History   Mail   Print   Edit
Address  E:\Temp\Authoring\JSB\examples\Ch12 - Working with Forms\textarea.html          Go  Links

How many grains of
sand are there in

The field type is: textarea
The name of this field is: ta1
The value of this field is: How many grains of sand are there in the Sahara desert?
The value of this field is: 20
The value of this field is: 2

Done                                                                        My Computer
```

1 Open the file `js-skeleton.html` in Notepad.

2 Before the `<script>` tags, add a form with a textarea box.

3 Add several `document.write` statements to display some of the `textarea` object properties.

4 Save the file as `textarea.html`.

5 Open the `textarea.html` file in a browser.

■ A textarea box is displayed with its property values.

Apply It

The `textarea` properties can be combined with an event to update the text within a textarea box. For example, imagine listing a riddle and showing the answer when the user clicks in the box. The code looks like this:

```
<form name="form1">

   <textarea name="ta1" rows="4"
onfocus="document.form1.ta1.value='I
have you covered.'">What did the rug
say to the floor?</textarea>

</form>
```

This form presents a textarea box with the riddle question displayed within it. When the user clicks in the textarea box or when it gets focus, the `onfocus` event is fired and the JavaScript statement is executed, which replaces the question with the appropriate answer.

USING A TEXTAREA BOX OBJECT METHOD

```
<html>
<head>
</head>
<body>
  <script language="javascript">
  </script>
  <form name="form1">
    <textarea name="ta1" rows="4"
onfocus="document.form1.ta1.select()">Independent forces can work together
if coerced in the right manner.</textarea>
  </form>
</body>
</html>
```

Independent forces can work together if coerced in the right manner.

■1 Open the file js-skeleton.html in Notepad.

■2 Add a form with a textarea box to the Web page.

■3 Add the onfocus event to the textarea box and assign it the select() method.

■4 Save the file as textarea2.html.

■5 Open the textarea2.html file in a browser.

■6 Click in the textarea box.

■ The text within the text box is selected.

USING BUTTONS

Using HTML, you may make form buttons in two different ways. The first way is to use the `<input/>` tag and set the `type` attribute equal to `button`, `reset`, or `submit`. The second way is to use the `<button>` tag.

Reset and Submit buttons have their own objects and are covered later in this chapter in the sections "Using a Reset Button" and "Using a Submit Button."

JavaScript includes a `button` object that includes properties and methods for controlling form buttons.

`button` properties include `enabled`, `form`, `name`, `type`, and `value`. The `value` attribute determines the text that appears on the surface of the button.

The `button` object methods include `click()` and `focus()`. Using the `click()` method, you can simulate the user clicking the button.

This example uses the `js-skeleton.html` file found on the book's CD-ROM, but you can apply these steps to any file.

DISPLAY BUTTON OBJECT PROPERTIES

```
button.html - Notepad
File Edit Search Help
<html>
<head>
</head>
<body>
  <form name="form1">
    <input type="button" name="button1" value="One Standard Button">
  </form>
  <script language="javascript">
    document.write("The field type is: " + document.form1.button1.type +
"<br/>");
    document.write("The name of this field is: " +
document.form1.button1.name + "<br/>");
    document.write("The value of this field is: " +
document.form1.button1.value + "<br/>");
  </script>
</body>
</html>
```

One Standard Button

The field type is: button
The name of this field is: button1
The value of this field is: One Standard Button

1 Open the file js-skeleton.html in Notepad.

2 Before the <script> tags, add a form with a button.

3 Add several document.write statements to display some of the button object properties.

4 Save the file as button.html.

5 Open the button.html file in a browser.

■ A button is displayed with its property values.

Apply It

Using the `<button>` tag is somewhat different than using an `<input/>` tag, but the results can be the same. The following code uses the `<button>` tag to create a button that updates a text box when it's ' "" clicked:

```
<form name="form1">

  <input type="text" name="text1">
</br>

  <button name="button1"
onclick="document.form1.text1.value=
'Settle down, count to 10 and take a
deep breath.'">Panic Button</button>

</form>
```

This button works the same as a button created using an `<input/>` tag.

REACT TO A CLICK EVENT

```
button2.html - Notepad
File  Edit  Search  Help
<html>
<head>
</head>
<body>
  <script language="javascript">
  </script>
  <form name="form1">
    <input type="text" name="text1" size="45"> </br>
    <input type="button" name="button1" value="Panic Button"
onclick="document.form1.text1.value='Settle down, count to 10 and take a
deep breath.'">
  </form>
</body>
</html>
```

E:\Temp\Authoring\JSB\examples\Ch12 - Working with Forms\button2.html - Microsoft Internet ...

File Edit View Favorites Tools Help

Back Forward Stop Refresh Home Search Favorites History Mail Print Edit

Address E:\Temp\Authoring\JSB\examples\Ch12 - Working with Forms\button2.html   Go Links

Settle down, count to 10 and take a deep breath.

Panic Button

Done   My Computer

1 Open the file **js-skeleton.html** in Notepad.

2 Add a form with a text box and a button to the Web page.

3 Add the `onclick` event to the button and assign it a statement to update the text box.

4 Save the file as `button2.html`.

5 Open the `button2.html` file in a browser.

6 Click the button.

■ The text specified by the `onclick` event is displayed in the text box.

197

USING A RESET BUTTON

Reset buttons are a special type of button that resets all the form elements to their initial default values. Reset buttons can be created using the `<input/>` tag with the `type` attribute set to `reset`.

The `reset` object includes properties for `enabled`, `form`, `name`, and `value`. Just like the `button` object, it also includes `click()` and `focus()` methods.

This example uses the `js-skeleton.html` file found on the book's CD-ROM, but you can apply these steps to any file.

Extra

The `form` object includes the `reset()` method. This method can be used to simulate the results of a Reset button, which resets a form.

USING A RESET BUTTON

```
reset.html - Notepad
File  Edit  Search  Help
<html>
<head>
</head>
<body>
  <form name="form1">
    <input type="reset" name="reset1" value="Reset Form">
  </form>
  <script language="javascript">
    document.write("The field type is: " + document.form1.reset1.type +
"<br/>");
    document.write("The name of this field is: " +
document.form1.reset1.name + "<br/>");
    document.write("The value of this field is: " +
document.form1.reset1.value + "<br/>");
  </script>
</body>
</html>
```

```
E:\Temp\Authoring\JSB\examples\Ch12 - Working with Forms\reset.html - Microsoft Internet Ex...
File  Edit  View  Favorites  Tools  Help
Back   Forward   Stop   Refresh   Home   Search   Favorites   History   Mail   Print   Edit
Address  E:\Temp\Authoring\JSB\examples\Ch12 - Working with Forms\reset.html

  Reset Form

The field type is: reset
The name of this field is: reset1
The value of this field is: Reset Form

Done                                                    My Computer
```

■1 Open the file js-skeleton.html in Notepad.

■2 Before the `<script>` tags, add a form with a Reset button.

■3 Add several `document.write` statements to display some of the `reset` object properties.

■4 Save the file as `reset.html`.

■5 Open the `reset.html` file in a browser.

■ A Reset button is displayed with its property values.

USING A SUBMIT BUTTON

A Submit button sends the form data to the server. The place where the data is sent is determined by the `<form>` tag's `action` attribute. Submit buttons can be created using the `<input/>` tag with the `type` attribute set to `submit`.

The `submit` object includes properties for `enabled`, `form`, `name`, and `value`, as well as the `click()` and `focus()` methods.

This example uses the `js-skeleton.html` file found on the book's CD-ROM, but you can apply these steps to any file.

Extra

The Submit button can be used to send form data to an e-mail address. You enable this functionality by adding the `mailto:` keyword and an e-mail address to the `action` attribute of the `<form>` tag.

The `form` object also includes the `submit()` method. This method can be used to simulate the results of a Submit button, which submits a form.

USING A SUBMIT BUTTON

```
submit.html - Notepad
File Edit Search Help
<html>
<head>
</head>
<body>
  <form name="form1">
    <input type="submit" name="submit1" value="Submit Form">
  </form>
  <script language="javascript">
    document.write("The field type is: " + document.form1.submit1.type +
"<br/>");
    document.write("The name of this field is: " +
document.form1.submit1.name + "<br/>");
    document.write("The value of this field is: " +
document.form1.submit1.value + "<br/>");
  </script>
</body>
</html>
```

E:\Temp\Authoring\JSB\examples\Ch12 - Working with Forms\submit.html - Microsoft Internet ...

Address E:\Temp\Authoring\JSB\examples\Ch12 - Working with Forms\submit.html

Submit Form

The field type is: submit
The name of this field is: submit1
The value of this field is: Submit Form

1 Open the file `js-skeleton.html` in Notepad.

2 Before the `<script>` tags, add a form with a Submit button.

3 Add several `document.write` statements to display some of the `submit` object properties.

4 Save the file as `submit.html`.

5 Open the `submit.html` file in a browser.

■ A Submit button is displayed with its property values.

USING CHECK BOX BUTTONS

Check box buttons are boxes that can be marked as checked or unchecked. They are typically used to set or unset options. Check boxes are created with an <input/> tag whose type attribute is set to checkbox.

The checkbox object identifies each separate check box element by its name attribute. For example, the value of a check box named check1 in a form named form1 could be referenced using the statement document.form1.check1.value.

The properties for the checkbox object include checked, defaultChecked, enabled, form, name, type, and value. The checked property is a Boolean value that is set to true if the check box is checked.

The methods for this object are click() and focus().

This example uses the js-skeleton.html file found on the book's CD-ROM, but you can apply these steps to any file.

DISPLAY CHECK BOX OBJECT PROPERTIES

checkbox.html - Notepad

```
<html>
<head>
</head>
<body>
  <form name="form1">
    <input type="checkbox" name="cb1">Computer Savvy?
  </form>
  <script language="javascript">
    document.write("The checkbox is checked: " + document.form1.cb1.checked
+ "<br/>");
    document.write("The checkbox type is: " + document.form1.cb1.type +
"<br/>");
    document.write("The name of this checkbox is: " +
document.form1.cb1.name + "<br/>");
  </script>
</body>
</html>
```

E:\Temp\Authoring\JSB\examples\Ch12 - Working with Forms\checkbox.html - Microsoft Intern...

Address: E:\Temp\Authoring\JSB\examples\Ch12 - Working with Forms\checkbox.html

☐ Computer Savvy?

The checkbox is checked: false
The checkbox type is: checkbox
The name of this checkbox is: cb1

1 Open the file js-skeleton.html in Notepad.

2 Before the <script> tags, add a form with a check box.

3 Add several document.write statements to display some of the checkbox object properties.

4 Save the file as checkbox.html.

5 Open the checkbox.html file in a browser.

■ The check box is displayed with its property values.

You can set up a function that executes statements based on which check boxes are selected. Such a function looks like this:

```
function check() {
    if (document.form1.check1.checked ==
true)
        document.write("Checkbox 1 is
selected");
    if (document.form1.check2.checked ==
true)
        document.write("Checkbox 2 is
selected");
    if (document.form1.check3.checked ==
true)
        document.write("Checkbox 3 is
selected");
}
```

This function runs the statements associated with each checked check box. If all three are selected, the browser displays all three statements.

CHECK MULTIPLE CHECK BOXES

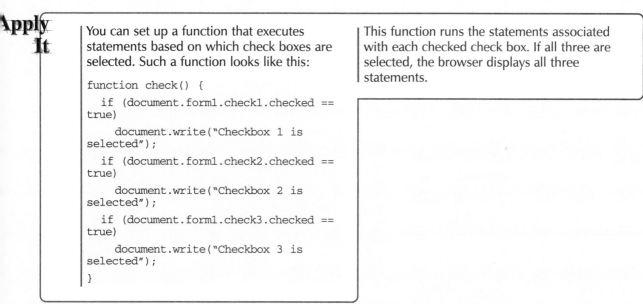

1 Open the file js-skeleton.html in Notepad.

2 Add a form with several check boxes and a button to the Web page.

3 Add the onclick event to the button and assign it a statement for each check box that checks the check box.

4 Save the file as checkbox2.html.

5 Open the checkbox2.html file in a browser.

6 Click the button.

■ All check boxes are checked (☑).

USING RADIO BUTTONS

R adio buttons come in sets. Only a single radio button in the set may be selected at a time. All the radio buttons within a set share the same name. Each individual radio button is indexed by the order that it appears in the form. The first radio button has an index value of 0.

For example, a set of four radio buttons named myradio could be referred to in order as myradio[0], myradio[1], myradio[2], and myradio[3].

Just like the other Web page elements, the object properties are similar to the attribute list for the <input/> tag, including checked, defaultChecked, enabled, form, length, name, and value. The length property returns the number of radio button elements in the set.

The radio button object also includes the click() and focus() methods.

This example uses the js-skeleton.html file found on the book's CD-ROM, but you can apply these steps to any file.

DISPLAY RADIO BUTTON OBJECT PROPERTIES

1 Open the file js-skeleton.html in Notepad.

2 Before the <script> tags, add a form with a set of radio buttons.

3 Add several document.write statements to display some of the radio object properties.

4 Save the file as radio.html.

5 Open the radio.html file in a browser.

■ The radio buttons are displayed with their property values.

Apply It

You can set up a function that executes statements based on which radio button is selected. Such a function looks like this:

```
function radio() {
    if (document.form1.radio1.checked ==
true)
        document.write("Radio button 1 is
selected");
    else if (document.form1.
radio2.checked == true)
        document.write("Radio button 2 is
selected");
    else
        document.write("Radio button 3 is
selected");
}
```

This function is a little different than the example for check boxes because radio buttons are mutually exclusive. This means that only one radio button at a time can be selected.

RESPOND TO A RADIO BUTTON SELECTION

```
radio2.html - Notepad
File  Edit  Search  Help
<html>
<head>
</head>
<body>
    <form name="form1">
        <input type="radio" name="radio1" onclick="document.form1.text1.value =
'easy care, elegant, short spring bloomer, grown from bulb'">Tulips
        <input type="radio" name="radio1" onclick="document.form1.text1.value =
'difficult to grow from seed, vibrant colors, two inch blooms, summer
bloomer'">Petunias
        <input type="radio" name="radio1" onclick="document.form1.text1.value =
'easy care, robust, autumn bloomer, good indoors, perennial'">Mums
        <input type="radio" name="radio1" onclick="document.form1.text1.value =
'easy care, summer bloomer, variety of colors'">Snapdragons
        <input type="radio" name="radio1" onclick="document.form1.text1.value =
'moderate care, summer bloomer, lasts to end of season'">Roses<br/>
        <input type="text" name="text1" size="75">
    </form>
    <script language="javascript">
    </script>
</body>
</html>
```

```
D:\JSB\examples\Ch12 - Working with Forms\radio2.html - Microsoft Internet Explorer
File  Edit  View  Favorites  Tools  Help
Back  Forward  Stop  Refresh  Home  Search  Favorites  History  Mail  Print  Edit
Address  D:\JSB\examples\Ch12 - Working with Forms\radio2.html          Go   Links

○ Tulips  ○ Petunias  ○ Mums  ○ Snapdragons  ○ Roses
easy care, elegant, short spring bloomer, grown from bulb

Done                                    My Computer
```

1 Open the file js-skeleton.html in Notepad.

2 Add a form with several radio buttons and a text box to the Web page.

3 Add the onclick event to each radio button and assign it a statement that updates the text box text.

4 Save the file as radio2.html.

5 Open the radio2.html file in a browser.

6 Click a radio button.

■ The text in the text box is updated.

WORK WITH SELECTION LISTS

The `select` object is used to create drop-down lists. Each item in the list is created with an `<option/>` tag. JavaScript includes a `select` object, as well as an `option` object, that can be used to control selection lists.

The `select` object includes the `name`, `length`, `size`, and `selectedIndex` properties. The `length` property returns the number of options in the selection list, and the `selectedIndex` property holds the index of the selected list item.

The `option` object is a sub-object of the `select` object. It is an array, and each object can be referred to by using its index value (with 0 being the first option).

For example, the first option of a selection list named `mylist` found in a form named `form1` is `document.form1.mylist.option[0]`. The `option` object also includes properties. These properties are covered later in this chapter in the section "Work with Separate Selection List Items."

The `select` object also includes the `blur()` and `focus()` methods.

This example uses the `js-skeleton.html` file found on the book's CD-ROM, but you can apply these steps to any file.

DISPLAY SELECT OBJECT PROPERTIES

1 Open the file `js-skeleton.html` in Notepad.

2 Before the `<script>` tags, add a form with a selection list.

3 Add several `document.write` statements to display some of the `select` object properties.

4 Save the file as `select.html`.

5 Open the `select.html` file in a browser.

■ The selection list is displayed with its property values.

6 Click an item in the list.

7 Click your browser's Refresh button.

■ The selected list item's property value updates.

Extra

If you try to reference an index value that doesn't exist, the browser produces an error and the JavaScript script quits. The error is indicated in the browser with a message that shows up on the browser's Status bar.

If no selection list item is selected, the `selectedIndex` property returns -1. You can check for this value to validate that the user has selected an item on the list.

You can use the `selectedIndex` property to mark which list item is selected by default. For example, if you set the `selectedIndex` to 2, then the third item in the list will be selected by default.

RESPOND TO A LIST SELECTION

select2.html - Notepad

```html
<html>
<head>
</head>
<body>
  <form name="form1">
    <select name="select1" size="4" onchange="travel()">
      <option name="option1" value="LON">London, England</option>
      <option name="option2" value="DUB">Dublin, Ireland</option>
      <option name="option3" value="AMS">Amsterdam, Holland</option>
      <option name="option4" value="PAR">Paris, France</option>
    </select><br/>
    <input type="text" name="text1" size="60"/>
  </form>
  <script language="javascript">
    function travel() {
      if (document.form1.select1.selectedIndex == 0)
        document.form1.text1.value = "London flight: Monday at 9:12 am";
      if (document.form1.select1.selectedIndex == 1)
        document.form1.text1.value = "Dublin flight: Tuesday at 10:14 am";
      if (document.form1.select1.selectedIndex == 2)
        document.form1.text1.value = "Amsterdam flight: Friday at 6:24 am";
      if (document.form1.select1.selectedIndex == 3)
        document.form1.text1.value = "Paris flight: Thursday at 9:47 am";
    }
  </script>
</body>
</html>
```

1 Open the file js-skeleton.html in Notepad.

2 Add a form with a selection list and a text box to the Web page.

3 Add the onchange event to the selection list and assign it a function.

4 Add a function that updates the text box based on the list item that is selected.

5 Save the file as select2.html.

6 Open the select2.html file in a browser.

7 Click one of the list items.

■ The text in the text box is updated.

WORK WITH SEPARATE SELECTION LIST ITEMS

The option object is a sub-object of the select object. Each selection list item is an element in an array, and each object can be referred to by using its index value. The first index value is always 0.

The option object also includes several properties that relate directly to the individual list items. The defaultSelected property returns the index of the list item that is marked to be selected initially. The selectedIndex property identifies the currently selected list

item, and the selected property is a Boolean that identifies if the current list item is selected. The text property returns the text that is in between the beginning and ending <option> tags.

Properties can be used for individual list items using their index values. For example, if the third item in a list is selected, document.form1.select1.options[2].selected returns a value of true.

DISPLAY OPTION OBJECT PROPERTIES

```
option.html - Notepad
File  Edit  Search  Help
<html>
<head>
</head>
<body>
    <form name="form1">
        <select name="select1" size="4">
            <option name="option1" value="LON">London, England</option>
            <option name="option2" value="DUB">Dublin, Ireland</option>
        </select>
    </form>
    <script language="javascript">
        document.write("The default selection is: " +
document.form1.select1.options[0].defaultSelected + "<br/>");
        document.write("The index for the first list item is: " +
document.form1.select1.options[0].index + "<br/>");
        document.write("The name of the first list item is: " +
document.form1.select1.options[0].name + "<br/>");
        document.write("The first list item is selected: " +
document.form1.select1.options[0].selected + "<br/>");
        document.write("The text for the first list item is: " +
document.form1.select1.options[0].text + "<br/>");
        document.write("The value for the first list item is: " +
document.form1.select1.options[0].value + "<br/>");
    </script>
</body>
</html>
```

```
D:\JSB\examples\Ch12 - Working with Forms\option.html - Microsoft Internet Explorer
File  Edit  View  Favorites  Tools  Help
Back  Forward  Stop  Refresh  Home  Search  Favorites  History  Mail  Print  Edit
Address  D:\JSB\examples\Ch12 - Working with Forms\option.html

London, England
Dublin, Ireland


The default selection is: false
The index for the first list item is: 0
The name of the first list item is: option1
The first list item is selected: false
The text for the first list item is: London, England
The value for the first list item is: LON
```

1 Open the file js-skeleton.html from the CD-ROM in Notepad.

2 Before the <script> tags, add a form with a selection list.

3 Add several document.write statements to display some of the option object properties.

4 Save the file as option.html.

5 Open the option.html file in a browser.

■ The selection list is displayed with the properties for a single list item, as specified by the document.write statements in this example.

Extra

Selection lists can accept only a single selection. If you add the `multiple` attribute to the `<select>` tag, the selection list allows multiple list items to be selected. If the `multiple` attribute is included, then the user can select multiple list items by holding down the Ctrl or Shift keys. The `multiple` attribute is covered in the next section, "Work with a Multiple-Selection List."

If the `size` attribute isn't specified, then only a single list item is initially displayed. The list will include an arrow to its right that will reveal the rest of the list items if it is clicked on. Because the selection list doesn't include any way to scroll horizontally, the width of the entire list is determined by the width of the longest list item element.

The `option` object includes other properties, such as `index`, `length`, `name`, and `value`.

I The `option` object doesn't include any methods.

CHANGE LIST ITEM TEXT

Notepad — option2.html:

```html
<html>
<head>
</head>
<body>
 <form name="form1">
   <select name="select1" size="4">
     <option name="option1" value="LON">London, England</option>
     <option name="option2" value="DUB">Dublin, Ireland</option>
     <option name="option3" value="AMS">Amsterdam, Holland</option>
     <option name="option4" value="PAR">Paris, France</option>
   </select><br/>
   <input type="button" name="button1" value="Update" onclick="update();"/>
 </form>
 <script language="javascript">
   function update() {
       document.form1.select1.options[0].text = "London flight: Monday at
9:12 am";
       document.form1.select1.options[1].text = "Dublin flight: Tuesday at
10:14 am";
       document.form1.select1.options[2].text = "Amsterdam flight:
cancelled";
       document.form1.select1.options[3].text = "Paris flight: Thursday at
9:47 am";
   }
 </script>
</body>
</html>
```

Browser display:

```
London flight: Monday at 9:12 am
Dublin flight: Tuesday at 10:14 am
Amsterdam flight: cancelled
Paris flight: Thursday at 9:47 am
[Update]
```

1 Open the file js-skeleton.html in Notepad.

2 Add a form with a selection list and a button to the Web page.

3 Add the `onclick` event to the button and assign it a function.

4 Add a function that updates the selection list items.

5 Save the file as option2.html.

6 Open the option2.html file in a browser.

7 Click the form button.

■ The list item text is updated.

WORK WITH A MULTIPLE-SELECTION LIST

Selection list boxes can be set to accept multiple selections. Including the `multiple` attribute in the `<select>` tag enables multiple selection.

The `select` and `option` object properties work the same for multiple selection lists as they do for single selection lists. The `selectedIndex` property, which for single selection lists the index of the selected item, returns only the index of the lowest selected item.

For example, if you have a selection list with seven items and the second, third, and fourth list items are selected, the `selectedIndex` property returns the index for the second item in the list, which is 1 because the index starts at 0.

This example uses the `js-skeleton.html` file found on the book's CD-ROM, but you can apply these steps to any file.

WORK WITH A MULTIPLE-SELECTION LIST

```
<html>
<head>
</head>
<body>
  <Form name="Form1">
    <select name="select1" size="4" multiple>
    <option name="option1" value="LON">London, England</option>
    <option name="option2" value="DUB">Dublin, Ireland</option>
    <option name="option3" value="AMS">Amsterdam, Holland</option>
    <option name="option4" value="PAR">Paris, France</option>
    </select>
  </form>
<script language="javascript">
    document.write("The first list item is selected: " +
document.form1.select1.options[0].selected + "<br/>");
    document.write("The second list item is selected: " +
document.form1.select1.options[1].selected + "<br/>");
    document.write("The third list item is selected: " +
document.form1.select1.options[2].selected + "<br/>");
    document.write("The fourth list item is selected: " +
document.form1.select1.options[3].selected + "<br/>");
</script>
</body>
</html>
```

```
London, England
Dublin, Ireland
Amsterdam, Holland
Paris, France

The first list item is selected: false
The second list item is selected: false
The third list item is selected: false
The fourth list item is selected: false
```

1 Open the file js-skeleton.html in Notepad.

2 Before the `<script>` tags, add a form with a multiple selection list.

3 Add several `document.write` statements to display the `selected` property for each of the list items.

4 Save the file as `multiple.html`.

5 Open the `multiple.html` file in a browser.

■ The selection list is displayed with none of the list items selected.

Apply
It

You can set up a function that executes statements based on which selection list item is selected. Such a function looks like this:

```
function list() {

  if
(document.form1.select1.options[0].
selected == true)

      document.write("Selection list
option 1 is selected");

  if
(document.form1.select1.options[1].
selected == true)

      document.write("Selection list
option 2 is selected");

  if
(document.form1.select1.options[2].
selected == true)
```

```
      document.write("Selection list option
3 is selected");

}
```

This function executes a different set of statements for each list item that is selected.

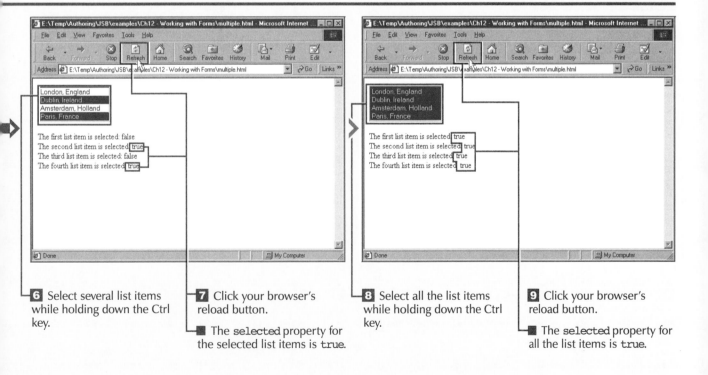

6 Select several list items while holding down the Ctrl key.

7 Click your browser's reload button.

■ The `selected` property for the selected list items is `true`.

8 Select all the list items while holding down the Ctrl key.

9 Click your browser's reload button.

■ The `selected` property for all the list items is `true`.

DISABLE FORM ELEMENTS

Form elements can be disabled if the disabled attribute is included. Disabled form elements are removed from the tab order, which assigns focus. They also become grayed out and cannot be interacted with until enabled again.

Almost all the form elements include a disabled property. This property returns a Boolean value, either true if the form element is disabled or false if the form element is enabled.

For example, if a form named form1 contains a text box named text1 that is disabled,

document.form1.text1.disabled equals true.

Form elements that include the disabled property include the button, checkbox, combo, password, radio, reset, select, submit, text, and textarea objects.

This example uses the js-skeleton.html file found on the book's CD-ROM, but you can apply these steps to any file.

DISABLE FORM ELEMENTS

1 Open the file js-skeleton.html in Notepad.

2 Before the <script> tags, add a form with a selection list, a text box, and a check box.

3 Add the disabled attribute to all form elements.

4 Add several document.write statements to display the disabled property.

5 Save the file as disabled.html.

6 Open the disabled.html file in a browser.

■ The form elements are all disabled.

Apply It

Using the `disabled` property, you can dynamically disable form elements. For example, if you have a form named `form1`, a text box named `text1`, and a button named `button1`, the following JavaScript statement disables these two form elements:

```
function disableElements() {
    document.form1.text1.disabled = true;
    document.form1.button1.disabled =
true;
}
```

This function disables the form elements whose `disabled` properties are set to `true`. The form elements can be enabled once again if the `disabled` property is set to `false`.

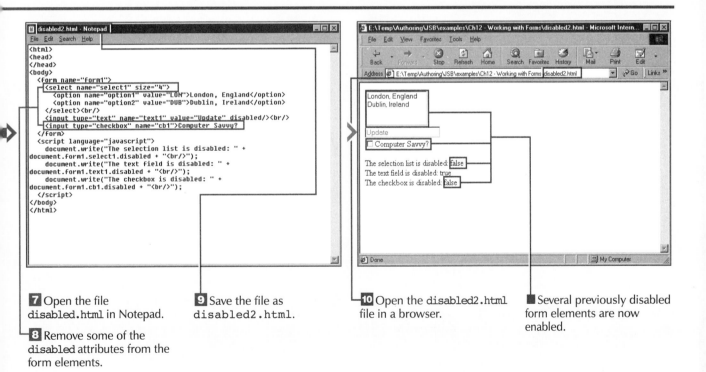

7 Open the file `disabled.html` in Notepad.

8 Remove some of the `disabled` attributes from the form elements.

9 Save the file as `disabled2.html`.

10 Open the `disabled2.html` file in a browser.

■ Several previously disabled form elements are now enabled.

RESET AND SUBMIT A FORM

The form object includes properties and methods for the entire form, including methods that can be used to reset and submit the form data to the server.

The form object properties include action, elements, length, method, and target. The action and method properties determine where and how the form data gets passed to the server. The elements property enables you to refer to any element within the form using an index that matches the order in which the element appears in the form. The length property returns the number of elements in the form. The target property

specifies which window name the form data is sent to. This property is explained in more detail in Chapter 13.

The form object methods that, like the Reset and Submit buttons, reset and send the form data to the server are reset() and submit(). Using these methods, you can reset or submit the form data using any JavaScript event.

This example uses the js-skeleton.html file found on the book's CD-ROM, but you can apply these steps to any file.

DISPLAY FORM OBJECT PROPERTIES

1 Open the file js-skeleton.html in Notepad.

2 Before the <script> tags, add a form with a text box.

3 Add several document.write statements to display some of the form object properties.

4 Save the file as form.html.

5 Open the form.html file in a browser.

■ The form is displayed with its properties.

Extra

The form object can accept the onReset and onSubmit events. Using these events, you can override the typical Submit and Reset button functions.

The form object holds an array of all the form elements. Using the form object, you can directly control all the form elements. The index values for the elements of a form are determined by the order in which they appear in the form. For example, if a single form named form1 includes two text boxes and a button, then the first text box can be referenced as document.form1.elements[0], the second text box can be referenced as document.form1.elements[1], and the button can be referenced as document.form1.elements[2].

DISPLAY FORM ELEMENT PROPERTIES

```
form2.html - Notepad
File Edit Search Help
<html>
<head>
</head>
<body>
<form name="form1" action="cgi-bin/validate.pl" method="post">
  <input type="text" name="text1" value="information, please">
</form>
<script language="javascript">
    document.write("The value of the first form element is: " +
document.form1.elements[0].value + "<br/>");
    document.write("The name of the first form element is: " +
document.form1.elements[0].name + "<br/>");
    document.write("The type of the first form element is: " +
document.form1.elements[0].type + "<br/>");
</script>
</body>
</html>
```

E:\Temp\Authoring\JSB\examples\Ch12 - Working with Forms\form2.html - Microsoft Internet E...
File Edit View Favorites Tools Help
Back Forward Stop Refresh Home Search Favorites History Mail Print Edit
Address E:\Temp\Authoring\JSB\examples\Ch12 - Working with Forms\form2.html

information, please

The value of the first form element is: information, please
The name of the first form element is: text1
The type of the first form element is: text

1 Open the file js-skeleton.html in Notepad.

2 Add a form with a text box to the Web page.

3 Add several document.write statements to display the properties of the first form element.

4 Save the file as form2.html.

5 Open the form2.html file in a browser.

■ The property values of the first form element are displayed.

VALIDATE FORMS

One of the useful ways that JavaScript can be used with forms is to validate the form data before it is sent to the server. If invalid values are identified and corrected before making a server request, then many unnecessary server requests can be eliminated.

CGI scripts on the server can be used to validate form data, but using JavaScript to validate forms saves an extra trip or two to the server and ensures the type of data the server will be receiving.

For example, you can validate a phone number to make sure that it doesn't include any letters.

The way to validate form data is different for every type of data, but JavaScript includes many operators that help you customize the validation routines.

This example uses the js-skeleton.html file found on the book's CD-ROM, but you can apply these steps to any file.

VALIDATE FORMS

1 Open the file js-skeleton.html in Notepad.

2 Add a form with a text box.

3 Create a function within the <script> tags that displays an alert dialog box if the value of the text box is unacceptable.

4 Add an onchange event to the text box and assign it the function name.

5 Save the file as validate.html.

6 Open the validate.html file in a browser.

■ A single text box along with some text is displayed in the browser.

Extra

Several operators are used in JavaScript as part of mathematical operations. In addition to the standard mathematical symbols for add (+), subtract (-), multiply (*), and divide (/), the != symbol means "not equal," && means "and," || means "or," <= means "less than or equal to," and >= means "greater than or equal to."

Several string functions can also be used to validate form data. For example, if you want to check to see if a specific word is contained within a text box or a textarea box, then you could use indexOf() to search for a string within a line of text.

7 Type an invalid value in the text box.

8 Press the Enter key.

■ An alert dialog box appears with a message for the user.

CONTROL FORM FOCUS

When a form element has focus, the user can enter values into the form using the keyboard.

For example, if a text box has the focus, you can type data by using the keyboard, and the typed characters will appear in the text box.

You can use the `focus()` method to change the focus between the various form elements. For example, if a form named `form1` includes a text box named `text1`, you can set the focus to this text box by using the statement `document.form1.text1.focus()`.

A similar method to `focus()` is the `blur()` method. Using this method, you can cause a form element to lose the focus. Associated with these two methods are two events that can be used to detect the focus and blur actions — `onFocus` and `onBlur`. These events are covered in the next section, "Using Focus Events."

This example uses the `js-skeleton.html` file found on the book's CD-ROM, but you can apply these steps to any file.

CHANGE FOCUS

```html
<html>
<head>
</head>
<body>
    <script language="javascript">
    </script>
    <form name="form1">
        <input type="text" name="text1" value="Where is your focus?"/><br/>
        <input type="text" name="text2" value="Is it here?"/><br/>
        <input type="text" name="text3" value="Or maybe here?"/><br/>
        <input type="button" name="button1" value="Text Box #1"
onclick="document.form1.text1.focus()"/><br/>
        <input type="button" name="button2" value="Text Box #2"
onclick="document.form1.text2.focus()"/><br/>
        <input type="button" name="button3" value="Text Box #3"
onclick="document.form1.text3.focus()"/><br/>
    </form>
</body>
</html>
```

■1 Open the file js-skeleton.html in Notepad.

■2 Add a form with a several text boxes and buttons.

■3 Add the onclick event to each button.

■4 Set the onclick event to change the focus to one of the text boxes.

■5 Save the file as focus.html.

■6 Open the focus.html file in a browser.

■7 Click one of the buttons.

■8 Type some text.

■ The text appears in the text box that has the focus.

Extra

Radio buttons and check box buttons don't include the blur() method because each individual radio button or check box button belongs to a group and the browser cannot determine when a single item loses the focus. Radio buttons and check box buttons both have the focus() method, though, and pressing the Enter key when a radio button or check box button has the focus selects or deselects the item.

The focus() method can be used to set the focus to a specific form element. This can be useful to automatically set the focus to the first form element where the user needs to enter information.

USING BLUR

1 Open the file focus.html in Notepad.

2 Change the focus() methods to blur().

3 Save the file as blur.html.

4 Open the blur.html file in a browser.

5 Click one of the buttons.

6 Type some text.

■ No text appears in any of the text boxes because they have lost the focus.

USING FOCUS EVENTS

When a form element has focus, you can enter the form data into the form using the keyboard. You can give any form element the focus by clicking on it with the mouse or by using the Tab key.

When the user presses the Tab key, the focus will move between the various form elements. The default order proceeds according to the order that the form elements appear in the form, but you can set the order that each form element receives the focus by using the tabindex attribute.

You can also detect when a form element receives or loses the focus by using the onFocus and onBlur events. The onFocus event can be used on every form element, but the onBlur event can only be used with the select, option, text, password, and textarea form elements.

This example uses the js-skeleton.html file found on the book's CD-ROM, but you can apply these steps to any file.

DETECT FOCUS

1 Open the file js-skeleton.html in Notepad.

2 Add a form with several text boxes.

3 Add the onFocus event to each text box.

4 Set the onFocus event to change the text in the text box.

5 Save the file as onFocus.html.

6 Open the onFocus.html file in a browser.

7 Click in one of the text boxes.

■ Some text is displayed in the text box that has the focus.

Apply It

One common use of the onFocus event is to select the text in a text box when it gets the focus. If you use onFocus to select text box text, the user doesn't need to delete the existing text; instead, the existing text will be replaced with the new text when the user begins to type. The functionality to select the text when it receives the focus can be placed within the text and textarea boxes form elements like ""this:

```
<form name="form1">

  <input type="text" name="text1"
value="default text"
onfocus="document.form1.text1.select()"
/>
```

```
  <textarea name="ta1" value="default
text"
onfocus="document.form1.ta1.select()"

</form>
```

When the various form elements get the focus, the onfocus event is fired causing the select() method to be executed, which selects the text within the text box.

DETECT BLUR

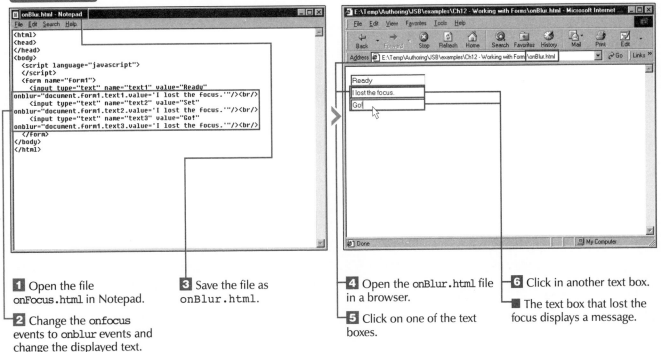

1 Open the file onFocus.html in Notepad.

2 Change the onfocus events to onblur events and change the displayed text.

3 Save the file as onBlur.html.

4 Open the onBlur.html file in a browser.

5 Click on one of the text boxes.

6 Click in another text box.

■ The text box that lost the focus displays a message.

WORK WITH THE FRAME OBJECT

rames enable you to split a Web page up into several different panes. The tricky part about working with frames is to determine which frame gets the focus and where the changes caused by the JavaScript code appear.

The `frame` object includes many properties that define the various frames. These properties include `frames`, `onBlur`, `onFocus`, `parent`, `self`, `top`, and `window`.

The `frames` property is an array of all the frames included in the frameset. These frames are sub-objects of the parent object, and you can reference them by an index value that matches the order that they appear in the

HTML file. For example, if a frameset includes three frames, then the first frame could be referenced as `document.frames[0]`, the second one as `document.frames[1]`, and the third one as `document.frames[2]`.

The `frame` object also includes several methods, such as `open()` and `close()`, which are the same as for the `document` object.

This example uses the `skeleton.html` and `js-skeleton.html` files found on the book's CD-ROM, but you can apply these steps to any file.

WORK WITH THE FRAME OBJECT

```
frameset.html - Notepad
File  Edit  Search  Help
<html>
<head>
</head>
<frameset cols="50%,*">
  <frame src="left.html" name="left">
  <frame src="right.html" name="right">
</frameset>
</html>
```

```
left.html - Notepad
File  Edit  Search  Help
<html>
<head>
</head>
<body>
  <h2>Old World</h2>
  <script language="javascript">
    document.write("Frame name: " + parent.frames[0].name);
  </script>
</body>
</html>
```

1 Open the file skeleton.html in Notepad.

2 Replace the <body> tags with a frameset page with two frames.

3 Save the file as frameset.html.

4 Open the file js-skeleton.html in Notepad.

5 Add a heading.

6 Within the <script> tags, add a document.write statement to display the frame's name.

7 Save the file as left.html.

Extra

If you create a frameset and cannot see the frames, then you need to make sure that the Web pages that you specify in the `src` attributes for each frame are available. You should also check to make sure that the `<frameset>` tags replace the `<body>` tags for the frameset file. If the `<body>` tags exist in the file, then the frames will not be visible.

Because individual frames are simply one of several windows that appear in the browser, `frame` objects can use all the properties and methods used by the `document` and `window` objects. For example, you can access document properties for a frame for the first frame on the page using the statement `parent.frame[0].document.title`.

---

right.html - Notepad

File   Edit   Search   Help

```
<html>
<head>
</head>
<body>
  <h2>New World</h2>
  <script language="javascript">
    document.write("Frame #2: " + parent.frames[1].name);
  </script>
</body>
</html>
```

D:\JSB\examples\Ch13 - Working with Frames\frameset.html - Microsoft Internet Explorer

File   Edit   View   Favorites   Tools   Help

Back   Forward   Stop   Refresh   Home   Search   Favorites   History   Mail   Print   Edit

Address   D:\JSB\examples\Ch13 - Working with Frames\frameset.html   Go   Links

Old World

Frame name: left

New World

Frame #2: right

Done   My Computer

8 Open the file js-skeleton.html in Notepad.

9 Add a heading.

10 Within the `<script>` tags, add a `document.write` statement to display the frame's name.

11 Save the file as `right.html`.

12 Open the `frameset.html` file in your browser.

■ Two frames appear with the frame name inside each.

Note: The left frame displays the file left.html, and the right frame displays the file right.html.

ACCESS FRAMES BY NAME

Although you can reference a frame using its index value such as parent.frames[0], you can also reference a frame using its name as defined by the name attribute of the <frame> tag.

For example, if you name a frame frame1, then you could reference the frame as parent.frame1.

You can also reference the frame using the frames array by replacing the index value with the name value in quotation marks like this: parent.frames["frame1"].

After you create the frame, it acts like a standard window. document objects and all the properties and methods of the standard document object are available. For example, you can reference the frame title of a frame named frame1 with a statement like this: parent.frame1.document.title.

This example uses the skeleton.html and js-skeleton.html files found on the book's CD-ROM, but you can apply these steps to any file.

ACCESS FRAMES BY NAME

framest2.html - Notepad
File Edit Search Help
```
<html>
<head>
</head>
<frameset cols="50%,*">
  <frame src="left2.html" name="left">
  <frame src="right2.html" name="right">
</frameset>
</html>
```

left2.html - Notepad
File Edit Search Help
```
<html>
<head>
</head>
<body bgcolor="orange">
  <h2>Old World</h2>
  <script language="javascript">
    document.write("Frame background color: " +
parent.left.document.bgColor);
  </script>
</body>
</html>
```

1 Open the file skeleton.html in Notepad.

2 Replace the <body> tags with a frameset page with two frames.

3 Save the file as frameset2.html.

4 Open the file js-skeleton.html in Notepad.

5 Specify a background color in the <body> tag.

6 Add a heading.

7 Within the <script> tags, add a document.write statement to display the frame's background color.

8 Save the file as left2.html.

Extra

The Status bar properties are only available for the parent frame. If specified for the other frames, the Status bar properties are ignored.

Although frames extend from a parent object, you can reference any child frame object from any other child frame object. For example, if you have a page with three frames named `frame1`, `frame2`, and `frame3`, then from the file that is loaded into `frame1`, you can reference the `title` property for `frame2` using the following statement:

```
parent.frame2.document.title;
```

and the title property for `frame3` using this statement:

```
parent.frame3.document.title;
```

Using this method, you can use one frame to control the other frames on the page.

```
right2.html - Notepad
File  Edit  Search  Help
<html>
<head>
</head>
<body bgcolor="yellow">
   <h2>New World</h2>
   <script language="javascript">
     document.write("Frame background color: " +
parent.right.document.bgColor);
   </script>
</body>
</html>
```

```
D:\JSB\examples\Ch13 - Working with Frames\frameset2.html - Microsoft Internet Explorer
File  Edit  View  Favorites  Tools  Help
Address  D:\JSB\examples\Ch13 - Working with Frames\frameset2.html

Old World                          New World

Frame background color: #ffa500    Frame background color: #ffff00
```

9 Open the file js-skeleton.html in Notepad.

10 Specify a background color in the <body> tag.

11 Add a heading.

12 Within the <script> tags, add a document.write statement to display the frame's background color.

13 Save the file as right2.html.

14 Open the frameset2.html file in your browser.

■ Two frames appear with the frame's background color in each.

Note: The left frame displays the file left2.html, and the right frame displays the file right2.html.

FIND THE NUMBER OF FRAMES

For a given frameset, you can determine the number of frames that it includes by using the length property.

You can reference this property from the parent object. This property returns the number of frames.

For example, for a frameset with three frames, the parent.frames.length property would return a value of 3.

This example uses the frameset2.html and right2.html files found on the book's

CD-ROM (or which you may have created in the section "Access Frames by Name"), but you can apply these steps to any file.

Extra

The length property can be used to determine the number of children frames that are contained within the current frame. For example, if a frame named myFrame includes three additional frames within it, then the statement self.length will return a value of 3.

FIND THE NUMBER OF FRAMES

```
right3.html - Notepad
<html>
<head>
</head>
<body bgcolor="yellow">
  <h2>New World</h2>
  <script language="javascript">
    document.write("Number of frames within this frameset: " +
parent.frames.length);
  </script>
</body>
</html>
```

Old World

Frame background color: #ffa500

New World

Number of frames within this frameset: 2

■1 Open the file frameset2.html in Notepad.

■2 Change right2.html to right3.html.

■3 Save the file as frameset3.html.

■4 Open the right2.html file in Notepad.

■5 Change the document.write statement to display the number of frames.

■6 Save the file as right3.html.

■7 Open the file frameset3.html in your browser.

■ Two frames and the value of the number of frames appear.

REFERENCE THE CURRENT FRAME

You can always reference the current frame using the `self` object. The `parent` object refers to the `frameset` object that calls the current frame, but the `self` object refers to the current frame.

For example, if you have a frame named `frame1` and you are writing the code for this frame, then you can refer to the title for this frame using `self.document.title` rather than `parent.frame1.document.title`.

Using the `self` object reference is shorter and more intuitive.

This example uses the `frameset2.html` and `left2.html` files found on the book's CD-ROM (or which you may have created in the section "Access Frames by Name"), but you can apply these steps to any file.

Extra

The top object is the same as the parent object for frames contained within a frameset. For nested framesets, though, the top object always refers to the top-most frameset.

REFERENCE THE CURRENT FRAME

```
left4.html - Notepad
File  Edit  Search  Help
<html>
<head>
</head>
<body bgcolor="orange">
  <h2>Old World</h2>
  <script language="javascript">
    document.write("Frame background color: " + self.document.bgColor);
  </script>
</body>
</html>
```

```
D:\JSB\examples\Ch13 - Working with Frames\frameset4.html - Microsoft Internet Explorer
File  Edit  View  Favorites  Tools  Help
Back  Forward  Stop  Refresh  Home  Search  Favorites  History  Mail  Print  Edit
Address  D:\JSB\examples\Ch13 - Working with Frames\frameset4.html              Go  Links

Old World                              New World

Frame background color: #ffa500        Frame background color: #ffff00

Done                                                              My Computer
```

■1 Open the file `frameset2.html` in Notepad.

■2 Change `left2.html` to `left4.html`.

■3 Save the file as `frameset4.html`.

■4 Open the `left2.html` file in Notepad.

■5 Change the `document.write` statement to display the background color using the `self` object.

■6 Save the file as `left4.html`.

■7 Open the `frameset4.html` in your browser.

■ Two frames and the value of the background color appear.

REFERENCE ACROSS FRAMES

Using the frame's array, you can access all the elements included on a separate page, such as form elements.

For example, if you have a frameset with two frames named `frame1` and `frame2`, then you can reference a text field contained within `frame1` from `frame2` with a statement such as this:
`parent.frame1.document.forms[0].text1.value`.

For nested framesets, this can become a little tricky. To access frames within the same frameset, you can use the `parent` keyword,

which contains all the child frames for the frameset. To access frames outside of the current frameset, you can use the `top` keyword to get to the top-most frameset. From the top frameset, you can access the children frames.

This example uses the `skeleton.html` and `js-skeleton.html` files found on the book's CD-ROM, but you can apply these steps to any file.

REFERENCE ACROSS FRAMES

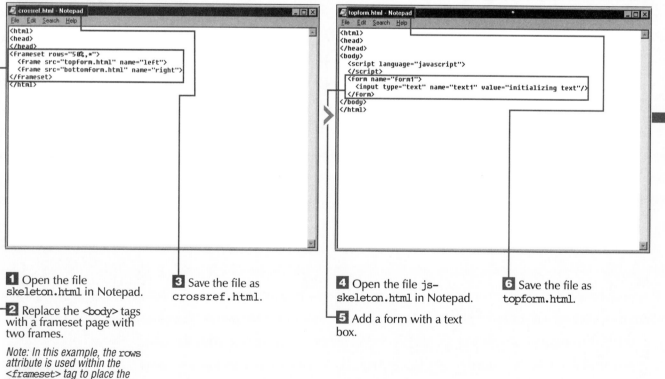

1 Open the file `skeleton.html` in Notepad.

2 Replace the `<body>` tags with a frameset page with two frames.

Note: In this example, the `rows` attribute is used within the `<frameset>` tag to place the frames on top of one another.

3 Save the file as `crossref.html`.

4 Open the file `js-skeleton.html` in Notepad.

5 Add a form with a text box.

6 Save the file as `topform.html`.

Extra

After you open a new window, you can name it. You can then use this name to access the properties and methods of the new window. For example, if you open a new window named `window1`, then you can get its title using the `window1.document.title` statement. Frames, on the other hand, are contained within framesets. Therefore, you need to access frames using their parent frameset, which is accomplished using a statement like `parent.frame1.document.title`.

The only real difference between frames that are side by side and frames that are above one another is the attribute that is included in the `<frameset>` tag. The first frame will always be on top for the `rows` attribute and to the left for the `cols` attribute.

7 Open the file js-skeleton.html in Notepad.

8 Add a form with a text box and a button.

9 Add the `onclick` event to the button and assign it to retrieve the text from the top frame.

10 Save the file as bottomform.html.

11 Open the crossref.html file in your browser.

12 Add some text to the text box in the top frame.

13 Click the button in the bottom frame.

■ The text in the bottom text box appears in the bottom frame.

WRITE TO A SEPARATE FRAME

Throughout the book, the document.write statement has been used to display text. This text appears within the current document window, but by using frame references, you can write text to another window.

For example, if you have a frameset with two frames named frame1 and frame2, then you could write the statement parent.frame2.document.write("welcome") within the code for frame1. This statement would write the word *welcome* in the second frame.

You could still use the document.write statement to display text in the current frame.

This example uses the frameset2.html and left2.html files found on the book's CD-ROM (or which you may have created in the section "Access Frames by Name"), but you can apply these steps to any file.

Extra

When you send text to be displayed in a frame, you need to make sure that the frame is created before you try to send text to it. If your browser cannot find the frame that you are referencing because you didn't create it, then the browser sends an error.

WRITE TO A SEPARATE FRAME

```
<html>
<head>
</head>
<body bgcolor="orange">
  <h2>Old World</h2>
  <script language="javascript">
    parent.right.document.write("This is a test of the emergency webcast
system.<br/>This is only a test.");
  </script>
</body>
</html>
```

1 Open the file frameset2.html in Notepad.

2 Change left2.html to writeframe.html.

3 Save the file as write.html.

4 Open the left2.html file in Notepad.

5 Change the document.write statement to reference the other frame.

6 Save the file as writeframe.html.

7 Open the write.html file in your browser.

■ Two frames appear, and the code for the left frame displays text in the right frame.

228

DETECT FRAME RESIZING

The frame object identifies standard events, including onBlur and onFocus. It also can be used with two unique events — the onMove and onResize events. These events can be added to the <frame> tags within the frameset file.

When referencing frames from the frameset file, you need to use self and the name of the frame because the frameset file is the parent.

This example uses the frameset2.html file found on the book's CD-ROM (or which you may have created in the section "Access Frames by Name"), but you can apply these steps to any file.

Extra

The onMove event fires whenever the window is moved. Because all frames are contained within a single browser page, all frames will detect an onMove event at the same time. The onResize event only occurs when you resize the frame. Two frames will always detect this event at the same time.

DETECT FRAME RESIZING

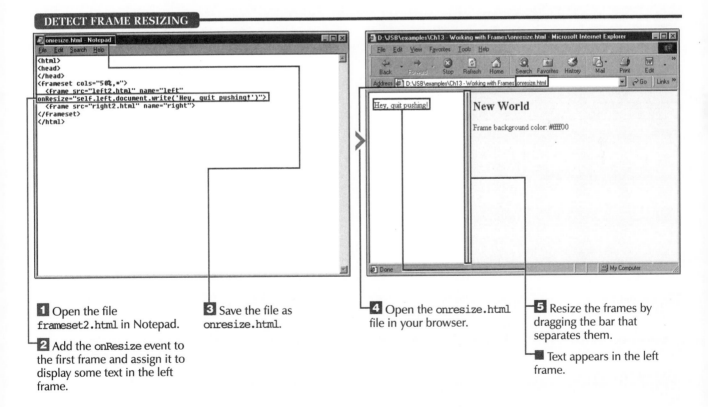

1 Open the file frameset2.html in Notepad.

2 Add the onResize event to the first frame and assign it to display some text in the left frame.

3 Save the file as onresize.html.

4 Open the onresize.html file in your browser.

5 Resize the frames by dragging the bar that separates them.

■ Text appears in the left frame.

SET THE TARGET FRAME

Web page elements including forms and links can include a `target` attribute. This attribute is the name of a frame where the results of the form or the link should be displayed.

Using JavaScript, you can view the `target` value using the `target` property of the `frame` object. You can also set the `target` value dynamically.

This example uses the `crossref.html` and `topform.html` files found on the book's CD-ROM (or which you may have created in the section "Reference across Frames"), but you can apply these steps to any file.

Extra

When working with links, you can set a target value where the Web link will load. This is useful for creating a navigation bar in one frame that contains a target to another frame where the link pages are loaded.

SET THE TARGET FRAME

1 Open the file `crossref.html` in Notepad.

2 Change `topform.html` to `targetframe.html`.

3 Save the file as `target.html`.

4 Open the `topform.html` file in Notepad.

5 Move the form above the `<script>` tags.

6 Add the `target` attribute to the form.

7 Add a `document.write` statement to display the target value.

8 Save the file as `targetframe.html`.

9 Open the `target.html` file in your browser.

■ Two frames and the target name appear.

Note: The target name identifies where the linked Web page will load.

PRINT A FRAME

Another useful method of the frame object is the print() method. This method enables you to print a single frame.

The print() method opens the print dialog box for your system. You need to click OK in this dialog box to actually send the page to the printer.

This example uses the crossref.html and bottomform.html files found on the book's CD-ROM (or which you may have created in the section "Reference across Frames"), but you can apply these steps to any file.

Extra

To print the entire page including all frames, you can use the following statement:

`parent.print();`

PRINT A FRAME

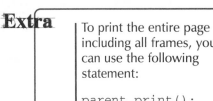

```
printframe.html - Notepad
File  Edit  Search  Help
<html>
<head>
</head>
<body>
  <script language="javascript">
  </script>
  <form name="form2">
    <input type="text" name="text2" value="ready"/>
    <input type="button" name="button2" value="Print Frame"
onclick="parent.right.print()"/>
  </form>
</body>
</html>
```

1 Open the file crossref.html in Notepad.

2 Change bottomform.html to printframe.html.

3 Save the file as print.html.

4 Open the bottomform.html file in Notepad.

5 Change the button's text.

6 Add a statement to the onclick event to print the frame.

7 Save the file as printframe.html.

8 Open the file print.html in your browser.

9 Click the button.

■ The Print dialog box opens.

USING THE NAVIGATOR OBJECT

Some of the most helpful objects enable you to detect the type of system that the user is using to view your page. By detecting these environment properties, you can customize your content appropriately.

For example, some JavaScript features are different between the Microsoft Internet Explorer and Netscape Navigator browsers. Detecting the browser that is being used lets you use different features, depending on the browser type.

The navigator object includes many properties and methods required to determine the user's system. The navigator object properties include appCodeName, appName, appVersion, platform, and userAgent.

The navigator object method is javaEnabled(). The properties of the navigator object are described in the section "Detect a User's Browser."

This example uses the js-skeleton.html file found on the book's CD-ROM, but you can apply these steps to any file.

USING THE NAVIGATOR OBJECT

```
navigator.html - Notepad
File  Edit  Search  Help
<html>
<head>
</head>
<body>
  <script language="javascript">
    document.write("<b>Navigator Object Properties</b><br/>");
    document.write("appCodeName: " + navigator.appCodeName + "<br/>");
    document.write("appName: " + navigator.appName + "<br/>");
    document.write("appVersion: " + navigator.appVersion + "<br/>");
    document.write("platform: " + navigator.platform + "<br/>");
    document.write("userAgent: " + navigator.userAgent + "<br/>");
  </script>
</body>
</html>
```

D:\JSB\examples\Ch14 - Determining Environment Properties\navigator.html - Microsoft Interne...
File Edit View Favorites Tools Help
Back Forward Stop Refresh Home Search Favorites History Mail Print Edit
Address D:\JSB\examples\Ch14 - Determining Environment Properties\navigator.html

Navigator Object Properties
appCodeName: Mozilla
appName: Microsoft Internet Explorer
appVersion: 4.0 (compatible; MSIE 5.0; Windows 98; DigExt)
language: undefined
platform: Win32
userAgent: Mozilla/4.0 (compatible; MSIE 5.0; Windows 98; DigExt)

Done   My Computer

1 Open the file js-skeleton.html in Notepad.

2 Add several document.write statements to display the values of the navigator object properties.

3 Save the file as navigator.html.

4 Open the file navigator.html in a browser.

■ All the properties of the navigator object are displayed.

Note: Internet Explorer version 5 will still return a version number of 4.0 because this is the version number for the last major engine release by Microsoft.

Extra

Many different pieces make up the user's environment, including the computer, the operating system, the browser, and the Web page. Each of these pieces can be controlled to an extent using JavaScript objects. The computer, operating system, and browser can all be detected using the `navigator` object, and the Web page URL can be detected using the `location` object. These objects are covered in the sections "Using the `navigator` Object" and "Using the `location` Object."

Some navigator object properties are read-only properties, such as the `language` property. If the `language` property were not a read-only property, then you would be able to change the scripting language at any time, which would confuse the browser.

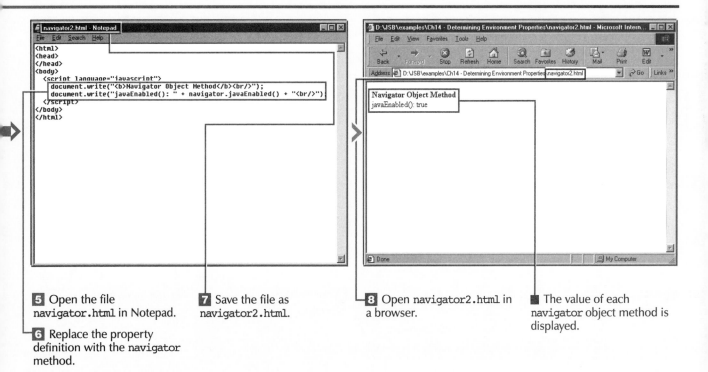

5 Open the file `navigator.html` in Notepad.

6 Replace the property definition with the `navigator` method.

7 Save the file as `navigator2.html`.

8 Open `navigator2.html` in a browser.

■ The value of each `navigator` object method is displayed.

DETECT A USER'S BROWSER

By detecting the user's browser, you can alter the content as needed for his or her specific format. For example, much of the Dynamic HTML syntax is different for different browser types.

The navigator object includes three properties that return the type of browser. The appCodeName property returns the code name of the browser. This is typically Mozilla, which is the standard code base. The appName property returns the actual browser name, such as Microsoft Internet Explorer. The appVersion property returns the version information or version number for the browser, such as 5.0.

Extra

The main two browser types are Microsoft's Internet Explorer and Netscape's Navigator, but other browsers exist, such as Lynx, a text-only browser, and AOL's custom browser. These other browsers will have a different identifying name, but the code name will probably be similar.

DETECT A USER'S BROWSER

```
appName.html - Notepad
File  Edit  Search  Help
<html>
<head>
</head>
<body>
  <script language="javascript">
    if (navigator.appName.indexOf("Microsoft") != -1) {
      document.write("You are using Microsoft's Internet Explorer browser");
    }
    else if (navigator.appName.indexOf("Netscape") != -1) {
      document.write("You are using Netscape's Communicator browser");
    }
  </script>
</body>
</html>
```

D:\JSB\examples\Ch14 - Determining Environment Properties\appName.html - Microsoft Interne...

File Edit View Favorites Tools Help

Back Forward Stop Refresh Home Search Favorites History Mail Print Edit

Address D:\JSB\examples\Ch14 - Determining Environment Properties\appName.html

You are using Microsoft's Internet Explorer browser

Done   My Computer

1 Open the file js-skeleton.html from the CD-ROM in Notepad.

2 Add an if statement to check for the word *Microsoft* within the navigator.appName value.

3 Include an else if statement that, if *Microsoft* is not found, checks to see if *Netscape* can be found.

Note: If the browser is neither a Microsoft nor a Netscape product, then nothing will be displayed.

4 Save the file as appName.html.

5 Open the file appName.html in a browser.

■ The browser type is detected and displayed.

DETECT THE BROWSER'S VERSION

The different browser versions support differing levels of HTML. For example, the early 3.0 browser versions only supported HTML Version 3.2.

Later versions supported later HTML specifications. If you use a feature in a later HTML version with a browser that doesn't support it, the results can be unexpected.

To eliminate any problems, you can check for the current browser version number using the `navigator.appVersion` property.

This example uses the `js-skeleton.html` file found on the book's CD-ROM, but you can apply these steps to any file.

Extra

The earliest versions to use JavaScript were the Netscape 2.0 and Internet Explorer 3.0 versions. Browsers prior to these versions cannot interpret JavaScript code.

DETECT THE BROWSER'S VERSION

```
<html>
<head>
</head>
<body>
  <script language="javascript">
    if (navigator.appVersion.indexOf("4.0") != -1) {
      document.write("You are using a version 4.0 compatible browser.");
    }
    else {
      document.write("This browser is not 4.0 compliant.");
    }
  </script>
</body>
</html>
```

You are using a version 4.0 compatible browser.

1 Open the file js-skeleton.html in Notepad.

2 Add an `if` statement to check for a specific version number.

3 Include an `else` statement that executes if the specified version number isn't found (including versions that have a higher version number).

4 Save the file as appVersion.html.

5 Open appVersion.html in a browser.

■ The browser version is detected, and a message is displayed.

DETECT A USER'S OPERATING SYSTEM

U nderstanding the user's operating
system helps you to know what type of
interfaces he or she is most comfortable
with. Macintosh interfaces are different from
Windows and UNIX interfaces.

You can detect a user's operating system using
the platform property of the navigator
object. This property returns the platform for
which the browser was compiled.

This example uses the js-skeleton.html
file found on the book's CD-ROM, but you can
apply these steps to any file.

Extra

JavaScript can identify the most
common operating systems,
such as Win32, which includes
all Windows 95, Windows 98,
Windows Me, Windows NT,
and Windows 2000
computers; Macintosh, which
includes older systems, Power
PC, and later versions; and
UNIX, which includes the
popular Linux version.

DETECT A USER'S OPERATING SYSTEM

```
platform.html - Notepad
File  Edit  Search  Help
<html>
<head>
</head>
<body>
  <script language="javascript">
    if (navigator.platform.indexOf("Win32") != -1) {
        document.write("You are using a computer running Windows 95 or
higher.");
    }
    else {
        document.write("This computer is not running Windows 95 or higher.");
    }
  </script>
</body>
</html>
```

D:\JSB\examples\Ch14 - Determining Environment Properties\platform.html - Microsoft Internet ...

Address D:\JSB\examples\Ch14 - Determining Environment Properties\platform.html

You are using a computer running Windows 95 or higher.

■1 Open the file js-skeleton.html in Notepad.

■2 Add an if statement to check for the platform to determine the operating system.

■3 Include an else statement that executes if the specified platform isn't found.

■4 Save the file as platform.html.

■5 Open the file platform.html in a browser.

■ The user's operating system platform is detected and displayed.

236

UNDERSTAND A USER AGENT

The userAgent property of the navigator object returns the header information that is sent to the server during a request by the browser.

The information in the header includes the same information in the appVersion property plus the information from the appCodeName property.

This example uses the js-skeleton.html file found on the book's CD-ROM, but you can apply these steps to any file.

Extra

When a request is sent to the server, part of the request includes a header. This header is information about where the request came from and what information is needed to satisfy the request.

UNDERSTAND A USER AGENT

```
userAgent.html - Notepad
File  Edit  Search  Help
<html>
<head>
</head>
<body>
  <script language="javascript">
    if ((navigator.userAgent.indexOf("MSIE") != -1) &&
(navigator.userAgent.indexOf("Windows 98") != -1)) {
      document.write("You are using Microsoft Internet Explorer on a Windows
98 computer.");
    }
    else {
      document.write("This computer is not running Internet Explorer
on Windows 98.");
    }
  </script>
</body>
</html>
```

D:\JSB\examples\Ch14 - Determining Environment Properties\userAgent.html - Microsoft Intern...
File Edit View Favorites Tools Help
Back Forward Stop Refresh Home Search Favorites History Mail Print Edit
Address D:\JSB\examples\Ch14 - Determining Environment Properties\userAgent.html

You are using Microsoft Internet Explorer on a Windows 98 computer.

Done   My Computer

1 Open the file js-skeleton.html in Notepad.

2 Add an if statement to check for specific environment properties.

3 Include an else statement that executes if the specified properties aren't found.

4 Save the file as userAgent.html.

5 Open the file userAgent.html in a browser.

■ The browser type and operating system are detected and displayed.

DETERMINE WHETHER JAVA IS ENABLED

*J*ava is a programming language that enables developers to program applications that work with the browser over the Web. Browsers have the option of enabling or disabling this feature. If Java is disabled, no Java content will run within the browser.

The `navigator` object includes a method for determining whether Java is enabled for the browser. This method is `javaEnabled()`. It returns either a `true` or a `false` value.

This example uses the `js-skeleton.html` file found on the book's CD-ROM, but you can apply these steps to any file.

Extra

Java can be enabled or disabled using the browser settings. The reason why you would want to check to see if Java is enabled is that Java components are typically rather large and downloading them could take a long time. If Java isn't enabled, you can save the user some trouble.

DETERMINE WHETHER JAVA IS ENABLED

```
javaEnabled.html - Notepad
File  Edit  Search  Help
<html>
<head>
</head>
<body>
  <script language="javascript">
    if (navigator.javaEnabled() == true) {
      document.write("Java is enabled for this browser.");
    }
    else {
      document.write("Java is not enabled for this browser.");
    }
  </script>
</body>
</html>
```

D:\JSB\examples\Ch14 - Determining Environment Properties\javaEnabled.html - Microsoft Inter...
File Edit View Favorites Tools Help
Back Forward Stop Refresh Home Search Favorites History Mail Print Edit
Address D:\JSB\examples\Ch14 - Determining Environment Properties\javaEnabled.html

Java is enabled for this browser.

Done   My Computer

1 Open the file js-skeleton.html in Notepad.

2 Add an `if` statement to check whether Java is enabled.

3 Include an `else` statement that executes if Java isn't enabled.

4 Save the file as javaEnabled.html.

5 Open the file javaEnabled.html in a browser.

■ The script detects whether Java is enabled on the browser and displays the results.

DETERMINE THE CODE NAME

The `appCodeName` property returns the name of the code used by the browser. This value represents a baseline of functionality.

Both Microsoft's Internet Explorer and Netscape's Navigator browsers return the value of `Mozilla` for this value. This is the developer's name for the browser code.

This example uses the `js-skeleton.html` file found on the book's CD-ROM, but you can apply these steps to any file.

DETERMINE THE CODE NAME

```
<html>
<head>
</head>
<body>
  <script language="javascript">
   if (navigator.appVersion.indexOf("Mozilla") != -1) {
      document.write("The code name for this browser is Mozilla.");
   }
   else {
      document.write("This code name for this browser isn't Mozilla.");
   }
  </script>
</body>
</html>
```

The code name for this browser is Mozilla.

■1 Open the file js-skeleton.html in Notepad.

■2 Add an if statement to check the code name.

■3 Include an else statement that executes if the specified code name isn't found.

■4 Save the file as appCodeName.html.

■5 Open appCodeName.html in a browser.

■ The script detects and displays the code name.

USING THE LOCATION OBJECT

The location object includes properties that hold every piece of information that makes up a URL. These properties are very similar to the link object properties.

These properties include hash, host, hostname, href, pathname, port, protocol, and search. All these properties return information about the current URL.

The first part of a URL is the protocol. The protocol property defines the protocol type, such as HTTP (Hypertext Transfer Protocol) or FTP (File Transfer Protocol). The hostname property returns the domain name, and the port property returns the port if one is included. The host property

returns the host name and the port number together. The path to the file is returned by the pathname property.

At the end of the URL comes the hash or search information. The hash property defines any anchor names included in the URL. These are identified with the numeric symbol (#). The search property returns any information passed to the server, which follows after the question mark (?).

The location object also includes the reload() method, which reloads the current URL.

This example uses the js-skeleton.html file found on the book's CD-ROM, but you can apply these steps to any file.

DISPLAY THE LOCATION OBJECT PROPERTIES

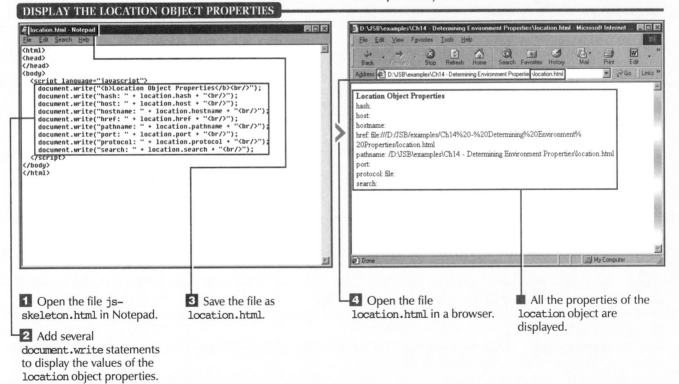

```
location.html - Notepad
File  Edit  Search  Help
<html>
<head>
</head>
<body>
    <script language="javascript">
    document.write("<b>Location Object Properties</b><br/>");
    document.write("hash: " + location.hash + "<br/>");
    document.write("host: " + location.host + "<br/>");
    document.write("hostname: " + location.hostname + "<br/>");
    document.write("href: " + location.href + "<br/>");
    document.write("pathname: " + location.pathname + "<br/>");
    document.write("port: " + location.port + "<br/>");
    document.write("protocol: " + location.protocol + "<br/>");
    document.write("search: " + location.search + "<br/>");
    </script>
</body>
</html>
```

D:\JSB\examples\Ch14 - Determining Environment Properties\location.html - Microsoft Internet ...
File Edit View Favorites Tools Help
Back Forward Stop Refresh Home Search Favorites History Mail Print Edit
Address D:\JSB\examples\Ch14 - Determining Environment Propertie\location.html

Location Object Properties
hash:
host:
hostname:
href: file:///D:/JSB/examples/Ch14%20-%20Determining%20Environment%20Properties/location.html
pathname: /D:/JSB/examples/Ch14 - Determining Environment Properties\location.html
port:
protocol: file:
search:

🔲 1 Open the file js-skeleton.html in Notepad.

🔲 2 Add several document.write statements to display the values of the location object properties.

🔲 3 Save the file as location.html.

🔲 4 Open the file location.html in a browser.

■ All the properties of the location object are displayed.

Apply It

Using the `location` object, entire URLs can be divided into their base components. This enables you to manipulate URLs as needed. A function to deconstruct a URL would look like this:

```
function decomposeURL() {

   address = location.href;

   prot = location.protocol;

   domain = location.hostname;

   prt = location.port;
```

```
   path = location.pathname;

   anchor = location.hash;

   search = location.search;

   document.write("Current URL: " +
prot + domain + prt + path +
anchor + search);

}
```

This function splits the URL into its separate components. Each separate component can be replaced as needed.

RELOAD A PAGE

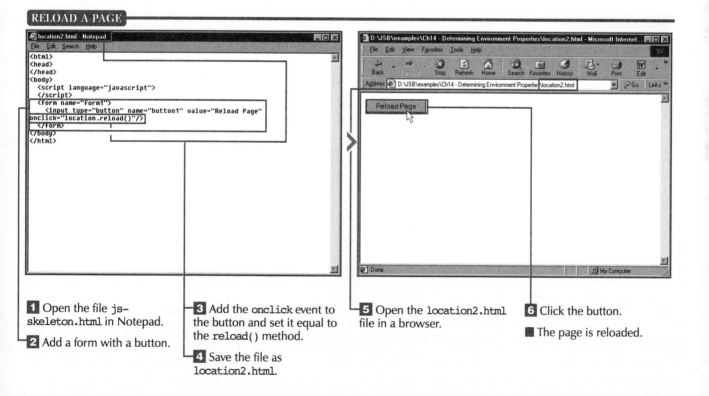

1 Open the file js-skeleton.html in Notepad.

2 Add a form with a button.

3 Add the onclick event to the button and set it equal to the reload() method.

4 Save the file as location2.html.

5 Open the location2.html file in a browser.

6 Click the button.

■ The page is reloaded.

USING COOKIES

*C*ookies are small pieces of data that help maintain the state of the browser. They are written to the user's computer and are indexed by the site that creates them. When the user returns later to the site, the data is retrieved and used.

One common use of cookies is to keep information about the user's preferences. Saving a user's preferences in a cookie will enable the browser to read the cookie and display the Web page according to the user's specifications the next time he or she returns.

To write a cookie using JavaScript, you use the document.cookie object. By setting this object equal to the piece of data that you want to save, the cookie is automatically written to the user's computer. Each piece of data saved in a cookie should have a name and an equal sign so that it can be identified and retrieved later.

This example uses the js-skeleton.html file found on the book's CD-ROM, but you can apply these steps to any file.

USING COOKIES

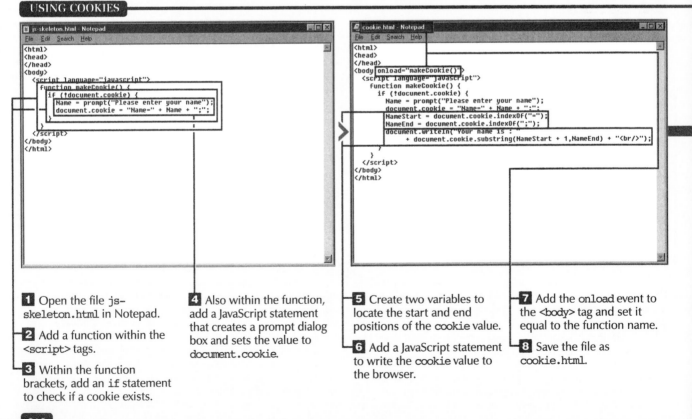

1 Open the file js-skeleton.html in Notepad.

2 Add a function within the <script> tags.

3 Within the function brackets, add an if statement to check if a cookie exists.

4 Also within the function, add a JavaScript statement that creates a prompt dialog box and sets the value to document.cookie.

5 Create two variables to locate the start and end positions of the cookie value.

6 Add a JavaScript statement to write the cookie value to the browser.

7 Add the onload event to the <body> tag and set it equal to the function name.

8 Save the file as cookie.html.

Extra

Browsers include settings for disabling cookies if you don't want them stored on your computer. For Internet Explorer, you can disable cookies by selecting the Tools⇨Internet Options command. This command opens the Internet Options dialog box. Select the Security tab and click the Custom Level button. Then select the Disable radio button under the Cookies heading (○ changes to ●).

Any string can be included within a cookie, but all cookies need to include a name and a value. The cookie file has a size limitation of 4KB. If the string saved to a cookie is larger than this, then a portion of the cookie data will be lost.

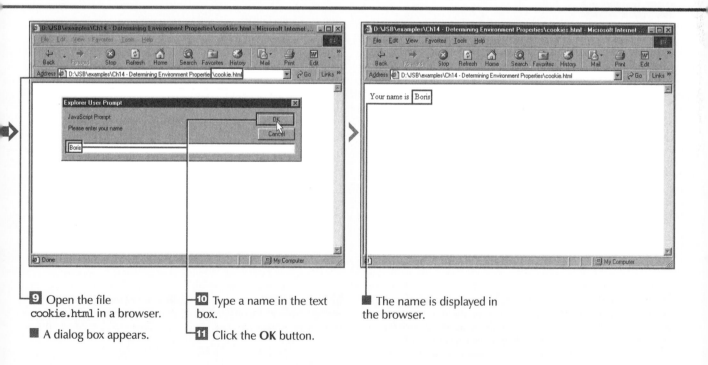

9 Open the file cookie.html in a browser.

■ A dialog box appears.

10 Type a name in the text box.

11 Click the **OK** button.

■ The name is displayed in the browser.

ENCODE CHARACTERS

When some characters such as spaces and certain symbols are passed to the server, they are confused for server commands. This can result in incorrect processing of data. JavaScript includes two statements that can be used to encode the characters before they are sent to the server. When the encoded characters are received by the server, they can be unencoded to retrieve the data. This process of encoding and decoding data ensures the integrity of the data.

The statement to encode a character is `escape()`. This statement accepts a single string, which is the text to encode.

The text is encoded by converting it to a percentage symbol (%) followed by a two-digit ASCII value. For example, a space is represented by the ASCII value of 20, and an ampersand symbol (&) is represented by the ASCII value of 26, so the statement `escape("& ")` would encode to "%26%20".

Text received in the encoded format can be decoded using the `unescape()` statement.

This example uses the `js-skeleton.html` file found on the book's CD-ROM, but you can apply these steps to any file.

ENCODE TEXT

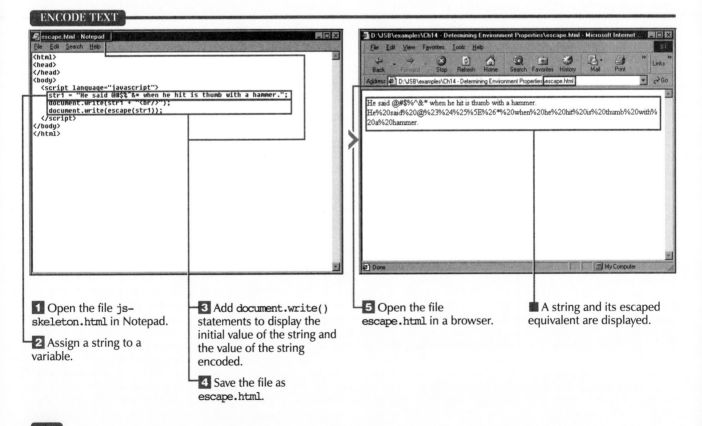

1 Open the file `js-skeleton.html` in Notepad.

2 Assign a string to a variable.

3 Add `document.write()` statements to display the initial value of the string and the value of the string encoded.

4 Save the file as `escape.html`.

5 Open the file `escape.html` in a browser.

■ A string and its escaped equivalent are displayed.

Extra

If your Web page filename includes any spaces, then links to the Web page will not be able to locate the Web page name. If you encode the URL by using the `escape()` statement, then you will be able to use the name with spaces.

The `escape()` and `unescape()` statements are not a part of any object, but are JavaScript keywords. They do not need any parent object in order to work correctly.

The `escape()` and `unescape()` statements can be used on single characters, full lines of text, or even paragraphs.

Because the type of encoding used by `escape()` is based on the ASCII character set, it cannot be used with Unicode characters.

DECODE TEXT

```
unescape.html - Notepad
File  Edit  Search  Help
<html>
<head>
</head>
<body>
  <script language="javascript">
    str1 = "He said @#$%^&* when he hit is thumb with a hammer.";
    document.write(str1 + "<br/>");
    document.write(escape(str1) + "<br/>");
    str2 = escape(str1);
    document.write(unescape(str2));
  </script>
</body>
</html>
```

Browser window — D:\JSB\examples\Ch14 - Determining Environment Properties\unescape.html - Microsoft Interne...

Address: D:\JSB\examples\Ch14 - Determining Environment Properties\unescape.html

He said @#$%^&* when he hit is thumb with a hammer.
He%20said%20@%23%24%25%5E%26*%20when%20he%20hit%20is%20thumb%20with%20a%20hammer.
He said @#$%^&* when he hit is thumb with a hammer.

1 Open the file escape.html in Notepad.

2 Assign the escaped string to a variable.

3 Add a `document.write()` statement to display the value of the string decoded.

4 Save the file as unescape.html.

5 Open the file unescape.html in a browser.

■ An encoded string and its unescaped equivalent are displayed.

DETECT JAVASCRIPT ERRORS

As scripts are created, the syntax must be followed exactly to avoid generating an error. *Debugging* is the process of identifying and eliminating errors.

Several different types of errors can happen. *Syntax errors* occur when you use syntax that the browser can't understand, such as misspelling a keyword or variable. *Runtime errors* are harder to detect. They occur when the script's syntax is correct but the program doesn't do what it should. An example of this is using a wrong equation.

Syntax errors are the easiest to detect because the browser lets you know that an error has occurred. Runtime errors are harder to find but can be found with some careful debugging techniques.

This example uses the `js-skeleton.html` file found on the book's CD-ROM, but you can apply these steps to any file.

DETECT JAVASCRIPT ERRORS

```html
<html>
<head>
</head>
<body>
    <script language="javascript">
    document.write("A syntax error follows");
    doc.write("A syntax error, document is misspelled.");
    </script>
</body>
</html>
```

A syntax error follows

Done, but with errors on page.

1 Open the file `js-skeleton.html` in Notepad.

2 Add a couple of `document.write` statements within the <script> tags.

3 Misspell the word *document* in one statement to cause a syntax error.

4 Save the file as `error.html`.

5 Open the file `error.html` in a browser.

■ The page loads, but the status bar displays an error.

Note: The error dialog box includes an Always Display This Message When a Page Contains Errors check box. If you checked this at some earlier time, then the error dialog box appears automatically.

Extra

In the error dialog box is a check box that you can check to cause the error dialog box to appear automatically every time the browsers detects an error on the current page.

If you view the details in the error dialog box, it includes the line and character where the syntax error appears. Using this information, you can locate exactly where the syntax error is.

The error dialog box has two buttons used to cycle through the errors. Click the Previous button to see the previous error or the Next button to the see the next error.

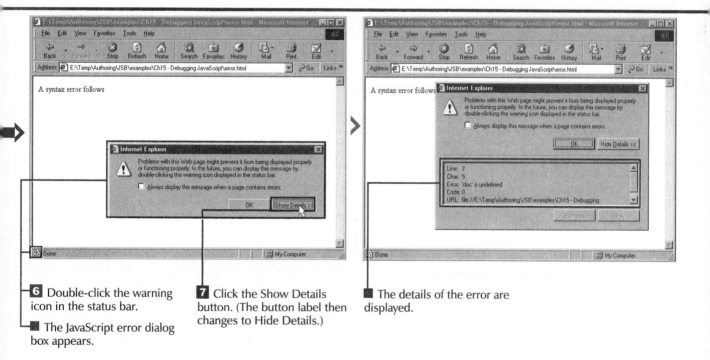

6 Double-click the warning icon in the status bar.

■ The JavaScript error dialog box appears.

7 Click the Show Details button. (The button label then changes to Hide Details.)

■ The details of the error are displayed.

DEBUG WITH COMMENTS

One of the first tasks when debugging your script is to determine what works and what does not. If you correctly identify the statements that are causing the error, then you can work to fix it.

The easiest way to locate JavaScript statements that work is to use *comments*. Comments are lines of the script that aren't executed. They are mainly used to document your script. If you comment out a statement with an error, the rest of the page should work fine.

Comments can be added to a single line by placing two slash marks (//) in front of the

line. These comment marks can be placed in the middle of the line, which comments out everything to the end of the line. Double slash marks (//) affect only the line they are on.

Another way to comment out several statements at once is to use the /* and */ marks. These marks comment out any statements within them, even over multiple lines.

This example uses the `js-skeleton.html` file found on the book's CD-ROM, but you can apply these steps to any file.

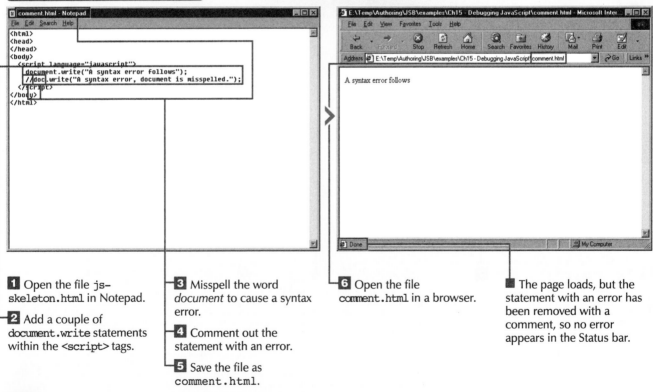

1 Open the file `js-skeleton.html` in Notepad.

2 Add a couple of `document.write` statements within the `<script>` tags.

3 Misspell the word *document* to cause a syntax error.

4 Comment out the statement with an error.

5 Save the file as `comment.html`.

6 Open the file `comment.html` in a browser.

■ The page loads, but the statement with an error has been removed with a comment, so no error appears in the Status bar.

Extra

If only one bracket of a function statement is included in a commented statement, the script produces an error. The same problem happens if you include only one end of a set of quotes or parentheses in a commented statement.

The copy and paste functions can be used to temporarily remove and replace lines of code, but if you use Notepad to write scripts, the copy buffer remembers only a single line of code. Also, if you remove a large section of code, you run the risk of losing the code.

USING MULTIPLE-LINE COMMENTS

```
comment2.html - Notepad
File  Edit  Search  Help
<html>
<head>
</head>
<body>
  <script language="javascript">
    document.write("A syntax error follows");
    /*doc.write("A syntax error, document is misspelled.");
    document.write('This line is correct.");*/
  </script>
</body>
</html>
```

```
E:\Temp\Authoring\JSB\examples\Ch15 - Debugging JavaScript\comment2.html - Microsoft Int...
File  Edit  View  Favorites  Tools  Help
Back  Forward  Stop  Refresh  Home  Search  Favorites  History  Mail  Print  Edit
Address  E:\Temp\Authoring\JSB\examples\Ch15 - Debugging JavaScript\comment2.html         Go   Links

A syntax error follows

Done                                                              My Computer
```

1 Open the file comment.html in Notepad.

2 Add another document.write() statement.

3 Comment out the document.write statements with multiple-line comment marks instead of the slashes.

4 Save the file as comment2.html.

5 Open the file comment2.html in a browser.

■ The page loads, but the statement with an error has been removed with a comment, so no error appears in the Status bar.

OUTPUT VALUES TO TEXT BOXES

Another common way to debug your script is to output the value of the variables that you are working with to a temporary text box.

This method gives you a chance to examine the value as the script is being executed. For example, if you include a `for` loop in your script, you can display the value of the loop variables each time the loop is encountered.

Text boxes can be easily included within any form on the page, or a new form can be

quickly added to the page to display the values.

You could add events to various elements within the page that display the values with the text box when fired. This enables you to interactively check variables as the script is run.

This example uses the `js-skeleton.html` file found on the book's CD-ROM, but you can apply these steps to any file.

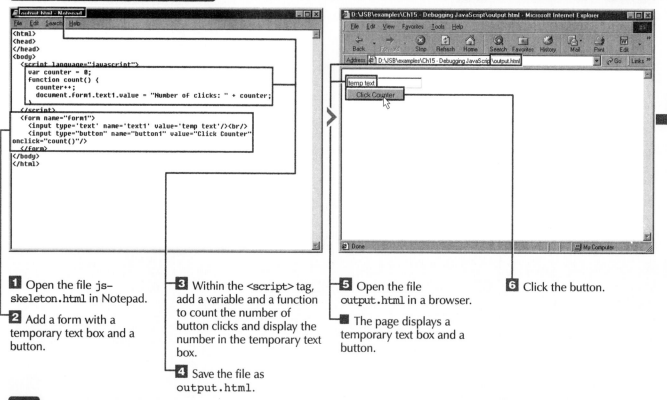

OUTPUT VALUES TO TEXT BOXES

1 Open the file js-skeleton.html in Notepad.

2 Add a form with a temporary text box and a button.

3 Within the `<script>` tag, add a variable and a function to count the number of button clicks and display the number in the temporary text box.

4 Save the file as output.html.

5 Open the file output.html in a browser.

■ The page displays a temporary text box and a button.

6 Click the button.

Apply It

Another common way to display variables in order to debug your script is to use *alert boxes*. Alert boxes are convenient because they only take a single-line statement that can be easily removed after the script is working. For example, if you have a script that computes an intermediate value such as the conversion of meters to millimeters, an alert box can be used to display the value of the variable like this:

```
meters =
document.form1.text1.value;

millimeters = meters*1000;

window.alert("meters converted to
millimeters = " + millimeters);
```

After the script is working, the single `window.alert` statement can be removed.

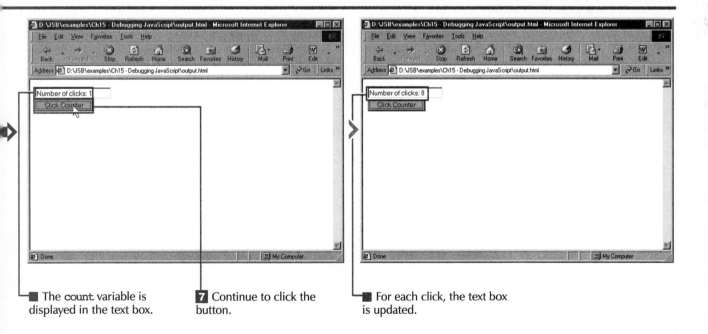

■ The count variable is displayed in the text box.

7 Continue to click the button.

■ For each click, the text box is updated.

COMMON JAVASCRIPT ERRORS

Scripts can generate errors many ways using JavaScript, but some errors are more common than others.

One common error that exists in `if` statements is to use the assignment operator (=) instead of the equality operator (==). `if` statements should always include two equal signs.

Another common way to err is to mismatch brackets, quote marks, and parentheses. You should especially watch when including quote marks (`'`) within double-quote marks (`"`).

Object properties and methods are case-sensitive, so a property like `bgColor` will not work if you forget to capitalize the C.

Another common error is to use properties, methods, and events that aren't associated with a specific object. For example, if you try to use the `onclick` event on a `form` object, the browser detects an error.

This example uses the `js-skeleton.html` file found on the book's CD-ROM, but you can apply these steps to any file.

COMMON JAVASCRIPT ERRORS

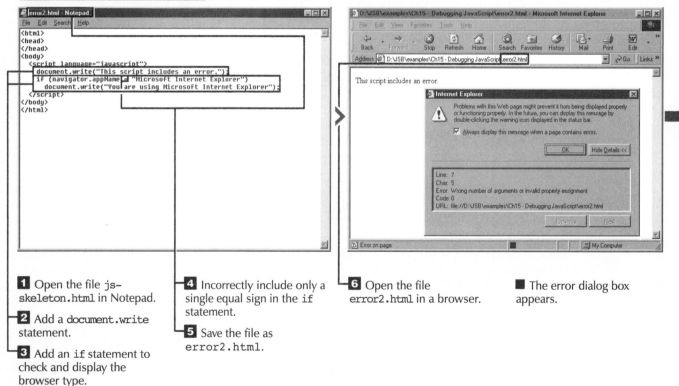

1 Open the file `js-skeleton.html` in Notepad.

2 Add a `document.write` statement.

3 Add an `if` statement to check and display the browser type.

4 Incorrectly include only a single equal sign in the `if` statement.

5 Save the file as `error2.html`.

6 Open the file `error2.html` in a browser.

■ The error dialog box appears.

Extra

Certain text editors such as Allaire HomeSite and Macromedia Dreamweaver can check for some common errors such as misplaced brackets. These editors keep track of every quote and bracket that you type, and when an ending bracket or quote is missing, the text appears red until it is entered. You can also select a single bracket or quote, press a key, and locate its partner. These editors also check the spelling of keywords to prevent spelling errors. Good scripting habits like aligning your brackets and indenting code help to make your code easier to debug and follow.

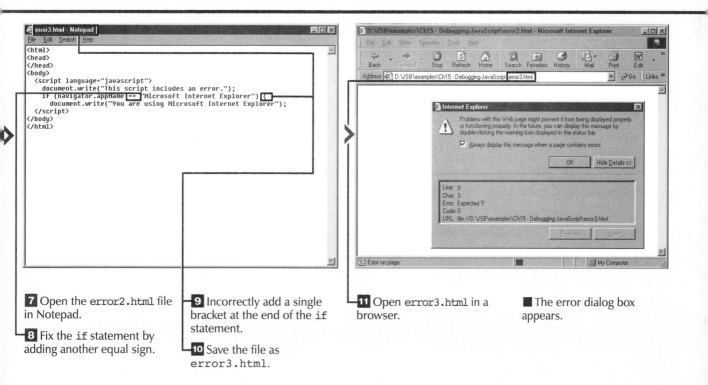

```html
error3.html - Notepad
File  Edit  Search  Help
<html>
<head>
</head>
<body>
  <script language="javascript">
    document.write("This script includes an error.");
    if (navigator.appName == "Microsoft Internet Explorer") {
      document.write("You are using Microsoft Internet Explorer");
  </script>
</body>
</html>
```

Internet Explorer

Problem with this Web page might prevent it from being displayed properly or functioning properly. In the future, you can display this message by double-clicking the warning icon displayed in the status bar.

☑ Always display this message when a page contains errors.

OK   Hide Details <<

Line: 9
Char: 3
Error: Expected ')'
Code: 0
URL: file://D:\JSB\examples\Ch15 - Debugging JavaScript\error3.html

Previous   Next

7 Open the error2.html file in Notepad.

8 Fix the if statement by adding another equal sign.

9 Incorrectly add a single bracket at the end of the if statement.

10 Save the file as error3.html.

11 Open error3.html in a browser.

■ The error dialog box appears.

JAVASCRIPT

This reference is based on the HTML 4.01 specification published online at www.w3c.org. This reference does not include the deprecated (or discontinued) elements. It also does not include frame definitions.

COMMON ATTRIBUTES

These common attributes are used across many different elements as indicated. They are divided into three groupings — core, language, and events.

Attribute	Description	Acceptable Values
	Core Attributes	
id	Element ID.	
class	Defines a style sheet class.	
style	Defines inline style sheets.	
title	Provides a title to the element.	
	Language Attributes	
lang	Indicates primary language.	
dir	Defines text direction.	ltr and rtl
	Event Attributes	
onclick	Element was clicked.	
ondblclick	Element was double clicked.	
onmousedown	Mouse button was pressed.	
onmouseup	Mouse button was released.	
onmouseover	Cursor was moved over an element.	
onmousemove	Cursor was moved.	
onmouseout	Cursor was moved off an element.	
onkeypress	Keyboard key was pressed.	
onkeydown	Keyboard key was pressed down.	
onkeyup	Keyboard key was released.	

DOCUMENT STRUCTURE ELEMENTS

These elements compose the major sections of a Web page, including the root <html> tags, the head, and the body.

Attribute	Description
	<HTML> . . . </HTML> (supports common language attributes)
version	Specifies a DTD.
	<HEAD> . . . </HEAD> (supports common language attributes)
profile	Locates separate meta data file.
	<BODY> . . . </BODY> (supports common core, language, and event attributes)
onload	Document was loaded.
onunload	Document was unloaded.

HEAD ELEMENTS

The following tags can be included within the head section of a Web page. These tags can appear multiple times within the head section.

Attribute	Description	Acceptable Values
	<TITLE> . . . </TITLE> (supports common language attributes)	
<BASE/>		
href	Location of base.	
	<META/> (supports common language attributes)	
http-equiv	Response header.	
name	Meta information name.	
content	Information for name.	
scheme	Meta data interpretation scheme.	
	<LINK/> (supports common core, language, and event attributes)	
charset	The browser's character set.	
href	Location of the link.	
hreflang	Language of the link.	
type	Content type of the link.	
rel	Forward link type.	
rev	Reverse link type.	
media	Specifies media type.	

Attribute	Description	Acceptable Values
	<SCRIPT> . . . </SCRIPT>	
charset	The browser's character set.	
type	Content type of the scripting language.	
src	Location of external script file.	
defer	Allows deferred execution of script.	defer
	<NOSCRIPT> . . . </NOSCRIPT> (supports common core, language, and event attributes)	
	<STYLE> . . . </STYLE> (supports common language attributes)	
type	Content type of the style language.	
media	Specifies the media type.	
title	Title for the style.	
	<OBJECT> . . . </OBJECT> (supports common core, language, and event attributes)	
declare	Declaration flag.	declare
classid	Identifies the class ID.	
codebase	The object's location.	
data	Data passed to the object.	
type	Content type of the object.	
codetype	Content type of the code.	
archive	Archived copy of the object.	
standby	Standby message to show while loading.	
height	Height of the object.	
width	Width of the object.	
usemap	Use client-side image map.	
name	Reference name for the object.	
tabindex	Tab order position.	
	<PARAM/>	
id	Parameter ID.	
name	Property name.	
value	Property value.	
valuetype	Defines value type.	data, ref, and object
type	Content type of the value.	

BLOCK ELEMENTS

These elements support common core, language, and event attributes.

Tag
```
<P>   . . .  </P>
<DIV>  . . .  </DIV>
<ADDRESS>  . . .  </ADDRESS>
```

PREFORMATTED TEXT ELEMENT

Attribute	Description
`<PRE> ... </PRE>` (supports common core, language, and event attributes)	
`width`	Width of the preformatted text.

QUOTE ELEMENTS

Attribute	Description
`<BLOCKQUOTE> ... </BLOCKQUOTE>`	
`<Q> ... </Q>` (supports common core, language, and event attributes)	
`cite`	Location of the quote source.

HEADING ELEMENTS

There are six heading levels from H1 (the most important) to H6 (the least important). These all share the same attributes. The heading elements support common core, language, and event attributes.

Tag
```
<H1>  . . .  </H1>
<H2>  . . .  </H2>
<H3>  . . .  </H3>
<H4>  . . .  </H4>
<H5>  . . .  </H5>
<H6>  . . .  </H6>
```

PHRASE ELEMENTS

These elements mark text as emphasis, strong, definition, code, sample, keyboard, variable, cite, abbreviation, and acronym styles. These elements support common core, language, and event attributes.

Tag
```
<EM>  . . .  </EM>
<STRONG>  . . .  </STRONG>
<DFN>  . . .  </DFN>
<CODE>  . . .  </CODE>
<SAMP>  . . .  </SAMP>
<KBD>  . . .  </KBD>
<VAR>  . . .  </VAR>
<CITE>  . . .  </CITE>
<ABBR>  . . .  </ABBR>
<ACRONYM>  . . .  </ACRONYM>
```

INSERTED/DELETED TEXT ELEMENT

These elements support common core, language, and event attributes.

Attribute	Description
`<INS> ... </INS>`	
`<DEL> ... </DEL>`	
`cite`	Location of the source.
`datetime`	Date and time of change.

TEXT STYLE ELEMENTS

These elements format text as teletype, italics, bold, big, or small. These elements support common core, language, and event attributes.

```
Tag
<TT> . . . </TT>

<I> . . . </I>

<B> . . . </B>

<BIG> . . . </BIG>

<SMALL> . . . </SMALL>
```

SUBSCRIPT AND SUPERSCRIPT ELEMENTS

These elements mark text as subscripts or superscripts. These elements support common core, language, and event attributes.

```
Tag
<SUB> . . . </SUB>

<SUP> . . . </SUP>
```

INLINE ELEMENT

This element supports common core, language, and event attributes.

```
Tag
<SPAN> . . . </SPAN>
```

BIDIRECTIONAL OVERRIDE ELEMENT

Attribute	Description	Acceptable Values
	<BDO> ... </BDO> (supports common core attributes)	
lang	Defines the language.	
dir	Defines the text direction.	ltr and rtl

LIST ELEMENTS

These elements are used to create lists including definition, ordered, and unordered lists.

Attribute	Description	Acceptable Values
	<DL> ... </DL>	
	<(DT)> ... </DT>	
	<(DD)> ... </DD> (supports common core, language, and event attributes)	
	<OL> ... </OL> (supports common core, language, and event attributes)	
type	Sets the numbering style.	1, a, A, i, and I
start	Sets the list start value.	
	<UL> ... </UL> (supports common core, language, and event attributes)	
type	Sets the bullet style.	disc, square, and circle
	<LI> ... </LI> (supports common core, language, and event attributes)	
type	Sets the numbering or bullet style.	1, a, A, i, I, disc, square, and circle
value	Sets the current list value.	

LINE BREAK ELEMENT

This element supports common core attributes.

Tag
  `<BR/>`

HORIZONTAL RULE ELEMENT

This element supports common core, language, and event attributes.

Tag
  `<HR/>`

THE ANCHOR ELEMENT

Attribute	Description	Acceptable Values
	`<A>` ... `</A>` (supports common core, language, and event attributes)	
charset	Character set to use.	
type	Content type for the link.	
name	Name of the anchor.	
href	Location of the link.	
hreflang	Language of the link.	
rel	Forward link type.	
rev	Reverse link type.	
accesskey	Shortcut key.	
shape	Client-side image map shape.	default, rect, circle, and poly
coords	Client-side image map coordinates.	
tabindex	Tab order position.	
onfocus	Element has received the focus.	
onblur	Element has lost the focus.	

IMAGE ELEMENT

Attribute	Description	Acceptable Values
	`<IMG/>` (supports common core, language, and event attributes)	
src	Location of image.	
alt	Alternative description.	
longdesc	Location of long description.	
name	Reference name of the image.	
height	Image height.	
width	Image width.	
usemap	Use client-side image map.	
ismap	Use server-side image map.	ismap

CLIENT-SIDE IMAGE MAP ELEMENTS

Attribute	Description	Acceptable Values
<MAP> . . . </MAP> (supports common core, language, and event attributes)		
name	Reference name for the map.	
<AREA/> (supports common core, language, and event attributes)		
shape	Client-side image map shape.	default, rect, circle, and poly
coords	Client-side image map coordinates.	
href	Location of the link.	
nohref	Specifies no link.	nohref
alt	Alternative description.	
tabindex	Tab order position.	
accesskey	Shortcut key.	
onfocus	Element has received the focus.	
onblur	Element has lost the focus.	

FORM ELEMENTS

Attribute	Description	Acceptable Values
<FORM> . . . </FORM> (supports common core, language, and event attributes)		
action	Server-side form handler.	
method	HTTP submission method.	get and post
enctype	URL encoding type.	
accept	Acceptable MIME types.	
name	Reference name of form.	
onsubmit	Form was submitted.	
onreset	The form was reset.	
accept-charset	Supported character sets.	
<LABEL> . . . </LABEL> (supports common core, language, and event attributes)		
for	Field ID value.	
accesskey	Shortcut key.	
onfocus	Element has received the focus.	
onblur	Element has lost the focus.	
<INPUT/> (supports common core, language, and event attributes)		
type	Type of input field.	text, password, checkbox, radio, submit, reset, file, hidden, image, and button
name	Reference name.	

FORM ELEMENTS CONTINUED

Attribute	Description	Acceptable Values
value	Value for the input field.	
checked	Marks when radio buttons and check boxes are selected.	checked
disabled	Disables the form element.	disabled
readonly	For passwords; allows read mode only.	readonly
size	Specifies the size of the field.	
maxlength	Maximum length of a text field.	
src	Location of the image.	
alt	Alternative description.	
usemap	Use client-side image map.	
ismap	Use server-side image map.	ismap
tabindex	Tab order position.	
accesskey	Shortcut key.	
onfocus	Element has received the focus.	
onblur	Element has lost the focus.	
onselect	Some text was selected.	
onchange	The element value was changed.	
accept	Acceptable MIME types.	

<SELECT> . . . </SELECT> (supports common core, language, and event attributes)

Attribute	Description	Acceptable Values
name	Reference name.	
size	Number of visible rows.	
multiple	Allows multiple selection items.	multiple
disabled	Disables the form element.	disabled
tabindex	Tab order position.	
onfocus	Element has received the focus.	
onblur	Element has lost the focus.	
onchange	The element value was changed.	

<OPTGROUP> . . . </OPTGROUP> (supports common core, language, and event attributes)

Attribute	Description	Acceptable Values
disabled	Disables the form element.	disabled
label	Labels the element.	

<OPTION> . . . </OPTION> (supports common core, language, and event attributes)

Attribute	Description	Acceptable Values
selected	Item is selected.	selected
disabled	Disables the form element.	disabled
label	Labels the element.	
value	Item value.	

FORM ELEMENTS CONTINUED

Attribute	Description	Acceptable Values
<TEXTAREA> ... </TEXTAREA> (supports common core, language, and event attributes)		
name	Reference name.	
rows	Defines the number of rows.	
cols	Defines the number of columns.	
disabled	Disables the form element.	disabled
readonly	For passwords; allows read mode only.	readonly
tabindex	Tab order position.	
accesskey	Shortcut key.	
onfocus	The element received the focus.	
onblur	The element has lost the focus.	
onselect	Some text was selected.	
onchange	The element value was changed.	
<FIELDSET> ... </FIELDSET> (supports common core, language, and event attributes)		
<LEGEND> ... </LEGEND> (supports common core, language, and event attributes)		
accesskey	Shortcut key	
<BUTTON> ... </BUTTON> (supports common core, language, and event attributes)		
name	Reference name.	
value	Button value.	
type	Type of button.	button, submit, and reset
disabled	Disables the form element.	disabled
tabindex	Tab order position.	
accesskey	Shortcut key.	
onfocus	Element has received the focus.	
onblur	Element has lost the focus.	

TABLE ELEMENTS

Attribute	Description	Acceptable Values
<TABLE> ... </TABLE> (supports common core, language, and event attributes)		
summary	Brief table summary.	
width	Table width.	
border	Defines border width.	
frame	Defines render frame.	
rules	Places rules between rows and columns.	
cellspacing	Spacing between cells.	

TABLE ELEMENTS CONTINUED

Attribute	Description	Acceptable Values
cellpadding	Spacing within cells.	

<CAPTION> ... </CAPTION> (supports common core, language, and event attributes)

<COLGROUP> ... </COLGROUP>

<COL> ... </COL> (supports common core, language, and event attributes)

Attribute	Description	Acceptable Values
span	Number of columns in a span.	
width	Column width.	
align	Horizontal alignment.	left, center, right, justify, and char
char	Alignment character.	
charoff	Character offset.	
valign	Vertical alignment.	top, middle, bottom, and baseline

<THEAD> ... </THEAD>

<TBODY> ... </TBODY>

<TFOOT> ... </TFOOT>

<TR> ... </TR> (supports common core, language, and event attributes)

Attribute	Description	Acceptable Values
align	Horizontal alignment.	left, center, right, justify, and char
char	Alignment character.	
charoff	Character offset.	
valign	Vertical alignment.	top, middle, bottom, and baseline

<TH> ... </TH>

<TD> ... </TD> (supports common core, language, and event attributes)

Attribute	Description	Acceptable Values
abbr	Header abbreviation.	
axis	List of headers.	
headers	List of header cells IDs.	
scope	Scope of header cells.	
rowspan	Number of rows spanned by cell.	
colspan	Number of columns spanned by cell.	
align	Horizontal alignment.	left, center, right, justify, and char
char	Alignment character.	
charoff	Character offset.	
valign	Vertical alignment.	top, middle, bottom, and baseline

WHAT'S ON THE CD-ROM

The CD-ROM included in this book contains many useful files and programs. Before installing any of the programs on the disc, make sure that a newer version of the program is not already installed on your computer. For information on installing different versions of the same program, contact the program's manufacturer.

SYSTEM REQUIREMENTS

To use the contents of the CD-ROM, your computer must be equipped with the following hardware and software:

- A PC with a Pentium 133 MHz or faster processor or a Mac OS computer with a 68040 or faster processor.

- Microsoft Windows 95 or later, Windows NT 4 or later or Mac OS system software 7.5.5 or later.

- At least 16MB of total RAM installed on your computer (we recommend at least 32MB).

- At least 150MB of hard drive space.

- A ten-speed (10x) or faster CD-ROM drive.

- A sound card for PCs.

- A monitor capable of displaying at least 256 colors or grayscale.

- A modem with a speed of at least 28,800 bps.

INSTALLING AND USING THE SOFTWARE

Shareware programs are fully functional, free trial versions of copyrighted programs. If you like particular programs, register with their authors for a nominal fee and receive licenses, enhanced versions, and technical support. Freeware programs are free, copyrighted games, applications, and utilities. You can copy them to as many PCs as you like — free — but they have no technical support. GNU software is governed by its own license, which is included inside the folder of the GNU software. There are no restrictions on distribution of this software. See the GNU license for

more details. Trial, demo, or evaluation versions are usually limited either by time or functionality (such as being unable to save projects).

For your convenience, the software titles appearing on the CD-ROM are listed alphabetically.

Author's sample files

For Mac and Windows 95/98/NT. These files contain all the sample code from the book. You can browse these files directly from the CD-ROM, or you can copy them to your hard drive and use them as the basis for your own projects. To find the files on the CD-ROM, open the D:\Author Samples folder.

Acrobat Reader, from Adobe

For Windows 95/98 and NT 4 or later and Macintosh. Evaluation version. Acrobat Reader is a program and plug-in that can be used to display, search, and print PDF files.

Aladdin Expander, from Aladdin Systems

For Macintosh. Freeware. Aladdin Expander can create expandable archive files that can be expanded as needed. This freeware version doesn't include all the features of the commercial version, but it will not expire.

BBEdit, from Bare Bones Software

For Macintosh. Demo version. BBEdit is an advanced HTML editor that can be used to create Web pages. This demo allows you to use the full version for an evaluation period.

BBEdit Lite, from Bare Bones Software

For Macintosh. Lite version. BBEdit Lite is a light version of the popular HTML editing package that can be used to create Web pages.

CoffeeCup HTML Editor, from CoffeeCup Software
For Windows 95/98 and NT 4 or later. Shareware. The CoffeeCup tools are a suite of tools that let you work with all aspects of HTML, Web images, and Java. These tools are shareware and need to be registered after a given amount of time.

CSE HTML Validator Lite, from Windows-Al Internet Solutions
For Windows 95/98 and NT 4 or later. Lite version. CSE HTML Validator Lite doesn't include all the features of the professional version, but it will not expire.

CSE HTML Validator Professional, from Windows-Al Internet Solutions
For Windows 95/98 and NT 4 or later. Demo version. CSE HTML Validator Professional can be used to validate your Web pages. This demo allows you to use the full version for an evaluation period.

CuteFTP, from GlobalSCAPE
For Windows 95/98 and NT 4 or later. Shareware. CuteFTP is an FTP client that can be used to transfer files to a Web server.

CuteMAP, from GlobalSCAPE
For Windows 95/98 and NT 4 or later. Shareware. CuteMAP is an image map editor. It can be used to create and save image maps.

Dot Planet ISP, from DotPlanet.com
For Windows 95/98/NT. Evaluation version. In case you don't have a connection to the information superhighway, the CD includes sign-on software for DotPlanet Internet Access, an Internet service provider.

During the sign-up process, you will need to enter the registration number: 502 CY.

After you are signed on, you can access the world wide Web from DotPlanet's home page. You need a credit card to sign up with DotPlanet Internet Access.

Dreamweaver, from Macromedia
For Windows 95/98 and NT 4.0 or later. Trial Version. Dreamweaver is a robust Web page creation tool. It allows you to dynamically edit HTML and JavaScript pages. This demo allows you to use the full version for an evaluation period.

GIF Animator, from Ulead Systems
For Windows 95/98 and NT 4 or later. Trial version. GIF Animator is a package that can be used to create animated GIF images. This demo allows you to use the full version for an evaluation period.

GraphicConverter, from Lemke Software
For Macintosh. Shareware. GraphicConverter is a graphic conversion program that can be used to convert images between different formats.

HomeSite, from Allaire Corporation
For Windows 95/98 and NT 4 or later. 30-day evaluation version. HomeSite is a Visual HTML editor. It can be used to create Web pages. The evaluation version will expire after 30 days.

HotDog Express, from Sausage Software
For Windows 95/98 and NT 4 or later. Demo version. HotDog Express is the easier-to-use version of Sausage Software's Web page creation program (see "HotDog Professional").

HotDog Professional, from Sausage Software
For Windows 95/98 and NT 4 or later. Trial version. HotDog Professional is Sausage Software's professional-level Web page creation program.

HTML Pro, from Niklas Frykholm
For Windows 95/98 and NT 4 or later. Shareware. HTML Pro is a Web page editing package that can be used to create Web pages.

Internet Explorer, from Microsoft
For Windows 95/98 and NT 4 or later and Macintosh. Commercial version. Internet Explorer is a robust browser that can be used to display Web pages.

Mapedit, from Boutell Communications
For Windows 95/98 and NT 4 or later. Shareware. Mapedit is an image map editor. It can be used to create and save image maps.

Netscape Communicator, from Netscape
For Windows 95/98 and NT 4 or later and Macintosh. Commercial version. Netscape Communicator is a popular Web browser that can be used to display Web pages.

Paint Shop Pro, from JASC
For Windows 95/98 and NT 4 or later. Shareware. Paint Shop Pro is a powerful image editing package. This demo allows you to use the full version for an evaluation period. Paint Shop Pro includes many tools for creating, editing, and working with Web images.

PowWow, from Tribal Voice Software
For Windows 95/98 and NT 4 or later. Freeware. PowWow Professional is an instant messaging communication package that includes voice chat capabilities.

RealPlayer, from RealNetworks, Inc.
For Windows 95/98 and NT 4 or later and Macintosh. Commercial version. RealPlayer is a browser plug-in that can be used to view audio and video files.

Reptile, from Sausage Software
For Windows 95/98 and NT 4 or later. Demo version. Reptile is a seamless tile creation package.

Shockwave and Flash Players, from Macromedia, Inc.
For Windows 95/98 and NT 4 or later and Macintosh. Commercial version. The Shockwave and Flash Players are plug-ins that can be used to display Flash and Shockwave content within a browser.

SiteCheck, from Pacific Coast Software
For Windows 95/98 and NT 4 or later. Shareware. SiteCheck is a set of utilities that can be used to check the links on your site's Web pages.

SmartSaver Pro, from Ulead Systems
For Windows 95/98 and NT 4 or later. 15-day trial version. SmartSaver Pro is a Web image-optimization package that allows you to visually select the file settings for creating optimized images. This demo allows you to use the full version for an evaluation period.

Spider, from InContext Systems
For Windows 95/98 and NT 4 or later. Evaluation version. Spider is a Web-authoring package for creating Web pages.

Stuffit Expander, from Aladdin Systems
For Macintosh. Commercial version. Stuffit Expander can create expandable archive files that can be expanded as needed.

Stuffit Lite, from Aladdin Systems
For Windows 95/98 and NT 4 or later and Macintosh. Freeware. Stuffit Lite can be used to compress and archive files. The lite version is freeware and will not expire.

Web Razor Pro, from Ulead Systems
For Windows 95/98 and NT 4.0 or later. Evaluation Copy. Web Razor Pro is a Web image-editing package that includes features for creating GIF animations and optimizing Web images. This demo allows you to use the full version for an evaluation period.

WinZip, from Nico Mak Computing
For Windows 95/98 and NT 4 or later. Evaluation version. WinZip is a file compression and archiving package.

TROUBLESHOOTING
I tried my best to compile programs that work on most computers with the minimum system requirements. Your computer, however, may differ, and some programs may not work properly for some reason.

The two most likely problems are that you don't have enough memory (RAM) for the programs you want to use, or you have other programs running that are affecting installation or running of a program. If you get error messages like Not enough memory or Setup cannot continue, try one or more of these methods and then try using the software again:

- Turn off any anti-virus software.

- Close all running programs.

- In Windows, close the CD-ROM interface and run demos or installations directly from Windows Explorer.

- Have your local computer store add more RAM to your computer.

If you still have trouble installing the items from the CD-ROM, please call the IDG Books Worldwide Customer Service phone number: 800-762-2974 (outside the U.S.: 317-572-3443).

USING THE E-VERSION OF THE BOOK

You can view *JavaScript: Your visual blueprint for building dynamic Web pages* on your screen using the CD-ROM disc included at the back of this book. The CD-ROM disc allows you to search the contents of each chapter of the book for a specific word or phrase. The CD-ROM disc also provides a convenient way of keeping the book handy while traveling.

You must install Adobe Acrobat Reader on your computer before you can view the book on the CD-ROM disc. This program is provided on

the disc. Acrobat Reader allows you to view Portable Document Format (PDF) files, which can display books and magazines on your screen exactly as they appear in printed form.

To view the contents of the book using Acrobat Reader, display the contents of the disc. Double-click the PDFs folder to display the contents of the folder. In the window that appears, double-click the icon for the chapter of the book you want to review.

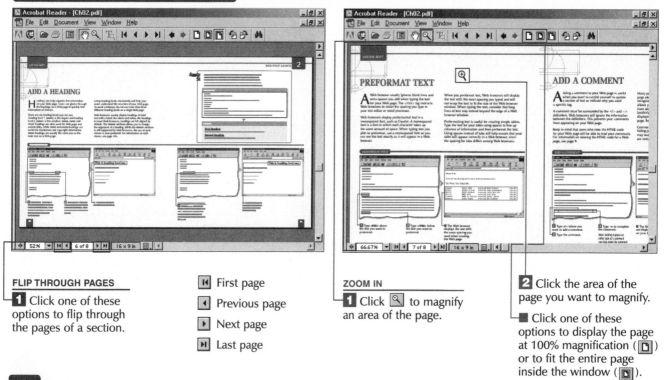

USING THE E-VERSION OF THE BOOK

FLIP THROUGH PAGES

■1 Click one of these options to flip through the pages of a section.

|◄| First page

|◄| Previous page

|►| Next page

|►|| Last page

ZOOM IN

■1 Click 🔍 to magnify an area of the page.

■2 Click the area of the page you want to magnify.

■ Click one of these options to display the page at 100% magnification (▢) or to fit the entire page inside the window (▢).

Extra

To install Acrobat Reader, insert the CD-ROM disc into a drive. In the screen that appears, click Software. Click Acrobat Reader and then click Install at the bottom of the screen. Then follow the instructions on your screen to install the program.

You can make searching the book more convenient by copying the `.pdf` files to your own computer. Display the contents of the CD-ROM disc and then copy the PDFs folder from the CD to your hard drive. This allows you to easily access the

Acrobat Reader is a popular and useful program. There are many files available on the Web that are designed to be viewed using Acrobat Reader. Look for files with the `.pdf` extension. For more information about Acrobat Reader, visit the Web site at `www.adobe.com/products/acrobat/readermain.html`.

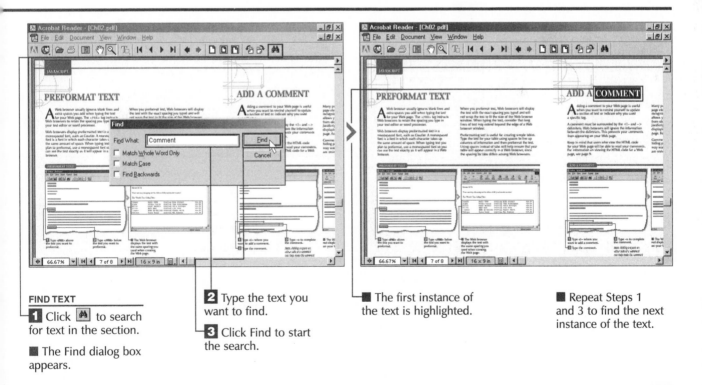

FIND TEXT

1 Click 🔍 to search for text in the section.

■ The Find dialog box appears.

2 Type the text you want to find.

3 Click Find to start the search.

■ The first instance of the text is highlighted.

■ Repeat Steps 1 and 3 to find the next instance of the text.

INDEX

JAVASCRIPT:
Your visual blueprint for
building dynamic Web pages

JAVASCRIPT:
Your visual blueprint for
building dynamic Web pages

INDEX

JAVASCRIPT:
Your visual blueprint for
building dynamic Web pages

INDEX

JAVASCRIPT:
Your visual blueprint for
building dynamic Web pages

N

INDEX

JAVASCRIPT:
Your visual blueprint for
building dynamic Web pages

INDEX

JAVASCRIPT:
Your visual blueprint for
building dynamic Web pages

INDEX

IDG BOOKS WORLDWIDE, INC.
END-USER LICENSE AGREEMENT

READ THIS. You should carefully read these terms and conditions before opening the software packet(s) included with this book ("Book"). This is a license agreement ("Agreement") between you and IDG Books Worldwide, Inc. ("IDGB"). By opening the accompanying software packet(s), you acknowledge that you have read and accept the following terms and conditions. If you do not agree and do not want to be bound by such terms and conditions, promptly return the Book and the unopened software packet(s) to the place you obtained them for a full refund.

1. License Grant. IDGB grants to you (either an individual or entity) a nonexclusive license to use one copy of the enclosed software program(s) (collectively, the "Software") solely for your own personal or business purposes on a single computer (whether a standard computer or a workstation component of a multi-user network). The Software is in use on a computer when it is loaded into temporary memory (i.e., RAM) or installed into permanent memory (e.g., hard disk, CD-ROM or other storage device). IDGB reserves all rights not expressly granted herein.

2. Ownership. IDGB is the owner of all right, title and interest, including copyright, in and to the compilation of the Software recorded on the CD-ROM. Copyright to the individual programs on the CD-ROM is owned by the author or other authorized copyright owner of each program. Ownership of the Software and all proprietary rights relating thereto remain with IDGB and its licensors.

3. Restrictions On Use and Transfer.

(a) You may only (i) make one copy of the Software for backup or archival purposes, or (ii) transfer the Software to a single hard disk, provided that you keep the original for backup or archival purposes. You may not (i) rent or lease the Software, (ii) copy or reproduce the Software through a LAN or other network system or through any computer subscriber system or bulletin-board system, or (iii) modify, adapt or create derivative works based on the Software.

(b) You may not reverse engineer, decompile, or disassemble the Software. You may transfer the Software and user documentation on a permanent basis, provided that the transferee agrees to accept the terms and conditions of this Agreement and you retain no copies. If the Software is an update or has been updated, any transfer must include the most recent update and all prior versions.

4. Restrictions on Use of Individual Programs. You must follow the individual requirements and restrictions detailed for each individual program in the "What's On The CD-ROM Disc" section of this Book. These limitations are contained in the individual license agreements recorded on the CD-ROM. These restrictions may include a requirement that after using the program for the period of time specified in its text, the user must pay a registration fee or discontinue use. By opening the Software packet(s), you will be agreeing to abide by the licenses and restrictions for these individual programs. None of the material on this disc(s) or listed in this Book may ever be distributed, in original or modified form, for commercial purposes.

5. Limited Warranty.

(a) IDGB warrants that the Software and CD-ROM are free from defects in materials and workmanship under normal use for a period of sixty (60) days from the date of purchase of this Book. If IDGB receives notification within the warranty period of defects in materials or workmanship, IDGB will replace the defective CD-ROM.

(b) IDGB AND THE AUTHOR OF THE BOOK DISCLAIM ALL OTHER WARRANTIES, EXPRESS OR IMPLIED, INCLUDING WITHOUT LIMITATION IMPLIED WARRANTIES OF MERCHANTABILITY AND FITNESS FOR A PARTICULAR PURPOSE, WITH RESPECT TO THE SOFTWARE, THE PROGRAMS, THE SOURCE CODE CONTAINED THEREIN, AND/ OR THE TECHNIQUES DESCRIBED IN THIS BOOK. IDGB DOES NOT WARRANT THAT THE FUNCTIONS CONTAINED IN THE SOFTWARE WILL MEET YOUR REQUIREMENTS OR THAT THE OPERATION OF THE SOFTWARE WILL BE ERROR FREE.

(c) This limited warranty gives you specific legal rights, and you may have other rights which vary from jurisdiction to jurisdiction.

6. Remedies.

(a) IDGB's entire liability and your exclusive remedy for defects in materials and workmanship shall be limited to replacement of the Software, which may be returned to IDGB with a copy of your receipt at the following address: Disc Fulfillment Department, Attn: *JavaScript: Your visual blueprint for Building Dynamic Web pages,* IDG Books Worldwide, Inc., 10475 Crosspoint Boulevard, Indianapolis, Indiana, 46256, or call 1-800-762-2974. Please allow 3-4 weeks for delivery. This Limited Warranty is void if failure of the Software has resulted from accident, abuse, or misapplication. Any replacement Software will be warranted for the remainder of the original warranty period or thirty (30) days, whichever is longer.

(b) In no event shall IDGB or the author be liable for any damages whatsoever (including without limitation damages for loss of business profits, business interruption, loss of business information, or any other pecuniary loss) arising out of the use of or inability to use the Book or the Software, even if IDGB has been advised of the possibility of such damages.

(c) Because some jurisdictions do not allow the exclusion or limitation of liability for consequential or incidental damages, the above limitation or exclusion may not apply to you.

7. U.S. Government Restricted Rights. Use, duplication, or disclosure of the Software by the U.S. Government is subject to restrictions stated in paragraph (c) (1) (ii) of the Rights in Technical Data and Computer Software clause of DFARS 252.227-7013, and in subparagraphs (a) through (d) of the Commercial Computer—Restricted Rights clause at FAR 52.227-19, and in similar clauses in the NASA FAR supplement, when applicable.

8. General. This Agreement constitutes the entire understanding of the parties, and revokes and supersedes all prior agreements, oral or written, between them and may not be modified or amended except in a writing signed by both parties hereto which specifically refers to this Agreement. This Agreement shall take precedence over any other documents that may be in conflict herewith. If any one or more provisions contained in this Agreement are held by any court or tribunal to be invalid, illegal or otherwise unenforceable, each and every other provision shall remain in full force and effect.

Read Less, Learn More™

![Visual]

with these two-color Visual™ guides

The Complete Visual Reference

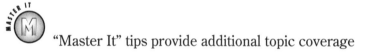

"Master It" tips provide additional topic coverage

Title	ISBN	Price
Master Active Directory™ VISUALLY™	0-7645-3425-4	$34.99
Master HTML 4 & XHTML 1 VISUALLY™	0-7645-3454-8	$34.99
Master Microsoft® Access 2000 VISUALLY™	0-7645-6048-4	$39.99
Master Microsoft® Office 2000 VISUALLY™	0-7645-6050-6	$39.99
Master Microsoft® Windows® Me Millennium Edition VISUALLY™	0-7645-3496-3	$34.99
Master Microsoft® Word 2000 VISUALLY™	0-7645-6046-8	$39.99
Master Office 97 VISUALLY™	0-7645-6036-0	$39.99
Master Photoshop® 5.5 VISUALLY™	0-7645-6045-X	$39.99
Master Red Hat® Linux® VISUALLY™	0-7645-3436-X	$34.99
Master Windows® 95 VISUALLY™	0-7645-6024-7	$39.99
Master Windows® 98 VISUALLY™	0-7645-6034-4	$39.99
Master Windows® 2000 Professional VISUALLY™	0-7645-3421-1	$39.99
Master Windows® 2000 Server VISUALLY™	0-7645-3426-2	$34.99

ORDER FORM

IDG BOOKS ®

TRADE & INDIVIDUAL ORDERS

Phone: **(800) 762-2974**
or **(317) 572-3993**
(8 a.m.–6 p.m., CST, weekdays)

FAX : **(800) 550-2747**
or **(317) 572-4002**

EDUCATIONAL ORDERS & DISCOUNTS

Phone: **(800) 434-2086**
(8:30 a.m.–5:00 p.m., CST, weekdays)
FAX : **(317) 572-4005**

CORPORATE ORDERS FOR 3-D VISUAL™ SERIES

Phone: **(800) 469-6616**
(8 a.m.–5 p.m., EST, weekdays)
FAX : **(905) 890-9434**

Qty	ISBN	Title	Price	Total

Shipping & Handling Charges

	Description	First book	Each add'l. book	Total
Domestic	Normal	$4.50	$1.50	$
	Two Day Air	$8.50	$2.50	$
	Overnight	$18.00	$3.00	$
International	Surface	$8.00	$8.00	$
	Airmail	$16.00	$16.00	$
	DHL Air	$17.00	$17.00	$

Subtotal _____

*CA residents add
applicable sales tax* _____

*IN, MA and MD
residents add
5% sales tax* _____

*IL residents add
6.25% sales tax* _____

*RI residents add
7% sales tax* _____

*TX residents add
8.25% sales tax* _____

Shipping _____

Total _____

Ship to:

Name _____

Address _____

Company _____

City/State/Zip _____

Daytime Phone _____

Payment: ☐ Check to IDG Books (US Funds Only)

☐ Visa   ☐ Mastercard   ☐ American Express

Card # _____ Exp. _____ Signature _____

M7074-C
94

maranGraphics™